D0090215

LETTERS FROM THE FRONT LINES

LETTERS FROM

To my good Friend Nigel. All the Best sir! Stuart F. Platt 2006 Vancouver BC

THE FRONT LINES

IRAQ AND AFGHANISTAN

Rear Admiral Stuart Franklin Platt, Ret.

with Duffrey Sigurdson

Granville Island Publishing

Publisher's Cataloging-in-Publication
(Provided by Quality Books, Inc.)

Letters from the front lines : Iraq and Afghanistan /
    Stuart Franklin Platt ; with Duffrey Sigurdson.
    p. cm.
    Includes index.
    ISBN 978-1-894694-48-3
    ISBN 1-894694-48-1

    1. Iraq War, 2003--Personal narratives, American.
    2. Afghan War, 2001--Personal narratives, American.
    3. War on Terrorism, 2001- 4. Soldiers--United States--
    Correspondence. 5. United States--History, Military--
    Sources. 6. United States--Armed Forces--Biography.
    I. Platt, Stuart Franklin, Rear Admiral. II. Sigurdson,
    Duffrey.

    DS79.764.U6L48 2006   956.7044'30922
                QBI06-600305

Editing: Graham Hayman
Indexing: Ann McTaggart
Cover and Book Design: Laura Kinder

First printing 2006
Printed in the United States

Granville Island Publishing
in the United States: 1574 Gulf Road, Point Roberts, WA 98281
in Canada: 212–1656 Duranleau, Vancouver, BC V6H 3S4
Tel: (604) 688-0320
Toll Free: 1-877-688-0320
www.GranvilleIslandPublishing.com

Distributed by Greenleaf Book Group LP
For ordering information or special discounts for bulk purchases,
please contact Greenleaf Book Group LP at 4425 S. Mo Pac Expwy.,
Suite 600, Longhorn Building, 3rd Floor, Austin, TX 78735, (512) 891-6100.

DEDICATION

I dedicate this book to the memory of those who have fallen in Operation Iraqi Freedom and Operation Enduring Freedom.

This book is also humbly dedicated to Harald Davidson, Christy and Jackson, Robin and Ethan, Cpl T.W. Stidham, USMC, Cpl Wm J. Keel, USMC, Maj. Jerry S. Stidham, US Army Air Corps, and Rachel Schmidt McCarthy.

TABLE OF CONTENTS

BOOK ONE: *Individual Letters*

PRELUDE: SEPTEMBER 2001

"I say to our enemies: we are coming.
God may show you mercy. We will not."

– Sen. John McCain

Dear Dad,

Well, we are still out at sea, with little direction as to what our next priority is. The remainder of our port visits, which were to be centered around max liberty and goodwill to the United Kingdom, have all but been cancelled. We have spent every day since the attacks going back and forth within imaginary boxes drawn in the ocean, standing high-security watches, and trying to make the best of our time. It hasn't been that fun I must confess, and to be even more honest, a lot of people are frustrated at the fact that they either can't be home, or we don't have more direction right now. We have seen the articles and the photographs, and they are sickening. Being isolated as we are, I don't think we appreciate the full scope of what is happening back home, but we are definitely feeling the effects.

About two hours ago the junior officers were called to the bridge to conduct Shiphandling drills. We were about to do a man overboard when we got a call from the LUTJENS (D185), a German warship that was moored ahead of us on the pier in Plymouth, England. While in port, the WINSTON S CHURCHILL and the LUTJENS got together for a sports day/ cookout on our fantail, and we made some pretty good friends.

Now at sea they called over on bridge-to-bridge, requesting to pass us close up on our port side, to say goodbye. We prepared to render them honors on the bridgewing, and the Captain told the crew to come topside to wish them farewell. As they were making their approach, our Conning Officer announced through her binoculars that they were flying an American flag. As they came even closer, we saw that it was flying at half-mast.

The bridgewing was crowded with people as the Boatswain's Mate blew two whistles – Attention to Port – the ship came up alongside and we saw that the entire crew of the German ship was manning the rails, in their dress blues. They had made up a sign that was displayed on the side that read "We Stand By You."

Needless to say there was not a dry eye on the bridge as they stayed alongside us for a few minutes and we cut our salutes. It was probably the most powerful thing I have seen in my entire life and more than a few of us fought to retain our composure. It was a beautiful day outside today.

We are no longer at liberty to divulge over unsecured e-mail our location, but we could not have asked for a finer day at sea. The German Navy did an incredible thing for this crew, and it has truly been the highest point in the days since the attacks. It's amazing to think that only a half-century ago things were quite different, and to see the unity that is being demonstrated throughout Europe and the world makes us all feel proud to be out here doing our job. After the ship pulled away and we prepared to begin our man overboard drills the Officer of the Deck turned to me and said "I'm staying Navy." I'll write you when I know more about when I'll be home, but for now, this is probably the best news that I could send you.

Love you guys

Author unknown

ACKNOWLEDGEMENTS

As with history itself, it is often the case when writing a book that key persons are overlooked. Authors get one final opportunity to correct the record. I will use mine to thank the following people who have done so much behind the scenes to make this book a reality:

First, my wife, Melonee Ann Daniels, whose presence at my side is one of my life's great pleasures.

Second, my daughters Elizabeth, Nancy and Jennifer. A man may accomplish many things, but none are so great as being a father.

My colleague Duffrey Sigurdson, who helped enormously in making the writing and research a pleasure rather than a task.

It has been a great pleasure to have the opportunity to seek insight on global events and to receive the collective wisdom of some of America's finest military minds. I am indebted to the former Chief of Staff of the Army, General Dennis Reimer, U.S. Army Ret.; Vice Admiral J.D. McCarthy, USN; Vice Admiral Robert Conway Jr., USN; Major General Kevin Kuklok, USMC, Ret.; Brigadier General Mike Regner, USMC; and Colonel Dan Hokanson, National Security Fellow at Harvard University.

I would also like to thank my good friend Gordon Christofferson, who reviewed parts of the book as a work-in-progress and whose comments and suggestions were gratefully received.

Lastly, I would like to thank my publisher, Jo Blackmore, and her staff, including Graham Hayman. We have done well and I thank you for your hard work.

Stuart Franklin Platt

FOREWORD

GENERAL DENNIS REIMER
first served his country as
a young Lieutenant in the
Field Artillery. After a long
and distinguished career, he
retired from the U.S. military
as the 33rd Chief of Staff of
the United States Army.

War is about people – on the ground, in the air, on the sea – fighting for their country and their way of life. It has always been that way in the American military experience and it always will be. From Concord to Fallujah, the United States has been represented by her most precious assets, which are her sons and daughters. These men and women have emotions just like the rest of us. Often they are happy, sometimes sad; most of the time they laugh, sometimes they cry. They fear the unknown but they take pride in their accomplishments. Most return home physically uninjured but some bleed and some die. All leave a little of themselves, either emotionally or physically, on the battlefield and are changed – some forever.

Admiral Stuart Platt in his book *Letters from the Front Lines* has captured their emotions and their inner-most feelings by letting them do their own talking. These letters and emails from soldiers, sailors, airmen, marines and coast guardsmen do more than any analytical study or research project to show the reader what combat operations are all about. If you are looking for theory and tactics, this is not the book you need to read. But if you want to know what young people who are thrust into battle really think about and what is really important to them, then this collection is a must-read.

I must warn you that you will have to read the entire book in order to understand what these young warriors are telling you, but that's not difficult, because once you pick it up you are not going to want to put it down. Each letter, every email and piece of correspondence, is a story in itself. This is a collection of many stories, of which the whole is greater than the sum of the parts.

I was impressed with the troops' sense of history, the pride they took in what they were doing and their vision of the future. They were too involved with the task at hand to get involved in the debate of whether the policy was right. They were too busy taking care of each other – making sure they didn't let their buddies down – to worry about whether the policy makers had the troop strength right or not. They remembered yesterday but their focus was always on making tomorrow better.

In this remarkable compilation of letters from the front lines, Stuart Platt has told their story. When you read this book you'll understand better why the decision to go to war is so important. You'll understand why it is important to make sure that those we ask to do the nation's bidding are properly trained and equipped before we put them in harm's way. You will understand that Operations Enduring Freedom and Iraqi Freedom, like any other war, are really all about people. These letters from the front reinforce the fact that this is the finest military in our history and we owe them a great deal. Do yourself a favor and read this great book – and then thank them in your own way.

General Dennis Reimer, U.S. Army Ret.

INTRODUCTION

"It is my hypothesis that the fundamental source of conflict in this new world will not be primarily ideological or primarily economic. The great divisions among humankind and the dominating source of conflict will be cultural. Nation states will remain the most powerful actors in world affairs, but the principal conflicts of global politics will occur between nations and groups of different civilizations. The clash of civilizations will dominate global politics. The fault lines between civilizations will be the battle lines of the future."

Samuel Phillips Huntington, 1993

ON JUNE 7, 1776, RICHARD HENRY LEE, a delegate from Virginia to the Continental Congress, read a resolution before that Congress "that these United Colonies are, and of right ought to be, free and independent States, that they are absolved from all allegiance to the British Crown, and that all political connection between them and the State of Great Britain is, and ought to be, totally dissolved."

The founding fathers of our nation expanded on that resolution by ordering the drafting of a document that would lay out the case for independence. That document, penned by a committee consisting of Thomas Jefferson, Ben Franklin, John Adams, Roger Sherman and Robert Livingston, is the cornerstone of our Nation to this day. It is the Declaration of Independence.

On September 11, 2001, America was rocked to the very foundations by the senseless murder of 2948 innocent civilians. America, the bastion of freedom and independence for over two hundred years, had been attacked on home soil. It was not an attack by a dictator bent on world domination, nor the long dreaded attack from the Russian bear, nor was it a blindside from the Chinese, whom we have watched arming themselves far beyond their security needs and obligations. It was an attack by Muslim zealots who despise the freedoms that are personified by the Declaration of Independence.

Within hours, and with hearts still heavy with grief, our Commander in Chief and personnel from every branch of the military were preparing for the task that lay ahead. They are still engaged in that task today, and it is for their honor and the honor of our Nation that I am compelled to write this book.

This book records the lives and experiences of America's fighting men and women in a conflict that is playing out on a global stage, a stage that has included not only Iraq and Afghanistan, but New York, Madrid, London, Bali, and numerous other cities around the world. An extremist sect within one of the world's great religions fuels this clash. Their fundamentalist aspirations will not tolerate a free and open society. Their leaders, along with a global network of supporters, have sworn the destruction of America and that of Western society as a whole. While controversy may continue to surround America's actions or motivation behind the conflict that is recorded here, the underlying fact is this: war was declared on us and it has been waged against us on our own soil.

The Background

The fight to destroy the terrorists' camps and to liberate Afghanistan from the grips of Bin Laden and the Taliban marked the beginning of the current conflict. Following on from that effort was the campaign in Iraq, whose goals were to eliminate the threat of weapons of mass destruction and to liberate the Iraqi people from the horrors of the Ba'athist regime of Saddam Hussein. Our men and women in uniform executed both campaigns with exceptional skill. The missions assigned to each branch of the military at the outset of Operation Enduring Freedom and Operation Iraqi Freedom were achieved with great success, using far fewer forces than might have been optimal. Even so, the speed and ease with which the battle was won may have surprised even the most optimistic military and civilian planners.

As a result, in the period that immediately followed the war, we stumbled in both concept and action. This period of post-war chaos allowed the insurgency to build its strength and thousands of fanatics poured into

Iraq, especially over the porous borders of Syria and Iran, which served as a conduit for the insurgents. However, as the American military adapts to their tactics, the insurgencies in both Iraq and Afghanistan will become less of a destabilizing threat. The first post-conflict elections held in Iraq and Afghanistan have demonstrated that democracy can grow in both nations and this, too, has been a severe blow to both insurgencies.

As the people of both nations become accustomed to electing and removing their leadership peacefully at the ballot box, they will be exercising a newfound right of self-determination they will not easily relinquish. This momentum will likely be irreversible and may serve as an example to other nations that democracy is not only possible but also essential to peace and security in the region. The magnitude of those elections will be proven out over time, but they simply could not have happened without the commitment of the people of the United States and the presence of the U.S. Military.

Although allied nations have begun to carry more of the load in Afghanistan, along with the Afghans themselves, and while it is apparent that each day the Iraqi people and the seeds of democracy planted there grow stronger, it will be some years before we will be able to stand down our entire military force in either Iraq or Afghanistan. Iraq will certainly continue to need our assistance into the foreseeable future, and we will be in both regions for the near term at least.

The Iraq and Afghanistan war operations have placed great stress on our Nation and our Armed Forces and their families. Our resources, especially our human resources, will continue to operate under considerable strain for some time and the frequent call-up to active duty of the National Guard and Reserves has placed a real hardship on them. This conflict is a real-life lesson for those who commit our military to action, that you cannot do more with less. Nevertheless, there is no fear of failure among the returning soldiers and they are receiving the welcome they deserve and have earned. Their morale is high and their fighting spirit lives on.

The future challenge for our nation will be to sustain the effort to restore peace to Iraq and Afghanistan (and other emerging democracies), while simultaneously maintaining a high level of global readiness to meet other potential threats. The foundation of success in meeting this challenge will be, as always, built upon the courage and morale of our troops and the courage and morale of our nation.

Much of the Islamic extremism we are now seeing is not new; what is new is the ability of extremists to operate globally. The United States and her allies are taking a bite out of a very big apple in this war, and the impact of this effort, whether success or failure, will affect future generations for centuries to come.

There are some elements within Islamic society and within Islamic governments who use their position of influence to call on the Islamic people to wage Jihad against the West. This tactic of creating mass hysteria and inciting mobs to burn down embassies and attack Western-owned interests is a clear example of the total loss of reason on the part of those members of society whom the people in the region look to for leadership.

Past centuries have seen great clashes of culture; there have also been long periods of peace and prosperity where people of all faiths and backgrounds have flourished while living beside and working with one another. Prosperity alone did not, and will not, create that peaceful environment; it required freedom then just as it does now.

The problems in the region involve more than a clash of cultures. There is no denying that oil is a factor. Not only oil for America, but oil for Europe, Asia and the Middle East. Oil is an essential commodity for every country, rich or poor. If a large percentage of the readily available sources of that commodity are in the hands of extremists who would cut off that supply, it will be disastrous for not only the United States, but the entire world. So yes, oil is a factor. It is not, however, the underlying motivation for this war. The real issue is freedom.

Freedom can have a very broad interpretation, but in fact it is easily understood. Freedom is the condition of being free or unrestricted; the power of self-determination. The freedom of all people to live, work, and raise their families in peace is an essential element of global security.

Freedom of speech, freedom to elect a government, freedom to attend school, freedom from tyranny and oppression, and freedom to practice religion without persecution are some of the fundamental building blocks our Founding Fathers felt are the right of every human being. As we know it, freedom is a very rare commodity in the world today. This is especially true in states under the influence of Islamic extremists.

In a war of ideas and ideals, victory requires not only courage and resolve, it requires patience. As a nation we must always seek to forge ahead and settle for no less than victory, not only to ensure the safety and well-being of our own citizens, but also those of the oppressed millions who endure the harsh rule of extremist ideology.

Americans are not Crusaders – we fight to ensure the survival of the ideas and ideals that are the underpinnings of our society. This war is about the survival of freedom. We have no choice but to see it through.

The Media and the Importance of War Letters

The recording of day-to-day life during wartime is especially important in an era when network news has become more infotainment than solid news reporting; it is often difficult to discern from these sources what is really going on in Iraq and Afghanistan. Media will continue to report on this war and future wars, and rightly so, but the current style or trend of reporting as entertainment (as opposed to reporting in depth) is disturbing.

The concept that war letters are historical documents and as such should be preserved is not recent or original; in fact, the many collections from previous wars have led us to this book. Two unique aspects of this collection, however, are the dominance of email over handwritten letters for communicating from the frontlines, and the recent invention of "blogging." Both forms of communication are well represented in this book.

Email has had an especially important role in recording this history. For future generations, the sheer volume of material will provide a treasure trove of insights and accounts of day-to-day life during wartime. It would be impossible to do the material justice in a single volume. This book can only examine that small corner of the war that was experienced by its contributors.

Blogging is a very recent innovation of communication using the internet; the online "diary" of a soldier can be a very revealing look at the individual. Most bloggers are educated and very much at home in the cyber world. This tool of public correspondence caused some stir in the military, as they were quick to respond to concerns that the public nature of a blog would compromise operational security or privacy issues.

I am blessed by a circle of friends and colleagues whose broad experience and great insight is often shared with me. Many have sons and daughters who have been on the ground in Iraq and in Afghanistan and their experiences there, conveyed in hastily written letters and email, often fly in the face of what I see and hear reported in the mainstream media. The letters home to parents and loved ones speak only rarely of the horrors of combat, but always speak to the small victories of life, in a world most of us cannot even imagine. I am retired now from active military service and I know that one of the duties of those who serve and wait is to record the history and tell the stories for those who fight for their honor and for the benefit of future generations. It is my honor as well as my duty to do this and I have sought out those words, written by America's sons and daughters, which tell the story best.

It is often difficult in war to find words that can express our feelings, or to convey what one is seeing; letters home from our men and women on the front lines are usually hastily written and don't often speak of the war, and yet they tell so much more than can be readily seen. On the modern battlefield, email is now replacing the pen and paper, but the letters are still written in haste, and they are still composed in the moment. Each war letter home, from the earliest days of America until today, is a part of our national treasure.

Stuart Franklin Platt
Bainbridge Island, WA
April 29, 2006

BOOK ONE

Individual Letters

1

THE VIEW FROM HERE — PART ONE

Sgt. Chris McCarthy
United States Marine Corps
MALS-11, MAG-11, 3DMAW
Kuwait – Iraq
January 2003 – May 2003

I STOOD THERE IN AWE of the largest aircraft I had ever seen. I have been on plenty of commercial jetliners in my day, but none of them could hold a candle to this monster. The C-5, I'm told, is the *second* largest aircraft on the planet. Apparently the Russians have something slightly larger. Guess they won that aspect of the cold war. Good for them. This thing is big enough. Were it just slightly wider, you could play a football game inside quite easily. It's certainly plenty long enough. The whole nose and tail sections lift up completely, leaving an enormous hollow tube to load all the equipment in . . . and we get to ride in it.

I was lucky enough to be volunteered to help fill up the belly of the beast. We call it being "voluntold." In retrospect, I am quite glad to have had the opportunity . . . once. Pallet after pallet of equipment, containers, objects of all shapes and sizes were loaded on. It didn't seem to end. As we filled every last bare space, I was really at a loss for where they were going to stick another hundred Marines. Then one of the loadmasters scaled the wall and pulled down a retractable staircase. Yup, there

C5 GALAXY PREPARING TO LOAD CARGO. *Photo courtesy Department of Defense*

was more room on this bird. We all climbed upstairs into what was remarkably similar to your typical 747, though just a clump of seats in the middle with the aisles on the outsides instead of down the center. There was a reasonable amount of legroom, too. Rather cozy, to be honest. Not typical of Marines . . . and then I realized it was an Air Force plane. Yeah, that explains it.

About half an hour later we were in the air and I could finally relax a little. The past month had been rather hectic. We're leaving. We're staying. We're going now. Wait another week. Get down to the flight line now. Go back to the barracks. Okay, now we're going. Just kidding. Okay, for real this time. Hah, got you again. Go back to your rooms. It went on like this for what seemed like forever. I was expecting something along these lines, but not quite this bad. I felt bad for the families that had to keep saying "goodbye" to their loved ones over and over again. I kissed my girlfriend goodbye the first time they said we were going and then didn't call her again. I didn't want her to go through all this. I was still in the same set of cammies I had been wearing all week. I had to do the laundry the day before we left by wrapping a bed sheet around myself like a toga, since all of my personal items had been TMO'd (packed up in storage by the Transportation Management Office) and my seabags for the deployment were all palletized (stacked with other bags, sealed with cargo netting, and staged at the flight line). It's all over now, though. Now we can focus on what's ahead instead of getting ready for it.

We stopped for several hours in Newark, NJ, and then in Moron, Spain for a four-hour layover before landing in Kuwait City. I believe it was close to 36 hours after we had actually taken off from MCAS Miramar, San Diego, CA – where I've called home the past three years of my life. This was my first deployment, and as it turns out, the only deployment of my enlisted career. "Operation Iraqi Freedom." Rumor has it they had originally wanted to call it "Operation Iraqi Liberation," but decided the acronym wouldn't lead to very good public relations. Can't say I blame them.

In addition to being my first deployment, it was also my first time off the continent besides a high school trip to Europe and Hawaii, my birthplace. The Middle East was quite different. We had some culture training before we left (for example, never shake a man's left hand. They often don't have toilet paper and that's the lucky substitute. On the other hand, the average Kuwaiti is considerably more wealthy than the average American, thanks to all of their oil, and they contract all of their unpleasant work to the neighboring countries, such as Egypt and Pakistan), but most of it was largely unnecessary because I never left the base. There were some supply convoys that went out a lot, but I stayed within the confines of Al Jaber. Ahmed Al Jaber Air Force Base was the full name, officially a Kuwaiti installation with part of it designated for the use of the United States military and its allies. This was to be my home for the next three months and change. Of course, I didn't know this at the time. I was anticipating six months to a year.

We arrived the last couple days of January 2003, and it was actually pretty chilly. It got down to the low 40's at night. I didn't think I needed the required sweater on the gear list but it certainly got used. I knew it wouldn't last, though. This was most certainly a desert, and winter was almost over.

Before we even stepped foot off of the aircraft, we had already been briefed time and time again, in addition to our regular annual training, on every aspect of the entire Nuclear, Biological and Chemical threat, including the actual NBC suit itself, rubber boots and gloves, and our ever-present gas masks. Once we left the plane we never spent a moment without our gas masks within arm's reach of us. It didn't matter if we were going to the bathroom or even taking a shower, our masks were hanging on the hook of our shower stall. These were explicitly enforced direct orders from higher than I care to think of. Eventually you got used to it. It was our only defense, really. We didn't get rifles. We were told we were going into what would be considered a combat zone, where we would get hazardous duty pay, but we weren't issued rifles. Now you have to understand, a Marine without a rifle is like a quarterback without a football. What's the point? So I went to the Exchange before we left and bought myself a nice Kabar. I'm not facing the enemy barehanded if I have anything to say about it.

CHRIS MCCARTHY LOCKED AND LOADED IN IRAQ. *Photo courtesy Chris McCarthy*

★ *I could hear a clicking sound that lasted for about a half-second often . . .*
but otherwise the voice was clear as a bell asking who I was. I made a com-
ment about him *calling* me *. . . and then he said "it sounds like my mother"*
    Chris?
    "Yeah, hi from Kuwait!"
I could hear him grinning through the rest of the conversation that lasted
about 8 minutes.

    He was calling on a free DSN line the military uses for business to mili-
tary installations only. As we live on base . . . it was transferred home to me
in Dad's absence at the office.

    Otherwise, he could not have gotten through. He said he gets to make a
short call occasionally with the command blessings . . . if he can just get a
phone available.

    He and his roommate Brian Dickert are safe and sound . . . and he empha-
sized safe *out of any threat. He said they are doing* exactly *what they were*
told they would be doing, (setting up camps/construction, etc) and that he
packed smart for this adventure. They work hard & steady . . . but not long
hours . . . and carry gas masks everywhere . . . no exceptions. "Dunno why,
there's absolutely nothing going on to even think about needing them." (as
he says). They were also issued head gear right off to wear in the sand storm
environment . . . and he said it was presently blowing up a good one. His
nose was stuffy like a cold due to the atmosphere he told me . . . but otherwise
fine.

    He shares a tent with 16 Marines . . . and needs a set of computer speakers
of max volume to share his tunes he says . . . (off the minidisc player he bought
before going). After being a professional DJ in college he has quite a collec-
tion. I inquired about the Exchange store he was supposed to have there . . .
and he laughed with the comment it was made to service 1,500 and there
were about 8,000 there now. So he also noted that "AA batteries" would

---

★ AUTHOR'S NOTE: Carol McCarthy kept the family informed of any news
she received during her son Chris's deployment.

keep the world a nicer place as well when I could send them. He still does not have desert camouflage issued yet . . . but the forest green kind work just fine for now. I am to look for a large Camelback for him in desert camouflage color that carries as much water as possible (3 liter?). They are drinking all bottled water, all they want. Also said they have Hagen Daas ice-cream... and enjoying it mightily.

No doubt in his mind that the food is far better than what they received in California.

I asked about his roommate Brian and he said he was in great spirits and goofing around. Something about his taking a white T-shirt over his head wrapped and people calling him the green snake or some such. Beyond me what sillies they get into for kicks . . . he thought it was great. He said it was good work . . . and good pay for it. He also told me he would try Dad's office number again next Monday when they said he would be off travel.

It was about 8:30am this morning when he called . . . and it took precious time from us to get all the transferring done. The route they flew was from Calif to New Jersey where he called here collect and talked to brothers one night when we were still in Colorado. Then they flew on to Spain to refuel and then to Kuwait.

I am relieved to know he is happy with conditions . . . and work he is doing. He has always loved to get something accomplished . . . and it sounds like he feels productive. He also said he has absolutely no access to computers or email. The few on base are for USAF personnel . . . and only if they have a code to enter. His brother Matthew is forwarding word to his on-line friends here as we get news.

That's the report for today . . . and my mind is more at ease. Keep our troops in your prayers,

. . . one Marine's Mom

But we weren't there to do the jobs we trained for, either in boot camp or in our MOS school. We were 9916s. The 9916 Military Occupational Specialty is used to "designate a billet to which any enlisted Marine may be assigned but will not be assigned to an individual." This translates into plain English as "grunt-work." We're there to do all the odd jobs that nobody has a permanent job doing. Let me assure you . . . there were plenty.

When we arrived at camp, there were already tents in the process of being built. We were one of the first groups to arrive, but others had been here for a good while working 12 hour shifts to build "tent city" for us: large General Purpose tents with a wood floor and skeleton and the heavy-duty green fabric over the top. Each GP tent was roughly fifteen feet across by 25 feet long. That's smaller than a lot of people's living room. We fit fourteen Marines in each one. They separated them by rank, so as a mighty Lance Corporal (E-3) I was as low as it gets. There weren't enough Privates and PFC's to have separate tents for them. By the time you get to the squadron in an Aviation MOS, everyone is a Lance Corporal unless you got busted down. Unfortunately, my MOS was extremely slow to promote, so it would be quite a while before I would see Corporal.

Our first major job after we got situated was to lay down a landing field for the Harriers. This was the most important task we had the entire trip. Apparently the entire "shock and awe" campaign was waiting on us laying this field. Now the quick-set concrete the Seabees had used to build all the landing strips for the normal jets work great when the engines are pointed parallel to the runway, but Harriers need to aim them straight down for extended periods of time to both take off and land. This requires a special "AM-2 matting" that can withstand the temperature.

AM-2 fields are built by interlocking sections of 144 pound slabs that are twelve feet long by two feet across and about an inch and a half thick. Before they can interlock, the ground has to be perfectly compressed beneath them with a steamroller and then dug out and smoothed by hand to match the level of the previous one nearly perfectly. Ah, the joys of technology. We worked in two shifts "twelve on – twelve off" meaning we worked for twelve hours straight and then were relieved by the other crew working the other twelve. Now add in the hour drive there; another hour back; grabbing some food before we left and after we returned; our morning and evening formations to make sure everyone is accounted for and so the bigwigs can run their mouths; and you can imagine we didn't have a whole lot of time left in our day. We had the option of A) laundry, B) shower or C) sleep. After laying 144-pound mats for twelve hours straight and being quite rushed in doing so, you can imagine option 'C' was the big winner.

It took fourteen days to finish the field with over a hundred people working on each shift. Apparently, we set some silly records for the largest AM-2 field as well as the fastest laid. I certainly didn't care. I was just glad it was over. What wonderful task lies ahead now? It certainly couldn't be worse than this.

I was certainly wrong. Now some Marines got lucky. My friend John Barnum managed to somehow secure a position driving an air-conditioned shuttle bus around the base all day. Some of the other Marines were sent to supplement the Air Force with overall base security, which meant they moved into the Air Force's air-conditioned barracks with cable TV as well. That was about it, though. The rest of us were stuck in the heat in the GP tents. It didn't make it through February before we started watching the thermometers outside top out at 140 degrees before noon every day, and there was no shade. The only shade was inside a tent, which acted like an oven making it worse. The nights weren't much better. I thought deserts got cold at night. Apparently, not in Kuwait. It didn't drop below 90 at the lowest point of the night. You had the option of sleeping in shorts and being eaten alive by invisible mosquitoes or you could wear your cammies and be too hot to sleep. Many Marines were issued mosquito netting, but most of those had gaping holes in them. Still, it was usually worth it to figure out some way to tie up and seal off the holes just to get some rest. Then you had to deal with the inevitable sounds of one of the fourteen members of your tent snoring, but most of us were too tired to care at that point.

The next task I pulled was to build bomb shelters all around the base to house the "gazillion" new personnel we now had. This consisted of four concrete U-shaped blocks dropped upside down to form the shelter (two on each side), and then cover the top, sides, and make an entrance as well with sand bags. In reality, this job wasn't all that bad, though once again we were on a really tight schedule. We worked three crews, ten hours each (they overlapped a bit), so it wasn't quite as bad. All we had was our mighty entrenching tool, or "E-Tool" to shovel the sand into sandbags, and then we all stacked them on the concrete shelters. It took a lot longer than you might imagine. It took approximately one minute to get a sandbag from the stack of them, open it up, shovel all the sand in, and then tie it off with this horrid twine they came with. Sometimes if you teamed up you could do it quicker, but it usually ended up not working efficiently. Somebody was always waiting on somebody else and us dumb Marines just couldn't quite get it right. I would try to point out better ways to do things, but nobody wants to listen to a Lance Corporal trying to give orders. I can't say as I blame them. It didn't take me too long before I decided to stop wasting time and just got back to filling sand bags as fast as I could until somebody ordered me to help out another inefficient team until they realized it wasn't working and I went back to going solo again. Physically, it was the easiest job I had out there, but mentally it was so frustrating. It seemed like everyone was fighting with everyone else more than getting work done. Plus, the time away from home had already begun to wear on some Marines, and they decided to start throwing rocks at other people that were filling sandbags to amuse themselves. The people working alone were the biggest target, and that meant me. The gravity of the situation was too hard to comprehend for them: we only had enough bunkers to protect 20% of the personnel on the base. At any point a successful attack would have left 80% of us completely unprotected. That was enough motivation for me to work harder, but the heat and work was just too much for a lot of them.

Out at the bunkers was not the only time the childishness of some of the men came out. Whenever we actually got a few moments of free time to ourselves, it was like little children at play. Some of these guys never grew up, I guess. One Marine was taking a shower when a duo decided to steal his shoes from him and run back to the tent with them.

They had extremely rocky gravel down before setting up all the tents to aide in liquid run-off and other reasons. This poor sap had to walk barefoot on those sharp rocks back to the tent, howling all the way. He threw a thirty-pound case of bottled water across the entire tent at no one in particular when he got back. He wasn't a small fellow.

Even I lost my cool once. One of the guys enjoyed flipping other people's cots over when they were sleeping in them, so I thought I'd show him how great it felt, though I wasn't going to flip it, just threaten to. Maybe it would be enough for him to stop. Apparently he was ready for this, and slept with a full two-foot long Mag-lite. When his cot started to move he pulled it out and knocked me upside the head with it. I stood there in shock for a brief moment that anyone would strike someone else, much less a fellow Marine, with such a weapon for nothing more than moving their cot, especially after they had done the same to so many before. That moment didn't last long, however, as I quickly grabbed the Mag-lite with lightning speed with the intent of wrenching it out of his hands and beating him to death with it. Lucky for him, he could see the fire in my eyes and held on to it for dear life as the other ten Marines or so in the tent all leapt on me at once. I was promptly subdued. Nothing became of the matter, but I never forgave him for the incident . . . at least not until several years later.

After three weeks sandbagging, I was about to lose my mind when they finally did a rotation of jobs. This time, the illustrious chow hall was the job that I managed to pull out of the imaginary hat. This was run by some senile Master Sergeant that apparently gave up sleeping years ago. He decided to use some clause in some rulebook somewhere that said he could work us eighteen hour shifts for a week during war-time if necessary for operational success. Then after the week was up we'd get perhaps a couple days working a 12 hour shift and then it was back to eighteen hour shifts again. In case you didn't get a chance to try out the wonderful "Math for Marines" course we all take, that leaves six hours total for bathing, laundry, and sleep. And working at the chow hall is not a walk in the park, nor is it only during meal times that work needs to be done. As soon as we finished cleaning up and everything that needed to be done from one meal, we were immediately getting ready for the next. Since work shifts ran all day and all night on the base, Marines needed to be fed all day and all night. We got to feed them. Oh joy.

My particular position was the "stocker." I would ensure that there was milk in the milk machines; soda in the soda machines; juice in the big reefers; bread in the bread machine; coffee, creamer, chocolate in the coffee machine; ice in the ice machine; and water in nearly every machine. The water had to be manually dumped from large five gallon drums outside. The water in Kuwait wasn't potable – we had crate after crate of bottled water brought in. We couldn't even brush our teeth with it. This complicated things immensely.

There were also other side items to keep replenished, specific to each meal, like peanut butter and jelly at lunch and yogurt for breakfast. Sometimes we'd get something special, like Starbucks cappuccino drinks one day and Snapple another. It was surprisingly extravagant, for an enormous tent in the middle of the desert. That's all the chow hall was – this large pink dome that was designed to be a portable hangar bay for a KC-130. They decided it would make a good chow hall. I thought they should change the last vowel to an 'e'.

So if you can imagine a tent large enough to fit the Marine Corps' largest personnel transport plane into, that was filled completely with Marines at every single meal, then you can guess how many people we fed . . . and I had to keep them all happy. I learned later that the stocker position is usually for four people in a much smaller chow hall. I was doing it all by myself. By the end of the first week I had a system down, though, and by the end of the second, it became a sixth sense to me. It was almost scary how I knew exactly what level everything was at without even checking it. My ears were so tuned in that I could hear the "fsssshh" of the soda machine as it ran out of syrup from the other side of the building. I could go run to the large trailers outside to grab the chocolate mix and run back in just as the first pilot was going "Hey, where's my café latte? I can't fly my mission without my hot café latte!" That might sound cynical, but in reality, the only way I kept myself sane was to keep telling myself that even the tiniest little thing that could keep one of them more focused on the task at hand was important enough for me to bust my tail end over. By the way, that Nestle coffee machine was incredible. You would not imagine how many different combinations of hot beverages you could make with just coffee, creamer, and chocolate mixes, all readily available at the touch of a button … but I digress. The fun is yet to come.

After the first two weeks of just our gas masks at our side, we were required to carry our entire NBC suits with us to be no more than fifteen minutes walking distance from them (much quicker running). We had a few drills as well, spending two hours with our gas masks on one day to encourage "confidence" in them, and "This is only a test. Alarm Red. MOPP level four," echoing from the loud speakers posted around the base from time to time. We all knew what it meant. Anybody could call it at any time, not just the speakers. You hear that, you put on your trusty gas mask as you're running to the bunkers, and then your full NBC suit goes on after that. Drill after drill, we get the point. We never really expected to use it. We were way off in Kuwait.

Chris said this is his last phone call … and there is some anticipation in his voice as well. It was hooked up between his Dad at work and us at home … so he spoke to everyone.

He says former roommate Brian needs that Arabic to English translation book more than ever these days. He sees very little of him as they are working in separate areas, and have been from shortly after they arrived. They can always use batteries that sell out fast in the NEX as well. Care packages are always welcome by all in the Group … from anyone! Send assortments of stuff … and anything is great, just avoid things that can melt down. Everyone needs "AA" batteries and the small maglite bulbs for those flashlights that take AA batteries are needed by most of them as well. Chris is still set with batteries sent by friends for now, but none would go to waste … and is waiting for the adaptor plugs we are shipping for using his systems on electrical hook-ups. It will be 4-5 weeks before he gets these however.

They are no longer allowed outgoing mail . . . but receive mail regularly. Initially written letters are already on their way from a couple weeks or more ago . . . but expect no more from them. We have rec'd nothing from him in the mail yet. Daytime temps are about 85 . . . with night down to 40's. He works the night shift, and is fine with that. He says he is the Camp Chess Champ presently . . . and tells his brother to prepare for a true contest when he gets home. Reading materials would be welcome for most of them, but he has no time for anything but his bible right now, which he is reading in earnest. He enjoys the Protestant Chaplain, who is teaching about the world in which they are working, and the history that put them there. To hear it without the media hype is refreshing to him, and he is learning. He is content enough about his work, with tough conditions, although he misses his computer immensely and friends back home. He dreads losing the phone calls home, as it is easier than writing by far. Not to worry he says, all is well. We aren't worrying . . . we're praying for all of our troops.

:o] Carol and Family

Then on Friday, March 21st, 2003, the "shock and awe" campaign began. We rocked the capital of Baghdad early that morning, before the sun came up. We actually had TV's in the chow hall, which were all tuned to Fox News, so we got to see what was going on. It's kind of sad to be getting our news from the TV no sooner than everyone back at home when we're in the combat zone, but we'll take what we can get. Breakfast was quite a buzz as we watched the explosions on TV, but everything kept going as normal. Lunchtime rolled around and we had just opened our doors about fifteen minutes ago when my highly-trained ears picked up a faint something over the roar of the full chow hall: " . . . red. MOPP level four. This is not a drill." I froze . . . why was I the only one freezing? The entire chow hall is full with over three hundred people, and I am the only one that heard this? Maybe I'm just hearing things . . . "I repeat: Alarm Red. MOPP level 4. This is not a drill." Still nothing. I'm the only one frozen. I heard it though, no doubt about it. At the top of my lungs, with the loudest Marine Corps voice this six-foot five-inch 250 pound Marine could muster, I screamed "ALARM RED!!!" They heard that. It was as though a rock had been lifted from over an ant-hill. Everyone immediately dropped what they were doing and scattered to find their NBC suits and get to the bunkers. I watched the ensuing chaos that I had created for at least five seconds before I realized, 'Oh yeah, that means me, too." I threw on my gas mask, ran for the table behind the extra juices where I kept my NBC suit, grabbed it and ran.

Thankfully, they had enough bunkers built by the time this all came about. I started to shimmy my way into my NBC suit while hunched over in the bunker as the air raid sirens kept blaring. I finally got my pants on by the time the sirens shut off. The gargantuan rubber boots and jacket took longer than I expected, and about fifteen minutes later I finally had my gloves on. Hmm, that was supposed to take two minutes. I'm going to have to work on that. As we sat there, I could tell one of the female Marines that worked in the chow hall with me was having a hard time. She was borderline on freaking out, and apparently, I was the only one that could see this. I talked to her in a calm, nonchalant tone and kinda made fun of her about freaking out – it was what she needed because she started to calm down. She did admit she was really nervous and I reassured her that Saddam is probably a bad shot anyway.

Turns out I was right. We had another four air raid sirens that day, and then one every hour all night long that night, but not a single one hit the base. Some of them went off into the ocean, others landed in the middle of the unpopulated desert, and the few that were actually on target got demolished by our patriot missile batteries. The only one that got close enough for us to see was hit with three different patriots – the first destroyed the missile, and the other two homed in on fragments of the remains. Man, those things are accurate. I sure felt safe after seeing that.

There was an occasional alarm red here and there throughout the next week or so, but it was nothing like the first night. We didn't get any sleep that night. I decided that was the strategy. He knew he couldn't hit us, so if he weakened us by forcing us to skip meals and sleep by diving for bunkers it was worth it. Too bad he vastly underestimates Marines if he thinks we can't snag an MRE on the run or go one night without sleep.

News at long last! The lines are finally back up again . . . and busy. Chris called at 6:30am our time to wake us on a Sunday morning . . . and so good to hear from him. He is fine . . . and receiving lots of mail and packages recently. A package from his Aunt Kyle's 4th grade class arrived 3 days ago finally . . . and he said there were pictures he liked and gum he shared, and mail!

He tries to answer what he can . . . but is falling behind with the very small breaks he gets. He says packages are coming in each week . . . and people are jealous . . . but since he shares it all with others . . . it is such a blessing. (for all) Sure makes life a nicer place with all of that . . . and he is not in a hurry to come home. We think he is happy with the high pay . . . and he is busy . . . which appeals to him.

They basically work him most all the time . . . with sleep, a long hike to shower, long chow lines . . . well . . . you get the idea. He does not have free time to amount to much. We know he plays chess when he can . . . and holds some sort of status as a top chess player. He sees his roommate, Brian D. from California often and says he is smiling and happy. They don't live in the same tent.

He gave us a "family only" email address . . . but there are only 3 machines in the area . . . so when others find out they can do that he suspects it to get busy and hard. He says it is hitting 110 degrees now . . . but he is still doing fine with it. He is still working the chow hall logistics . . . and may still be night shift . . . don't know.

Our call was cut off before finishing this morning . . . about half-way through the normal 12 min time. Dan rolled back over to sleep . . . but here I am.

Mail can be sent out again . . . but no one should be in a hurry to get it . . . as plenty of time goes by before it arrives on the mainland. (5 wks when we got a letter). He sounded in great spirits . . . some of that is the excitement of getting through after such a long time. He is very grateful for all the mail and packages from all points. Anything I hear I will pass on as I can. He says he is not needing anything in particular right now . . . what with the package stuff he has received. I'll keep everyone posted.

Take care . . . and a special thanks to all who sent things out to him . . . it is such a lift. It is not bad to be the envy of camp . . . with everyone watching to see what may come next to brighten their day as well. He loves to help others . . . so this gives him a real lift personally. It makes a difference . . . trust in that.

God bless all for their thoughts and prayers for all over there. Keep it up for them all as time gets old, and routines get harder to handle, they will need it. Thanks from us . . . and we'll keep the notes coming.

So many have inquired often . . . and it is appreciated.

Hugs to all, Carol and Dan (and especially Chris!)

I spent nearly two months at that beloved chow hall, until a salty old Master Gunnery Sergeant with a thick New York accent by the name of Suarez rescued me. He was always the first one in at 0400 to grab a cup of solid espresso and talk to me, his caffeine source, about how he'd managed to trade a tire for a hundred feet of coax cable, or a couple crates of two by fours for an air-conditioning unit. Where he got the tire or the crate in the first place was always a mystery, but this man was incredible. He could turn one completely useless thing into something extremely useful better than anyone I had ever seen in my life. He worked in G-6, which hooked up all the computers and network for the base. I mentioned my background in computing and he decided he had a much better use for me than working in the chow hall. He pulled the strings that only the most senior enlisted in the Marine Corps can pull and I finally said goodbye to that place, and moved into a cushy job setting up computers. Basically, my job turned into creating computers out of old junk that the Air Force had thrown out so that we could use them. This meant we had the most high-tech equipment out there. I actually got to watch a few DVDs on a small projection screen on my time off. Unfortunately, I only got to enjoy that job for a few days before the "shock and awe" was over. It was time to go home.

Just a quick note to let everyone know that Chris is scheduled to return on May 15th.

He is wishing he could stay on . . . but not likely he says. He plans to get some eye adjustments done surgically once back so he can put in for the aviation opportunities the Marine Corps offers to officers. His one eye needs only a slight adjustment to be eligible . . . it is not laser.

Any packages that have not arrived thus far will probably get to him before he leaves . . . or catch up once he is home. At any rate . . . they can still be shared with others.

His old address is San Diego . . . and we'll send that along once we know for sure it is a working one. He has so appreciated the mail and packages in an otherwise miserable atmosphere . . . about which we hear little for complaints (You've read that much).

About 3 1/3 weeks left . . . and he will be back to his computer and friends stateside.

His Dad sends notes to him every other day or so now . . . so nice to be back in touch.

I am grateful for those on the front lines who are able to reach home again. Theirs has been the toughest wait . . . and my prayers have been with all of them.

"Happy Easter" as we celebrate His love for us, and the blessings shared with all.

It is a sunny, bright morning here . . . with forsythia, tulips and daffodils blessing our yard. Trees are all tipped with color as they push forth again in splashes of color.

Temps are due to reach 80 today . . . we just don't seem to experience spring *anymore . . . but go directly to summer feel. *sniff* Have a wonderful week . . . and blessings to all.*

Hugs, Carol and family . . . which includes my brother-in-law and his daughter (my niece) this weekend. :o) Happy family days! Daze? Ah well.

I shipped out of there the first week of May. A lot of Marines had to stay longer, but most of us back in the states by mid-May. Not even a week went by before we had all our things out of TMO's storage, and life was pretty much back to normal ... though I certainly appreciate it a lot more. Those late nights at work don't seem quite so long, these little barracks rooms seem considerably roomier, and the cool breeze of southern California's summers has never felt so good.

Christopher N. McCarthy
Sergeant, United States Marine Corps
MALS-11, MAG-11, 3DMAW
MCAS Miramar, San Diego, CA

2

LAW & ORDER

Captain Brian Baldrate
3d ACR U.S. Army
Al Anbar Province, Iraq
May 2003 – March 2004

MAY 2003

Hey everyone – hope you all are doing well. We just recently got up limited email service so I figured I would send an update. Iraq is certainly an interesting place and I have had the opportunity to do some unique stuff since I have been here. As we drive through Iraq many of the people (especially children) smile and wave --- most are thrilled to be free from Saddam. That being said others aren't so happy with U.S. forces arrival so we also have our share of rocks and bricks fired from slingshots mixed in with the smiles and waves to keep things exciting. In the early days there was lots of gunfire and occasional grenades but in general things are calming down quite a bit, and other than convoys life is pretty safe. After a few weeks in the very harsh desert we have moved onto slightly nicer confines. We are currently living in one of Saddam's blown-up palaces just west of Baghdad on the Euphrates river.

Lest you think life is too luxurious the place was bombed and looted almost to oblivion. There is no running water, electricity, furniture, light fixtures, faucets, windows, doors, etc. Looters even smashed all of the porcelain in the bathrooms, and removed much of the marble off the floors. I guess they figure Saddam owed them that much. For us at least there is a roof over our head and some protection from the beating sun.

While my original "legal" mission focused mainly on rules of engagement and who we could and couldn't shoot we are now doing a lot of other quasi-legal work. We spent a few days working at the Coalition Forces detainee camp interrogating people in order to try and determine if the detainees were soldiers, innocent civilians, criminals or something else. We saw everything – Iraqi Colonels who worked on Weapons of Mass Destruction, 14 year old Syrian kids who crossed the border to support the Jihad, and even a Baghdad garbage man whose boss made him work during the attack – he was collecting trash when he got shot in the butt. Seems "the man" is always keeping someone down!

Additionally we spent some time helping work out the terms of the surrender of an Iranian terrorist group (MEK) living in our area. Lately we are moving on to the more daunting challenge of helping restore law and order. This involves everything from helping establish procedures to control looting, to sitting down with judges, prosecutors, and members of the Iraqi bar association in order to assess their legal system, monitor their prisons, and begin to get the courts up and running. This has many challenges including security, interpreters, and separating the judicial system from the Ba'ath party who heavily controlled it. Needless to say with our limited resources we are more like a band-aid on the problem until groups like OHRA, the state department, and the UN become more actively engaged. It is interesting work nonetheless; kind of like an urban renewal project on a massive level.

Due to security there is not much leisure activity so when we are not working we spend our time baking in the 110°+ sun, swatting flies and mosquitoes, waiting for mail to arrive, and speculating about how quickly we will return home. (Rumors run everywhere from an August return to late 2004 after attacking Iran, Syria and the rest of the Middle

East. We, of course, are hoping for the former but who knows. Being a lawyer gets us out of some of the worst taskings like all night guard duty, or worse yet, burning human feces…our younger paralegals aren't always so lucky…

Oh well, I hope everyone is doing well. While we don't expect email to be too consistent neither is the mail system so feel free to try either one. Take care and God Bless.

Brian

JUNE 2003

Hello everyone,

I thought I would send out another update on life in Iraq. For me, and I think most of us "Iraqi Freedom" has been characterized by both incredible emotional highs and absolute rock-bottom lows. The low points stem mostly from the lack of safety, security, and comfort here. Some days it really does feel like we are living in a Mad Max film. During some weeks not a night goes by without machine gun fire or RPG attacks. Staff officers like me remain relatively safe, although the last RPG attack on our compound hit about 20 meters from where we sleep and gave us all quite a scare. Others are not so fortunate and it's been extremely difficult watching dozens of soldiers, officers, and friends in my unit get killed or injured over the last few weeks. Not to mention the many other troops who have died or been injured since "major combat" ended back in April. Add that to the relentless heat, awful living conditions, and uncertainty of when we will return home, and at times morale runs pretty low.

That being said there are days when our work is not only exciting, but somewhat valuable as well. In recent weeks we have been investigating numerous war crimes and allegations. One incident involved the arrest of several Iraqis illegally transporting over 200 RPGs and grenade launchers in an Iraqi ambulance. Another involved the murder of one of our soldiers by an Iraqi civilian at a traffic control point. It appears the Iraqi pulled up to the checkpoint asking for a doctor because his friend was injured. When our young sergeant turned away to shout for a medic the Iraqi shot him in the head and then sped off before being chased down and captured by our troops. While we are still working out the when and where of these trials (Iraqi court, court martial, military tribunal, international court, etc.) investigating these cases helps keep me busy and aware of the gravity of our current situation.

Working with the judges and lawyers in getting the Iraqi courts up and running is also fascinating, and frustrating work. My unit, the Third Armored Cavalry Regiment, is occupying (pronounced "liberating") the Al Anbar Province, which is the largest province in Iraq. It spans from 30 miles west of Baghdad, all the way out west to the Syrian and Jordanian borders. Because of the huge space and difficulty of traveling, getting the justice system up and running has been a full time job. It is a strange experience going to work with Iraqi lawyers, judges, and clerks while wearing a bulletproof vest, a Kevlar helmet, and wielding an automatic weapon. Nonetheless, we are making some slow and steady progress. One recent example is a murder case we are working on. The murder occurred in April when no police, hospitals, or other government services were up and running. As a result the family buried the body without an autopsy or a death certificate. In order to get the case moving this week we had the judge order the exhumation of the body, met with the family, had the body dug up and transferred to the local morgue. Today we supervised the autopsy, which determined a single gunshot wound to the back was indeed the cause of death. Needless to say this was not a pleasant task on a 3 month old body in a country that doesn't use any embalming procedures. In any event, the coroner's report is done and the case should go to trial next week.

We try to find time to balance our local law and order missions with more relaxing and intellectual pursuits. To that end we attend weekly meetings up in Baghdad with the Coalition Provisional Authority (CPA), the interim government led by Ambassador Bremer. Saddam's main palace, where CPA is headquartered, is stunningly beautiful and full of amenities we are without like running water, hot meals, and air conditioning! They also have celebrities come to their palace including most recently Robert De Niro and Alyssa Milano. Additionally, CPA's Ministry of Justice is busy working on long-term judicial solutions like revamping the Iraqi criminal code, establishing a war crimes tribunal, and drafting a new Iraqi constitution. The weekly meeting is a welcome break for me from the daily chaos of life out in the field and I think having CPA hear about the less exalted aspects of justice-building like performing an autopsy without soap, or finding a generator to power the jailhouse lights helps keep their perspectives in check as well.

Anyway, I hope everyone is doing well. Thanks to all of you who have sent email, cards, letters, and packages or simply kept me in your thoughts. I can't express how much your thoughts and letters all mean, especially in light of recent rumors that our return home is not as fast-approaching as we had previously hoped (Christmas is the latest rumor). Please feel free to email this letter to any friends whose email address I forgot or do not have. I also enclosed my address below because I have received some delayed letters that were sent to the wrong APO address. Again thanks for all your support and take good care. I hope to see all of you before too long.

Sincerely, Brian

JULY 2003
Hello again,

Thought I would send out the latest update. Life here in Iraq remains steady, but still quite violent. Regrettably, this past week alone our unit has lost two more soldiers, and suffered almost a dozen more injuries. One of those killed was a fellow captain and friend from Colorado. Additionally, the nightly rocket propelled grenade attacks on our base have lately turned into mortar attacks, which are both louder and a bit more lethal. While I had been sleeping outside to catch whatever breeze the Euphrates river offered, the nightly attacks have moved me inside our cement "palace" for the time being. Other than the mortars, life on the base camp is slowly improving. A civilian contract team built us a dining facility so we have at least one real meal a day. They are also working on eventually trying to install electricity and air conditioning, which would be a blessing.

The death of Saddam's sons was of course an encouraging development, and although you hate to describe any killing as positive, I imagine few will shed tears for these two men in particular. Of course it is proving difficult to convince regular Iraqis that the Hussein brothers are dead and for that reason alone we would have been better off capturing them. In any event their death demonstrated some much-needed progress in what has often felt like a string of near misses and partial let downs. Our unit had such an experience a few weeks back when we thought we had identified and killed Saddam, himself. It happened around midnight one night at our tactical operation center (TOC) where we were briefed on the 'positive' identification of Saddam and his escorts driving in our area towards the Syrian border. Over the next several hours our troops raced toward the border while we staff officers huddled around satellite imagery advising the commander on different courses of action including bombing the vehicles with air strikes, sending troops into Syria, and countless other issues. It is hard to describe the emotion we experienced when the commander gave the order to "engage and destroy Saddam Hussein" but it was certainly unlike anything I have ever felt. Of course subsequent evidence indicating that whomever we engaged that night was probably not Saddam brought equally sobering emotions.

The legal work remains quite a challenge as we seem always to be taking one step forward and two steps back. For example, recently we hired several hundred new policemen in the town of Ar Ramadi (where I live) and had been helping teach new Iraqi criminal laws. One afternoon, less than an hour after we left the police station and the courthouse, a bomb went off at the station killing 8 Iraqi police recruits and injuring over 50 more.

Not surprisingly many of our remaining police recruits quit. Similarly, last week in Al Haditha (another town where our 3d ACR troops live and work) the mayor and his two sons were murdered for their cooperation with our soldiers. I think these two incidents personify how difficult it is for Iraqis to align themselves with coalition forces and demonstrate how hard it is for us to help the Iraqis restore peace, law, and order.

We also supervised Ar Ramadi's first criminal trial last week – a murder trial. It was also a mixture of good news/bad news. Iraqi law right now is a combination of an old Iraqi criminal code with recent coalition modifications. For example, our recent changes require that the accused have a defense attorney, and prohibit the use of torture to obtain confessions. Well, an hour into our first trial the newly appointed Iraqi defense attorney requested the judge throw out the confession because the police obtained it by pulling out the accused man's finger and toenails! (Nice country, huh.) Anyway, the legal dilemma was that the "confession" happened prior to the adoption of the coalition policy against torture. Our Iraqi judge (with our prodding) wisely decided to delay the trial and have a doctor examine the allegations and extent of the injuries ... More to follow.

Well, I guess that is all the highlights I have for now. I have been sending out this letter by group email as internet access is very limited and I often don't have time to write back everyone who writes me. I assume some people have been forwarding my email to others as I have received several nice letters or emails from people I do not know, which is incredibly kind. At the same time the intent of these letters is certainly not to clog up anyone's email so if you wish, please feel free to email me back requesting to unsubscribe. Thanks & take care.

Brian

AUGUST 2003

Hello again, I hope everyone remains well. Life in Iraq remains fast and furious. On a positive note our living conditions are finally getting better.

AN UNUSUAL BUT HEARTFELT ANNIVERSARY WISH FROM IRAQ FOR CHRISTY BALDRATE.
Photo courtesy Captain Brian Baldrate

We got air conditioning into our work areas this week, which was much needed as temperatures have been in the 130s with lows often around 90 degrees at night. Sadly the AC in the workspace hasn't prevented us from losing a couple of soldiers out on patrols due to heat-related deaths. But between the air-conditioned building and the mess hall serving 3 meals a day our life is pretty tolerable. Our biggest difficulty living wise was the recent attack on the oil pipeline contaminating the Euphrates river (our water supply) for a while. Even that is slowly returning to normal.

The atmosphere here remains somber as 5 soldiers have died and several more have been injured (including 3 guys losing their legs) in our unit since I last wrote. Despite this, the recent headlines are on the many other victims who've lost their lives in recent weeks—the Jordanian Embassy and UN Headquarters bombings, the mortar attack on the Iraqi prison, and the recent shooting of a journalist by one of our troops. This week I flew to the Abu Ghraib prison where 6 Iraqi prisoners were killed and 59 injured when mortar rounds hit their prison. Why fellow Iraqis are shooting mortars at an Iraqi prison is beyond me ... Maybe they're warning the prisoners against cooperating with US forces? In any event, we checked on the conditions of the prisoners and helped ensure the families were being notified about the dead and wounded.

Later that day, as I left Abu Ghraib, outside the front gate one of the Regiment's soldiers (and a friend of mine) mistook a journalist with a camera for an enemy with an RPG and shot and killed him. We currently have the unenviable task of investigating this high profile incident. These tragedies create defensiveness and anxiety amongst our soldiers, as no one likes being second-guessed on split-second life or death decisions. At the same time it is understandable that when an innocent journalist dies people demand answers and want accountability. Trying to ensure this investigation is neither a "witch hunt" nor a "white wash" is one of the least enjoyable tasks I am working on in Iraq.

Down at the Ramadi courthouse my Iraqi judges finally started working hard and pushed forward a case to trial. Of course the case they pushed forward was by an Iraqi farmer against Donald Rumsfeld for $200 million dollars alleging his wife, 10 children, 7 grandchildren, and 100 sheep were killed in a Coalition bombing attack during the war. Of course, I needed to get the case dismissed because the Iraqi courts lack jurisdiction over the Secretary of Defense (or any coalition forces), but we are trying to verify if his claim is true and if so, find another way to compensate him. No matter, this is a scenario where everybody loses.

This new Iraqi Central Criminal Court, a nationwide Iraqi-run court established by Ambassador Bremer to prosecute Iraqis committing war crimes, made history this week. The court tried its first ever case and for the first time U.S. soldiers testified in Iraqi court. Fortunately for me it was the case I investigated where our guys caught 3 Iraqis transporting over 500 rockets and missiles in a hospital truck. Watching the trial we were thrilled when the Iraqi judges convicted all three men of weapons trafficking, which carries a minimum 7 year sentence. Thus you can imagine our surprise when the judges somehow sentenced one man to 1 year in jail and the other two to 6 months! Turns out the judges claim to have "misunderstood" the new coalition laws making the maximum punishment for possession of a weapon 1 year, but keeping the punishment for weapons distribution between 7-10 years. The notion that these guys will be back on the streets again selling RPGs within months, while we are still here protecting Iraq, doesn't sit well – especially with the troops out doing raids everyday. I guess it just further highlights the difficulties that exist in turning over Iraq too quickly to the Iraqis. That is about all of an update I have for now. I look forward to the time when Iraq is calm enough that I having nothing more significant to write about than the mundane details of daily life in the desert. Better yet will be when we get word on our return date home. Maybe next month we will know more, if as the Iraqis say, Insha Allah (God's willing).

Take Care, Brian

SEPTEMBER 2003
Greetings,

Sorry I haven't got a chance to write sooner but life this past month seems busier then usual. It seems every day our guys are involved in a half-dozen attacks. The other week as I was flying on a Blackhawk to a meeting in Baghdad we flew right over an army truck that just got hit by an improvised explosive devise (IED). As we circled helplessly in the helicopter we watched the Iraqis scatter, the soldiers evacuated, and the vehicle burn to the ground in flames. Returning home that next night we were greeted with the horrific scene of the mangled body of a suicide bomber who blew himself up at the Ramadi university we were guarding; miraculously only injuring two soldiers. That same week troops discovered a large cache of high tech "suicide vests" equipped with a backup device that detonates if an Iraqi raises his hands as if to surrender.

It is hard to describe the toll these attacks and these techniques leave on the psyche. It takes deliberate effort to not harden your heart too much and try to convince yourself that the vast majority of Iraqis disapprove of these attacks as much as we do. Still, the frequency of such attacks in the towns where we live, and around the very people we help everyday, can't help but make our soldiers suspicious of everyone. This uneasiness and uncertainty has led to an increase in accidental killings, and over the past month our troops have accidentally shot journalists, school children, and even Iraqi policemen. These killings are not only tragic but create an increasing cycle of violence and revenge killings. The worst incident occurred last week as our guys were turning over the town of Fallujah to a new unit from the 82d Airborne Division. The 82d, who was unfamiliar with the neighborhood, mistakenly shot and killed 10 Iraqi police and a Jordanian hospital guard. This incident, the worst fratricide in Iraq so far, has further deteriorated our already tense relationship with the locals.

The good news, at least for my unit, the 3d ACR, is that after 6 pretty intense months in the heart of the Sunni Triangle this past week we packed up our bags and moved out further west. Sadly it wasn't west toward the United States but rather deeper into the Iraqi desert to concentrate more of our forces on the Syrian and Jordanian borders. In doing so we moved out of our tattered palace and into a modern Iraqi air force base that is complete with buildings, air conditioning, electricity, and even running water. Showering every day, even with only cold water, goes a long way toward boosting morale. It was actually difficult leaving Ramadi and the courthouse behind after having invested so much time and energy building trust with the locals and making progress with the courts. Luckily, there is still plenty of legal work to be done in the towns of Ruhtbah, Hit, Haditha, and Al Qaim still under our unit's control. In fact, for those of you who can tolerate magazines with scantily clad women, there is a great article on the 3d ACR, and our border mission, in September's issue of Maxim.

Well, as always, I have probably written too much. We're hopeful that the new move out west brings not only an improved quality of life, but a continued decrease in the violence and attacks in western Iraq. We will see.

CAPTAIN BRIAN BALDRATE WITH SOME OF THE LETTERS OF SUPPORT HIS UNIT RECEIVED FROM SCHOOL CHILDREN. *Photo courtesy Captain Brian Baldrate*

Again, thanks to all of you who are sending letters, cards, emails, and packages. They are all greatly appreciated even if I don't always have time to reply. Hope you all remain safe, healthy and very well. I look forward to seeing everyone before too long.

Brian

OCTOBER 2003

Happy Halloween! Hope everyone is doing well and enjoying autumn. While there are no leaves or fall foliage to enjoy out here, temperatures dropping down to highs in the 80s and lows in the 60s has been blessing enough. While we are grateful to be out of Ramadi and Fallujah and the worst parts of the Sunni Triangle, we are finding our mission out west towards Syria equally challenging.

Lately Iraqis and foreign terrorists have intensified their efforts to attack both coalition forces and those cooperating with us. Recent attacks against the Red Cross, the Iraqi Ministries, and the Al Rashid Hotel (the hotel where I stay when I go to Baghdad) vividly make that point. Out where we work, we have seen increased resistance mainly in Al Qaim, a major border crossing into Syria. Just weeks after a new Iraqi Police Chief took over and actually started arresting criminals, he was gunned down in broad daylight. In the days following his murder the police station was attacked by armed men in masks threatening to kill anyone caught cooperating with US forces. Despite enormous efforts by our guys to control the situation, many of the Iraqi police have quit or refuse to work, and not a day has gone by without our soldiers or the police station being attacked with bullets, rocket propelled grenades (RPGs), mortars, or incendiary explosive devices (IEDs). Nonetheless, we keep fighting the good fight and are investing enormous amounts of time and energy training new Iraqi police, civil defense workers, former army soldiers, and security forces. The dilemma we face daily is how to capture and kill terrorists without alienating ourselves from the Iraqi people. This is proving a difficult task, especially with our limited cultural understanding. While our daily raids into houses and neighborhoods net lots of very bad guys, it no doubt deteriorates our already tense relations with locals. Not sure there is a good solution (at least militarily), although working with the Iraqi police and security forces is a step in the right direction . . .

As we head into our 8th month in Iraq without a firm redeployment date (other than the generic "about a year promise") a few of our soldiers are growing restless, leading to a spate of criminal activity. Currently we are investigating, or prosecuting, everything from minor fights and skirmishes, to serious charges like stealing money from Iraqis, drug distribution, rape, suicide, even attempted murder. Unfortunately, one of our soldiers, overwrought with stress, grabbed his rifle and fired a few shots at two fellow soldiers. The psychiatrist who evaluated the soldier claims he went insane and is not competent to face court martial. If there is a silver lining to this incident (which is often all we look for out here) it is that no one was seriously hurt, and I may even get a trip to Germany in order to interview the doctors and conduct a hearing to determine his sanity to stand trial. This would be especially welcome news as it looks like I, along with about half of the guys in our unit, will not get mid-tour leave to go home and see our families. Anyway, adding criminal prosecution to my work with the Iraqi judicial system certainly helps ensure I remain busy and gainfully employed. Incidentally, a recent US News & World Report article discusses both the Red Crescent trial I brought before Iraqi's Central Court and our mixed results in restoring the Iraqi judicial system. I enclosed the article for anyone interested.

Lest I lead you to think life here is always hectic and dire (which is how it is portrayed in the media and often how it feels), rest assured there is indeed some time for relaxation and fun. Living on the Iraqi Air Force Base instead of downtown Ramadi now allows time for an occasional run, a game of basketball, or football. Armed Forces Network began broadcasting television over satellites giving us the chance to catch an occasional World Series game. To help pass time, a handful of fellow captains have taken to a nightly ritual of making the mile long walk to and from dinner and discussing every topic imaginable unrelated to Iraq. Though seemingly inconsequential, these evening meals have grown into the days most anticipated event. The wide-ranging and diverse dialogue during dinner and on our trek 'home' while smoking an occasional cigar (our only legal vice), would make for a great story if anyone had the ambition to take notes. Perhaps that is just as well.

Anyway, thanks again for all the letters, cards, and emails. While I continue to miss home and everyone terribly, I am staying safe, doing well, and keeping very busy. I hope everyone back home stays healthy and remains well. Looking forward to seeing you all before too long.

Take good care.
Brian

NOVEMBER 2003

Hello again.

I hope everyone had a Happy Thanksgiving. We haven't had Thanksgiving yet, as it was delayed until December 3rd due to ongoing missions. We are scheduled to have a big turkey dinner with all of the works on that date, but I am not holding my breath – only in the Army! Good thing the President didn't visit us as he would have been celebrating Thanksgiving by eating burritos!

This month I experienced both more severe lows and intense highs than any previous month in Iraq. November started out horribly. The Chinook helicopter that was shot down was transporting soldiers in our unit, the Third Armored Cavalry Regiment. This attack killed 16 of our fellow soldiers and injured many more. Six days later, the general in charge of the JAG corps was traveling in Iraq after arriving from Washington D.C. to meet with me, and all the other army lawyers in Iraq, when one of the Blackhawk helicopters in his party was shot down killing the sergeant major of the JAG corps and other members of the JAG family. It's hard describing the sadness and gloom we felt around here, losing so many friends and colleagues in such a short period of time. Most of the troops killed in the Chinook attack were young kids heading home on well earned R&R; one en route to see his newborn baby, another to get married, a third to attend his mother's funeral. In fact, last week President Bush went to our base at Fort Carson, CO to visit with some of the family members who lost loved ones in this Chinook attack. The loss of so many people in the Third Cavalry, and members of the JAG family, left me, and everyone, a bit shaken. Nonetheless, after many memorial services, and lots of reflection, life continues to move along...

Fortunately for me shortly after these attacks I went on a week-long trip to Germany for a court martial hearing. The purpose of the hearing was to determine if one of our soldiers, who went crazy and shot at a fellow soldier with his rifle, was fit to stand trial. The judge determined that the accused was indeed "legally incompetent to stand trial," so we committed him to the federal bureau of prisons and sent him to an inpatient psychiatric ward, much like the one where John Hinckley resides. Although the sanity hearing itself went fine, the highlight of the trip was my wife, Christy, flew out to meet me in Germany. Seeing Christy, eating schnitzel, and drinking a stein or two of German ale, brightened my mood considerably, and was, without question, the best week I have had in the last eight months since being deployed.

Back in Iraq, the pace of operations intensified as we (the Army and the 3d ACR) went on a major offensive to try and eliminate enemy forces – the reason for our Thanksgiving delay. Out on the western front, we've been focusing our efforts on killing and capturing foreign fighters infiltrating across the Syrian border and establishing terrorist camps in the Iraqi desert. These offensive operations have been largely successful and seem to have provided our guys with a greater sense of purpose and focus than we have had the past few months. (After all, our unit is trained to engage and destroy the enemy). As the pace of this operation winds down, we plan to launch another massive humanitarian effort to try and restore goodwill with the local population. The intent is for this stick & carrot approach to convince the general Iraqi population, who is understandably playing both sides, to cooperate with coalition forces. Like many people, it seems most Iraqis simply want to be left alone and live peacefully. Thus, convincing regular Iraqis that we will be successful, and they should cooperate solely with us, is crucial to creating a safe and secure environment. Of course, this is much easier said than done, and we will have to wait and see how things turn out.

I appreciate everyone who continues to keep us in their thoughts and prayers, or sends emails, letters, and packages. Although I don't always have the time (or internet access) to write and thank everyone individually, the gifts and food you send are greatly appreciated and are shared with all the other soldiers in our unit. Thanks again for all of your care and support.

Take Care, Brian

DECEMBER 2003

Happy Holidays.

As I am sure you can imagine, December has been a very busy and emotionally charged month, with Saddam's capture occupying most of our time and energy. The anticipation and uncertainty we felt in the first hours after learning of Saddam's supposed capture (again) was palpable, as were the feelings of excitement and relief when we learned in fact "we got him!" Unfortunately our exuberance was disrupted just hours later when we lost another soldier from the Third Cavalry who died while out on a convoy. As a result, the cheering and celebration over Saddam's capture was quickly tempered with the knowledge that someone back home was getting that dreaded knock on the door informing them that another loved one had passed on. I guess these conflicted emotions are a common theme of my emails. They certainly are a prevailing sentiment in my daily life out here.

For me, Saddam's capture created such intense feelings because it was the first time in many months I let down my normally cautious guard and allowed myself any real feeling of optimism and hope. The greatest frustration we've felt over these last 9 months in Iraq is that our soldiers really want to be appreciated and liked by the Iraqi people. Whatever the politics, our soldiers on the ground don't have grand or nefarious foreign policy objectives. They spend their days building schools, paving roads, training policemen, trying to catch 'bad guys,' and working to improve the lives of local Iraqis. I can't tell you how many times I've heard soldiers complain that "these people don't get it," or question "why Iraqis don't understand we are trying to help them." In frustration, I have probably expressed similar sentiments myself. Prior to Saddam's capture many of us clung to this wishful, perhaps overly-idealistic belief, that once Iraqis no longer feared Saddam they would be more welcoming of U.S troops, and peace and stability would follow.

Of course the truth is a good deal more complicated, and even after Saddam's capture Iraqi resentment toward Americans remains high.

Iraqis have understandably mixed feelings toward U.S. soldiers. The most rewarding part of training Iraqis border guards, policemen, and soldiers is I get to witness Iraqis undergo an attitude transformation from resentment and disdain for the United States to respect and appreciation. Iraqis are amazed that our troops follow orders, and accomplish missions without resorting to fear, threats, and physical violence. They are awestruck that we treat all people, even their 'lowly' privates, or suspected criminals, with respect and dignity, and are amazed when we train them to do the same. It is refreshing and gratifying watching the satisfaction these Iraqis feel simply by being treated humanely. At the same time, our other daily missions of conducting raids to route out "extremists" and "terrorists" is a very imprecise art, at best. As a result innocent Iraqis are often swept up in our arrests and subjected to degrading treatment at our hands. Having their doors kicked in and being pulled from their houses in handcuffs and blindfolds, or being shot at a traffic control checkpoint for driving too fast can't help but harden Iraqis hearts in the same way that roadside bombs and suicide attacks continue to harden our soldiers' hearts against the Iraqi people.

A perfect illustration of Iraqis conflicted feelings occurred last week at our detention cage when two teenage brothers admitted to setting roadside bombs (IEDs) in attempts to kill U.S forces. The teens claimed they were setting the IEDs not only to get the whopping $10 reward money being paid by foreign fighters, but also because Americans were evil occupiers who were trying to destroy Saddam and ruin Iraqi pride. When we brought in the boys' father and uncle, who were also being detained (perhaps unwisely), and told them what the teenagers did, the father broke down sobbing and the uncle needed to be restrained from strangling the two teens. It turns out the uncle had been ruthlessly tortured by Saddam's regime and couldn't believe his own relatives would be working against the freedom he had spent his whole life hoping for. I like to think that the uncle's sentiment is the prevailing view in Iraq, but there is no doubt that the teenagers' view is alive, perhaps, even growing. While Saddam's capture may someday lead to more peace and stability in Iraq, regrettably, right now the effect of his capture has been marginal, and life on the ground remains largely unchanged.

On the personal side, I have nothing too exciting to report. Truth be told, Christmas in Iraq was perhaps as depressing as you would imagine. It was almost better that the day passed without much notice as it left less time to dwell on how much we all missed our families and friends. Luckily, for me, I received more kindness and generosity from people back home than I could have ever imagined possible. I received gifts, cards, and letters from dozens of people – my family and friends; cousins, aunts, and in-laws; classmates and teachers from grade school through law school; childhood neighbors who'd lost touch and I assumed had long since forgotten me. I received even more letters and packages from friends I have never met, people who share mutual friends with me, and wanted to send something to brighten my day. It really meant a lot to feel so loved and cared for when we were all feeling as lonely as we were. Your letters and packages were shared with my whole troop and put smiles on the faces of many soldiers. Thank you.

Well, please have a safe, happy, and healthy New Year. I promise we are doing our best to make sure this New Year is more peaceful and joyful than this past year. I am looking forward to seeing you in it. Stay well.

Love, Brian

JANUARY 2004

Hello Everyone. Hope you all remain well.

Another month has crept by since I last wrote and I am now past my three hundredth day in Iraq. As we are expected to be home at the end of one year we are at least starting to see the tunnel, if not the actual light. Of course this past month has been as difficult as many previous ones. Two of the several helicopters shot down in Iraq this month belonged to my unit, the Third Cavalry. In the worst incident one of our medical helicopters was shot down near Fallujah, killing all four crew members and the five patients it was carrying. While the fact that Iraqis attacked a helicopter bearing the Red Cross symbol didn't necessarily surprise us, it was disheartening nonetheless. And while there is lots of well-deserved focus lately on helicopter attacks, ground transportation remains as dangerous as ever with frequent IEDs and roadside bombings, which we are reminded of every time we convoy to Ramadi or throughout Al Anbar province. In any event I spend most of my days inside the relative safety of our base at Al Asad and am much more fortunate than those troopers out in the towns doing patrols every day.

Lately there has also been a great deal of scrutiny on the thousands of detainees being held throughout Iraq. Because of the large number of detainees Ambassador Bremer recently announced a massive detainee release program. While the policy is probably prudent and necessary, it certainly isn't popular with the troops on the ground. Unlike conventional warfare, insurgency and occupation operations yield dozens of detainees who fall into a sort of gray status – perhaps an unlawful combatant, a common criminal, a sympathizer, an innocent civilian, or an enemy soldier. A typical raid finds several males in a house with a few RPGs and bomb-making equipment stashed in a back bedroom. While that alone isn't enough evidence to prosecute them in court (even if the courts were properly functioning), nor do our soldiers want to let these people go free. Accordingly, we often detain every military aged male in the house in the hopes that interrogation will sort out insurgent from innocent bystander. Of course blood ties run deeply and loyalty and fear of retribution makes turning families and tribes against one another difficult and complicated work. Regrettably, respecting dignity and upholding the rule of law doesn't always square neatly with the aggressive interrogation and prolonged detention that may yield valuable information on terrorist networks. Gauging the appropriate behavior is not always as black and white as we would hope. Thus, down in the weeds we are left balancing the need to investigate and punish our soldiers who cross the line without creating so many restrictions and judicial protections that interrogations become futile and meaningless. As I am quickly learning, interrogation and detention operations can be complex, dark, exhausting, graduate level stuff.

With all of these difficulties it is great when our guys can be part of something positive. These past few weeks our troops, along with the newly trained Iraqi Border Police, safely transferred thousands of Iraqi citizens through the Iraqi-Saudi Arabian border along the Hajj pilgrimage route to Mecca. The Hajj is the holiest time of year for Muslims and helping Iraqis participate in this journey to Mount Arafat was extremely rewarding. Prior to last year only a few privileged members of Saddam's Ba'ath party were allowed to leave Iraq and travel to Mecca. This year thousands of Iraqis made the pilgrimage across the border based on selection during a nationwide lottery. Our troops modernized border outposts, trained and equipped the Iraqi Border Police, and assisted as they stamped passports, and provided food, water, and medical care to the pilgrims. All and all the Hajj was a terrific success and a tangible example of how our presence can indeed help the Iraqi people. Moreover it provided a much-needed antidote to the frustration we feel on the days when we are unable to provide safety and security throughout the Sunni triangle. As always, I continue to receive lots of great emails, packages, and letters. Christy has also received many kind calls from people checking in on both of us. We really are fortunate to have so many great friends across the country. It is odd – in a typical year I am lucky to see many of you a couple times a year due to everyone's hectic schedules and our geographic dispersion. Yet as I enter my 11th month in Iraq I can't begin to describe how much I miss those occasional gatherings – a friend's wedding, a surprise visit, sporadic phone calls, a weekend tailgate, or a family reunion. My disappointment in missing so many significant events this past year is tempered by my determination to get together with all of you in this upcoming year and meet with the new friends I have picked up along the way. Looking forward to seeing you all soon.

Sincerely, Brian

FEBRUARY 2004

Hi again. Hope everyone remains healthy and well. February, like past months, has passed quickly even though life remains quite hectic. As the plan to restore Iraqi sovereignty continues to evolve, so does the situation on the ground. The push toward 'Iraqization' has made progress and decreased the number of U.S. casualties. (Although we in the Third Cavalry still lost 3 soldiers and had a dozen more injured this month). Despite limited successes, the violent attacks against Iraqi Security Forces continue to create instability and thwart significant progress. These attacks also depict the difficulty we face in transferring power to the Iraqi people while simultaneously engaging in combat operations. My friend Ryan and I recently made a trip to Baghdad to participate in an Iraqi criminal trial. Our trip highlights some of the complexities we face in trying to restore the Iraqi government in the current environment.

Ryan is tank platoon leader, charged with leading soldiers in the fight against enemy forces. While I commanded tanks years ago, now I'm a lawyer focused on helping restore the Iraqi judicial system. Ryan is ordered to Baghdad to testify before the Central Criminal Court (CCC), a Coalition-created Iraqi court established to prosecute Iraqis caught attacking our forces. Although Ryan can't remember the incident in question, he is told it involves an attack against him last summer when we lived in Ar Ramadi. Being familiar with the Iraq courts, I was sent to assist him.

Although we have detained thousands of Iraqis for attacking our soldiers this case will be only the fifth case to appear before the CCC. Thus, for me, and civilian authorities in Baghdad, this trial marks an important step toward empowering the Iraqi judicial system and helping restore Iraqi law and order. Ryan doesn't see it that way. To him, our trip is a dangerous, misguided, 400-mile trek through the dusty Iraqi desert and the hostile city of Fallujah, taking him away from where he is needed most – leading his soldiers on raids against the enemy.

When we arrive in Baghdad I meet up with some friends in an Iraqi cafe in the "Green Zone," a highly secured area surrounding Coalition

Headquarters. While the Green Zone covers only about a 5-mile area, I am excited and amazed to be able to walk the streets, interacting with Americans and Iraqis without wearing my Kevlar helmet, vest, and automatic rifle. This is a freedom not possible in the Sunni Triangle where I lived these last eleven months. While I walk the streets and talk with friends, Ryan enters the Coalition Headquarters, gets directions to a bay of beds, and goes straight to sleep.

The next morning we meet with a Coalition official who explains that Ryan is not testifying at an actual trial, but instead at a pretrial hearing before an Iraqi judge to determine if there is enough evidence to proceed to court. I understand, reminded of the similarity to the American system. Ryan is less patient and becomes agitated at the prospect they may call him back to Baghdad to testify again. The official hands Ryan a statement purported to be written by him last July after the attack. After a few minutes of reading Ryan begins to remember the night in question,

"While patrolling Ramadi around 0100 rockets fly from an open field lighting up the sky and flying over one of our vehicles. Our guys lay suppressive machine gun fire toward the open field while I direct them to form a 360-degree perimeter. Over the next several hours we search the field and find one dead Iraqi, one injured, and a third Iraqi laying in a hole about 120 meters from the RPGs point of origin. We take the two prisoners, briefly interrogate them (they admit nothing), and we move on to our next mission."

Ryan provides the Iraqi judge with vivid details and descriptions of the night, talking with pride as he describes his soldiers' bravery, tactics, and techniques under fire. Yet the Iraqi judge seems uninterested, instead asking what Ryan feels are all the wrong questions: "Did you see him fire the RPG?" (No, it was pitch black out); "Did he have any weapons on him when you captured him?" (No, he was hiding in a hole); "How do you know he wasn't an innocent bystander?" (Because it was one in the morning in Ramadi, in July, in an open field, and my guys secured the entire perimeter just after the shooting). The Iraqi judge asks Ryan "Who else witnessed the incident?" Ryan's eyes flash ... He remembers a few weeks after that attack when his vehicle was again hit with an RPG in the same area. Ryan was in the front seat and survived, but his troop commander was killed and his platoon sergeant lost both of his legs, now an amputee from the waist down. Although Ryan was promoted to captain back in January he continues to wear his lieutenant bar, waiting until he gets back home to give his platoon sergeant the honor of pinning on his new captain's rank. Ryan answers the judge coolly, "The only other witness is back in Colorado, titanium from the waist down." While something gets lost in the translation, the judge senses something in Ryan's tone and decides to move on.

When the hearing is over Ryan is visibly upset. Although no decision has been made, Ryan feels his men did their job well, and showed professionalism and restraint. He thinks the Iraqi judge has unrealistic expectations for Ryan's guys to gather 'evidence,' when they are in the middle of fighting a war. Ryan fears that rather than restoring law and order, this hearing encourages chaos by helping a legitimate prisoner of war go free. The Coalition official tries comforting Ryan explaining that if the accused is found not guilty it will show the Iraqi system is independent and Iraqi judges are not American pawns as the critics suggest. This is little comfort to Ryan and his guys out on patrols. In frustration, Ryan says he wishes his troops just shot the Iraqis and wonders aloud what they would do in future situations.

What was most striking about this hearing was that everyone involved was trying their best to do the right thing: Ryan, fighting and capturing enemy forces; Coalition administrators, enabling the Iraqi government; and the Iraqi judges, enforcing the standards of justice we are teaching them. Yet, despite the good intentions our trip seemed like a failure, hardening both American and Iraqi hearts. Even in hindsight, I am not certain what we should have, or could have, done differently. Instead, I share this story only to illustrate the many difficulties we face in pursuing combat operations while rapidly transitioning sovereignty to the Iraqi people.

Fortunately, for me, these challenges will soon pass to the many Marines who are gradually arriving into western Iraq and taking over Al Anbar

Province. With luck, next month's letter will be a brief note letting all of you know I am safely back home in the United States. Of course, as our helicopter crash earlier this week killing two reminds me, there are still many roads to cross between now and then. At least I am now counting the time in weeks, and no longer in months. Thanks again for all of the support. I am looking forward to seeing you all soon.

Brian

MARCH 2004
Hello and Happy Saint Patrick's Day!

I hope this is the last mass email I ever send. I returned back to Colorado safely and the remainder of my unit is either with me, or arriving in the coming weeks.

Our plane touched down in the United States in Maine at 8 am on Monday morning before heading home to our families in Colorado that afternoon. As we stepped off the plane we were greeted by hundreds of people – old World War II vets in wheelchairs, young children screaming and waving banners, and many regular folks simply waiting to shake our hands, give us a hug, or buy us our first beer to welcome us back home. As we choked back our emotions of gratitude, I could not stop thinking about how fortunate and lucky we all are compared to those veterans of the last generation.

As you all know, my time in Iraq witnessed some truly incredible achievements as well as some pretty dismal setbacks. Although opinions differ, I like to think we had more successes than failures, and I hope that continues to be the case for the soldiers taking our place. In any event, whatever success we did have was due in large part to the incredible support we received from people back home.

I am very lucky to have so many caring and concerned friends who stayed in touch with me and kept me updated on life while I was gone. Your thoughts, letters, prayers, and packages certainly kept me close to home and carried me through this difficult year. Many of you even sent cards, flowers, and balloons for my return home. Thank you! I also appreciate your patience in reading and responding to my monthly emails. Although my letters were often hastily written (as the spelling and grammar mistakes indicate), writing them and receiving your thoughtful replies was a wonderful and much needed escape from the day-to-day chaos in Iraq. Your questions and comments gave me a much greater insight into how people here are viewing the war. Perhaps the kindest and most perverse compliment I received was from a friend who wrote: "I am sad you are leaving Iraq as I am really going to miss your monthly updates." She is obviously no longer on my Christmas card list. Seriously though, while my perspective as a lawyer in the Sunni triangle can't pretend to represent the diverse experiences all of our soldiers face on a daily basis, I hope my random thoughts added something to your personal picture of the situation in Iraq.

While I am thrilled to be back home, I am anxious for the rest of my unit to return. The 49 soldiers from the Third Cavalry who never made it home, including one soldier we lost yesterday, continue to weigh heavily in my thoughts. Christy thinks the war can't have changed me too much as all I have been doing since I got home is eating pizza, lying on the couch, and watching college basketball. Luckily for me (maybe not for her) she is probably right.

Now that I am back home I look forward to remaining in closer touch with all of you, hopefully in a more personal medium than email. Christy and I are spending this spring relaxing in Denver, before shipping off this summer to wherever the Army decides we are needed most (it is looking like Savannah, Georgia). With the Army being stretched as it is, our biggest concern is that my fellow soldiers and I will be sent back to Iraq as early as next year. Here is hoping that is not the case.

In any event, thanks again for everything. Please feel free to call, or if you are near Colorado, to drop by and visit. Our contact information is below. We hope to see you soon.

Love,
Brian

3

THE OTHER SIDE OF THE SANDBOX

SSG Bryan Catherman
3d ACR U.S. Army
Al Anbar Province, Iraq
October 2003 – April 2004

FROM: Catherman, Bryan D. SGT
SENT: Thursday, October 09, 2003 3:36 PM
TO: Lisa Catherman
SUBJECT: Leaving Camp Wolf

Lisa,

I love you so much. Please let our friends and family know I am doing
fine. I thought I would leave you the Catherman perspective on the
Camp Wolf latrines.

I am preparing to depart Camp Wolf, Kuwait, to move north, so I
would like to share my thoughts on one not so talked about item here
– the latrine. The latrines are your typical porta-potty. They are like the ones
you would see at a fair or construction site. There is an oversize sand bag in
the bottom to keep it from moving around or blowing away in the fierce
winds. Inside, there is toilet paper, which is light and fluffy and appears to be
very loosely hand rolled onto the cardboard tube. It really is nice, I must say.

On the outside is a stand made of 2-by-4s and has a hand sanitizer dispenser fixed to the top of it with nails or zip-ties. If you're lucky, there is still some sanitizer left. The locals keep them clean so most of the time they are pleasant; however, if you have to use it during the high point of the sun, when it is over 100 degrees, take caution.

The most unique thing about these toilets is not that they are in Kuwait or are pitch-black at night, but rather, the graffiti inside. Here you won't find naked ladies or "for a good time . . ." Patriotism is the main theme. You will find latrine artists' pictures of eagles, the twin towers, and Lady Liberty.

While conducting your business, you should be able to enjoy quotes from the past and present Commanders-in-Chief, Martin Luther King Jr., Mickey Mantle, and many others. You can read speeches or parts of the Declaration of Independence. There are also phrases like "Iraq, you are free – no thanks needed!"

The Brits too have gotten involved. They like to draw pictures of their flag. It's interesting to note that I have not seen one American Flag gracing the walls of the plastic latrines.

Various units have also boasted their pride. "319th drillers, we've got the biggest rods." "101st, enough said!" And my favorite, "don't f**k with the Cav!" It's great. There is absolutely no need to take any reading material into the latrine; it's all right there for you.

Some of it even makes you a little sad. "I'm going home today. I have to leave my brothers because I was injured in battle. Take care boys, give 'em hell. PFC Stephen Bell."

It is truly remarkable what the power of positive vandalism can have. It's almost motivating to visit the latrine. The only thing I have seen thus far that could be taken as offensive was a well-done rendering of what looked like Saddam being kicked by a soldier. The trooper's boot was lodged well up Saddam's can and it looked like there was a large amount of force involved. Under the drawing, it read "Cause it's the American way!"

The next time you make a visit to a public bathroom, remember what is happening at Camp Wolf Kuwait. God bless.

Catherman

FROM: Catherman, Bryan D. SGT
SENT: Tuesday, October 21, 2003 3:36 PM
TO: Friends and Family
SUBJECT: What a Day!

Hey everybody. I am doing okay.

I went on a mission to teach classes to the Iraqi Civil Defense Corps. It's new recruit training at FOB Eden (Forward Operations Base Eden, Hit, Iraq). I was very nervous to be more than 6 feet away from a latrine, so I was very scared to convoy. Between that and IEDs (those are roadside bombs) or possible ambushes, I was not looking forward to the trip. I packed up early this morning, and in full "battle rattle," I rolled with an artillery unit going that direction.

On the way out of the wire, we locked and loaded live ammo and prayed we didn't hit an IED. I am in awe that so many troopers go through this every morning and have been doing it for 6 months or more.

Being my first time outside the wire, it was overwhelming. The Iraqis kept many of their planes off the airstrip. They hid them in U-shaped dirt piles. There are planes about every 300 or 400 feet for a good two miles outside the perimeter. I guess that is so it would be tougher to bomb them. Like everything else in Iraq, the locals have looted them, mainly focusing on scrap metal and wiring.

The first town we hit was Bagdadhi, a little village along the skinny highway. It reminded me of the movie Blackhawk Down. Things are not in good shape. The place just looks poor and filthy. The local shopkeepers just stared at us as we drove by. The locals driving on the road were scary. The Iraqis, they are the craziest drivers and there is no standard use of signals. Some use head lights, while others use their horn. Some drive with the 4-way flashers. My personal favorite is when they try to tell you where to go with their turn signals.

We arrived at FOB Eden, which had been mortared heavily over the past few nights. The signs of attack were eerie. Iraqis were working to make it a little better. Americans and Iraqis were working side by side to improve security and the general living conditions. I also noticed that one of the trucks in my small convoy delivered breakfast in the green marmite cans. FOB Eden is dependent on the success of the convoy for breakfast and dinner. They eat MREs (Meal Ready to Eat) for lunch. The line was long and staggered in a style that would prevent people from standing too close together, becoming a target of opportunity for a skilled mortar man. I was too afraid to eat because I had not yet located the best place to relieve myself. I would only have 30 to 40 seconds from the first bite until I would need a latrine. I had a class to teach and that was a distraction I didn't want.

I quickly marked my location on my GPS receiver and started off for one of the open bays in the mud-brick building being used as a classroom. When I walked in, the American soldier and instructor (somewhat like a Drill Sergeant) yelled, "On your feet!" They all leapt to the position of attention. I felt like I was back at a Basic Training camp. These guys were going through some of the same stuff I did! I quickly caught on and shouted, "Take, Seats!" To my surprise, the recruits, in unison, blasted back with, "ROCK STEADY!" and all sat down at the same time. Holy crap! This was basic training, in Iraq.

The entire platoon of 60 ICDC members, all wearing the Iraqi brown uniform (because you know there were some left in a warehouse somewhere), was staring at me. I greeted them through the two translators, which was awkward. They still just stared at me. My first class was The Rules for the Use of Force. Once we got into the subject, they became less like robots and started participating. When they got involved or answered questions correctly, I would hand them a Mug root beer hard candy. (I learned that tossing it back to them was seen as a sign of disrespect. I apologized and they laughed at my lack of cultural understanding.)

During the break, we told jokes. I didn't really get any of theirs, but I laughed anyway. That, in itself was probably the joke. They gave me a very small handleless-glass of boiling hot Chi tea that was mostly sugar. I gave them the rest of the candy from my care package. It was fun. They had never had root beer flavored candy before. I tried to explain that the shape was a barrel; but when they asked why candy would be made in the shape of a barrel, I had no answer. (Why do those things look like a barrel anyway?) The tea may cause more digestive trouble, but my hope is it will bring me back to solid again. I have moved through the solid stage to the liquid, and now to what I think is vapor. My body has become a living science project.

My next class was Human Rights. I had a prepared class that I worked on all week. It sucked. It made it look more like America's way we were trying to force on them. I bagged it and went with a big prayer and a feeling in my gut. These people have never really been given the chance to understand these rights, so how do you teach them?

We began with the United Nations' Universal Declaration of Human Rights, a document Iraq signed prior to Saddam. We discussed a base for many of the ideas that framed this document – religion. The focus was on peace and respect for one another. They told me about their religious beliefs and I shared mine. There were many similarities. We also discussed the constitutions of many free and democratic nations.

Then I shared with them a story about a time when America was wrong. I told them about Martin Luther King Jr. They heard about his non-violent protests, marches, and sit-ins. They learned about his ability to change minds with speeches, not guns or dictator type takeovers. The students were intrigued. They asked dozens of questions. One recruit asked me where this man was now. They were all angry when they learned he was assassinated.

The class was set up like a normal classroom with square rows. I had them create a circle (that was more of a gaggle). I sat on one side with them. At one point, I felt like I could get up in the middle and give "I have a Dream." It was one of the most amazing experiences of my life. It was somewhat like the end of Rocky IV. "If I can change, and you can change, we all can change!" They were with me. We then discussed the importance of being a champion of human rights, of tolerance, and of understanding.

These men, Iraqi men, are the new hope for Iraq. I told them, in Arabic (I'm trying to learn some), "God willing, peace will come to Iraq." They

SSG BRYAN CATHERMAN AND "TIMMY", AN IRAQI TRANSLATOR, AT RIFLES ACADEMY, A TRAINING FACIL-ITY FOR THE IRAQI CIVIL DEFENSE CORPS. *Photo courtesy Bryan Catherman*

erupted with cheers and "In-Sha Allah!" (Arabic for "God willing.") They put their hands on their hearts and then quickly moved them skyward in sincere cheer.

When they were marching back to their housing, they passed by me. Their Drill Sergeant was getting angry because they were turning and giving me the thumbs up (they really like our "thumbs up" hand gesture). They were telling me "thank you" in English and I was responding with the appropriate Arabic response ("ahf-when") and a smile.

We drove back to Al Asad on the highway. It was later in the day. Children continually waved at us, and of course, we waved back. The best part of all: we didn't get shot at or run across an IED. I left FOB Eden with a new hope for Iraq. It was like a drug, knowing there are pioneers for a new nation here. And I got to meet them!

I will be going back every week to teach classes to the new cycles. It is odd, but the translators and recruits I will have the privilege of working with may one day become Iraq's Benjamin Franklin, Alexander Hamilton, or Martin Luther King Jr. These dirty-faced Iraqi might just have a profound impact on a free Iraq. How cool is that!?!

It is funny what a difference one day can make. I have been here two weeks and have seen the best and worst in this country. Both the good and the bad have had a strong impact on me. I can't imagine what 6 months will do.

Tomorrow is the first ICDC class graduation in Al Anbar. The 82nd General and a bunch of other high-ups will be there. Security will be tight so we don't have a repeat of the police graduation suicide bombing. I will have the JAG digital camera. God willing (a phrase the Iraqis love to say), I will make the trip with no problems and be able to send some digital photos.

If you are still reading, thanks for taking an interest in what's going on in Iraq.

SGT Catherman

FROM: Lisa Catherman
SENT: Tuesday, October 21, 2003 7:22 PM
TO: Catherman, Bryan D. SGT
SUBJECT: Re: What a Day!

Bryan,

I love you. It's going okay here, but I can't wait for you to come home to me. I really liked your e-mail about the ICDC guys. All I see on the news is the fighting and where they think Saddam Hussein might be. Have you seen him? Just kidding. I should stop watching because it makes me worry too much, but I still watch it. I hope it is getting better for you. Are you making friends?

Love,
Lisa

FROM: Catherman, Bryan D. SGT
SENT: Wednesday, October 22, 2003 11:02 PM
TO: Lisa Catherman
SUBJECT: Re: Re: What a Day!

Maybe you should stop watching if you get really worried. Don't worry;
I'll be fine. No I haven't seen Saddam, but I really hope it's the 3d ACR
that catches or kills him. We are trying to help the good people here. If
not us, who? Remember that always.

Yes, I am making friends. Mooney is still on mid-tour leave and I
think SGT Ona hates that I am here, but there are some others that are
all right. I miss Bennett and the team at Carson but my duty has me
here, so here is where I need to keep my mind. I am really proud to be
part of the 3d ACR and maybe when some of them see that, they will
accept me.

I did make a new friend however. He is one of the Iraqi translators.
He works with the ICDC and has been assigned as my interpreter for
the classes. He is from southern Iraq. He was a college student studying English. With the war and his money problems, he decided it was
time to take a break to save money to marry his girlfriend if "he is not
killed before that." His would be mother-in-law HATES him because he
is poor. I can't remember his Iraqi name, but that is okay; he wants us
to call him Jeff because it's an American type name. He really wishes he
was an American and wants to visit the states someday. He is working
for us for pay (really good compared to what he could get anywhere else
right now: $20 a day, when the average salary is $40 a month), but he
mainly does it because he feels he can make a positive difference for his
country. I believe him. I think he will have a profound effect on Iraq. He
and his positive attitude have already had a serious impact on me. He
loves the Martin Luther King thing and can't wait for the next cycle to
discuss it next week. He likes to live and hang out with us Americans,
but I suggested to him that he pal around with the students more so
that maybe he infects them with the same passion for freedom that's

on fire within him. I hope one day he will be able to visit the states, and maybe visit us. That would be cool, yes?

I love you tons and will be dreaming about you.

B—

FROM: Catherman, Bryan D. SGT
SENT: Monday, November 10, 2003 3:40 AM
TO: Lisa Catherman
SUBJECT: Another Bad Day

Jeff is dead. He was my Iraqi friend and translator. His mangled body was found early this morning. They don't know how to contact his family or where exactly he is from, so they may let the locals or the students bury his body somewhere between Hit and the school. He was the best translator and an amazing patriot for freedom. I am going to miss him.

They think it was a small group of Iraqis that got through the screening. There was some fighting as well, more mortars than normal, so maybe this day was planned. The school is in a bad way right now. It was a real shitty day.

FROM: Catherman, Bryan D. SSG
SENT: Thursday, February 5, 2004 9:23 PM
To: Friends and Family
Subject: Ruth's

There is a little restaurant outside of Salt Lake City. Ruth's Diner. Some time ago, back in the 30's or 40's, Ruth opened this little joint in a trolley car and fed patrons recipes that still do well today. The trolley car sits in a wide spot around a bend far up in one of the many mountainous canyons that feed into the Salt Lake valley.

Hungry breakfast goers can still sit in the trolley car, but the real atmosphere of the place, and one of the main gravitational forces, is the outside patio. It rests under large trees and acts as a gateway to the wildlife and serenity that the canyon has to offer. Outside, there is a bar and a small stage. From time to time, an aspiring musician and her guitar belt out tunes for the morning patrons and their coffee. Mimosas and Bloody Marys are served after 11 on Sundays. The patio tables have retractable umbrellas to fend off the morning dew; and the service is comprised of the non-traditional employees that seem to have been there forever, maybe because they just like the laidback work environment.

Lisa and I used to take late morning motorcycle rides up the canyon for a Saturday breakfast and relaxing sit down. Although the wait was long, it was nice to be away from real life. The place has become a hangout for bikers, hippies, youthful college types, and even high-ranking Mormon leaders alike. It is diversity at its best.

We would order coffee and enjoy the fluffy mile-high biscuits, Ruth's trademark. Breakfast would take forever, but we welcomed the chance to chat and leisurely enjoy the morning. It was our time. We enjoyed this about once a month throughout the late spring, summer, and fall.

Breakfast in Iraq is shared with 2,000 other diners – mostly gun packing killers. It is rushed. The building is drafty and flies seem to find their way in and never leave. Stray animals, mostly cats now that the dogs have been killed and removed from Al Asad, prowl around the trash area, waiting to attack. The coffee is terrible and the contracted Indian and Iraqi workers don't really understand bacon or sausage. (They don't eat pork.) The food is scooped onto the plate with a spoon the size of a shovel and the plate is then passed down the line. It's no Ruth's.

In a couple of months, I hope to be home. I can't wait to fire up my bike. The rumble of the engine thunders in my dreams. I long for the fresh mountain air blasting my face. I wonder what Lisa and I will talk about while we wait for a table. What will I order? I am almost thinking that coffee and a huge mile-high biscuit sounds perfect. Ruth's Diner is calling me. I am looking forward to coming home.

SSG Bryan D. Catherman

FROM: Catherman, Bryan D. SSG
SENT: Friday, January 16, 2004 12:12 AM
TO: Friends and Family
SUBJECT: Just me, in Iraq

I have been thinking about the life we live in the US. We complain because we have to pay insurance, and then fight with the doctors and auto insurance when we have to pay a deductible. We complain about our electric, phone, and cable bills. We hate having to get our cars emission inspected. We gripe about almost everything. I'm sure you already see where I'm going with this – don't get me wrong, a year back in the states and I will be right back in the American groove.

I read that President Bush is talking about putting a man or woman on Mars. I'm sure there will be all kinds of discussions and criticisms about this on the news, in living rooms, colleges, and on the floor of Congress. Here in Iraq, they are trying to get electricity to at least 75% of all Iraqis. I am not trying to make the "what is the appropriate role of government" argument here, I have just been thinking about the stages of the life of a nation and its priorities at each stage. I am thankful that I live in a country were we get fired up over taxes, college admission policies, and the price of fake boobs. In Iraq, the problems are AK-47s being fired on every block, no place for children to go to school, no electricity or running water, and no plumbing and water treatment plants (they just dump raw sewage into the same river they get their water from). I am sure there are places in the US where they don't care about going to Mars. In these places, they only want a safe place to life and a good school for the children, but these are the places we don't talk about. We just hide them in the back of our mind and instead think about going to Mars and face-lifts.

Sorry about the soapbox. It's just hard to see how people live here compared to how we live in the States.

My work has been mentally taxing lately. I guess that is better than physically, because this work doesn't require me getting shot at. I don't even have to wear my flack vest. I am looking forward to changing gears when I get home. I am entertaining the idea of taking up real estate again, part time, while I'm in school. I can't see any job as tough as what I have been doing out here. I think this experience has been a great education for me.

Take care,
SSG Bryan Catherman

FROM: Catherman, Bryan D. SSG
SENT: Thursday, March 4, 2004 8:27 AM
TO: Friends and Family
SUBJECT: Let Us Not Forget

Staff Sergeant Stephen Bertolino, a Cavalry Trooper, was a good guy. He would come by, drink coffee, and tell jokes with us. He always called the lawyer I worked for "Boss." Not much ever seemed to bother him. He was the guy you would like to have as a neighbor. He was a good guy and he gave freedom to Iraq with his life. He died in November during Rifles Blitz under enemy fire. Those that survived likely still have nightmares of a well-planned ambush that led to a 40-minute firefight, 2 deaths, and a large number of wounded.

George Leigh Mallory, from England, tried to be the first man to summit Mount Everest back in 1924 (29 years before Sir Edmund Hillary stood on top of the world). Some felt he and his companion, Andrew Irvine, might have made it to the top of the world's largest mountain. They were spotted some 900 feet from the top. They never returned to the base camp. For some time, there was strong debate if they made it to the summit. After a while, people quit thinking about Mallory and life went on. He was here, and then he was not. We try not to forget those who have left us, but over time, it just happens. Then, after a little passing of time, dead men find ways to remind us again. In 1999, an American climber named Conrad Anker found Mallory's body resting at 27,000 feet in a location that appeared to be where he stopped after a tragic fall. And 75 years later, we remember George Leigh Mallory.

Stephen Bertolino didn't leave behind anything as dramatic as Mallory, but he still reminds us just the same. A file here, an old joke there, and we think of him again. I didn't know him well enough to send him a Christmas card, but I still think about him and what he did here in Iraq. He still reminds me.

Countless men and women have lost their lives in the name of freedom and human advancement. Some are remembered with memorials. Some rest in Arlington. Some have to remind us in ways like Mallory. The important thing is that we understand what they gave and why. I am sharing this thought with you because I want you to be able to put a name on a number. The 3d ACR has lost 48 troopers. Forty-eight troopers have gone to Fiddler's Green rather then coming home to their loved ones. Forty-eight – this is the number, Staff Sergeant Stephen Bertolino is a name. Let us not forget.

SSG Bryan D. Catherman

FROM: Catherman, Bryan D. SSG
SENT: Thursday, March 4, 2004 10:35 AM
TO: Friends and Family
SUBJECT: Moon Pie

Back when I was a young kid, my father would take me camping, fishing, and snowmobiling. There were a few stops along the way, you know, for donuts and orange juice. Before the big chain stations like Chevron replaced them, we would stop at these little mom-and-pop places. I'm sure if you have ever traveled around in the hills, you know them. They have great names like "Last Chance," "Cougar Mountain Lodge," or "Packer John's." I bet the ones in Utah and Idaho are the same as anywhere. You can get gas, donuts, a greasy hotdog that has been rolling around all morning on the cooker and a stale bun, a Dare Devil fishing lure, and a county road map. If you were really unprepared, you could buy a fishing license, jumper cables, a boat battery, and get the latest gossip on the town drunk that happens to be fixin' up burgers and wedge-shaped fries over in the joint next to the gas stations. That's the place that also serves up coffee as black as a cold night on the Syrian border. They were great places!

I remember some of the stuff they had on the shelves. It was not at all like today. One thing that really caught my eye as a kid was the Moon Pie. Nobody really knew how long that sandwich cookie snack had been sitting there, but that added to its charm. I never used to get one because we always got a box of 6 old-fashioned style donuts and a carton of pulpy O.J. Then it was back on the road. The lonely Moon Pie would just have to wait for the next dad and kid to come by. You don't see Moon Pies much any more. Then I went to Iraq.

About a week ago, an entire truckload of Moon Pies came to Al Asad. They were distributed out to the units. For the last few days, we have gorged ourselves full of Moon Pies. What a great treat! Not only is it pure sugary goodness, it is so full of memories. The older guys, like the First Sergeant open up the pies and say, "Man, I use to eat these as a kid all the time. Too bad we don't have an RC cola."

Now that I think about it, this place is not all that unlike going to the hills. We have guns, we stink, and we all sleep in sleeping bags. This is like one big camping trip! The Iraqi shops are much like those old pit stops on the back-hill highways. They have strange stuff sitting on rusty shelves in haphazard ways. You won't find a barcode or a computer cash register anywhere. They don't have old-fashioned donuts, but they do have O.J. I don't think they have fishing tackle, but a guy can buy a fat Cuban cigar. (We all bought one to smoke when we crossed the border into Kuwait.)

Moon Pies and Cuban smokes while camping in Iraq – what more could a trooper ask for?

I have had a little more time on the Internet than I thought I would have in these last days. I will be moving soon and you may not hear from me for a while. If that's the case, I'll see you back in the States!

SSG Bryan D. Catherman

FROM: Catherman, Bryan D. SSG
SENT: Sunday, March 7, 2004 3:35 AM
TO: Friends and Family
SUBJECT: Update from Iraq

I have just endured the long, painful line to get my 15 minutes on the lethargic Internet. I was lucky; I had time to shoot an E-mail off to Lisa. Now it is a race against time to get an update to you.

Things are going well here. We are getting most everything handed over to the Devil Dogs (also known as Marines). Last night, we did a dry run of our convoy plans for the jump to Kuwait. Although some of us (me included) have been out on convoys, conducting missions regularly, most of RHHT has been working strictly at Al Asad for the last 5 or 6 months. Many have not left the wire in half a year. The CO (commanding officer) and 1SG (1st Sergeant) want to ensure everybody gets a refresher and that we all make it to Kuwait alive. It is important that we all confidently know the plan and our role in that plan.

I can't give you the convoy date for security reasons, so no more asking please. As it stands right now, I will be driving a large truck and trailer, or manning a 240 (that's a big 7.62mm fully automatic machine gun in top hole of our rig), and TCing (that's like riding shotgun). I will also be mentoring the squad leader of Red-2, our squad. Some younger up and coming specialists have been made squad leaders so they receive some leadership experience. They will be the NCOs for OIF 3 and OIF 4. It's somewhat like putting in the freshmen players for the last three minutes of a winning football game. I have been assigned as the mentor for one of these squad leaders. He seems like a good guy and I believe he will do fine.

Yesterday, Hunter, the squad leader, drove and I ran the radio in a night practice run. A PFC worked the gun, but he was a stand in. We will have another NCO on our truck if this plan holds true. Hunter really doesn't want to deal with a radio, he just wants to drive; but with a little more practice with the communication, I think he will enjoy it. He seems like a natural leader and should do outstanding.

This should be a good convoy. Six hundred and fifty miles, sand, heat, and people that want to kill us – if Six Flags could re-create this, they would own the ultimate thrill ride. It's going to be uncomfortable and painful, but the reward at the end will be like a pot of Irish gold at the bottom of a rainbow. (I've been to Ireland but I didn't see any rainbows or gold. It did however smell like Irish Spring bar soap, which restores my faith that advertisers ARE telling us the truth.)

This is the best update I can muster in the 1 minute I had to write this. My time is up and the Internet Nazi is telling me I have to log off. I don't know when I will be able to log on again. Take care; see you soon!

SSG Bryan D. Catherman

FROM: Catherman, Bryan D. SSG
SENT: Sunday, March 14, 2004 1:24 AM
TO: Friends and Family
SUBJECT: Road Trip

Sometimes I wish I could hook up a VCR to my experiences. I want so badly to share events and emotions with you, but it is just impossible. Right before most convoys travel around the AO, there is a convoy briefing. We go over the plan, the order of march, enemy activity, medevac procedures, rules of engagement, radio frequencies, the route, and some other stuff. For this convoy, we have been doing this on a much larger level. There have been rehearsals and inspections, test fires and radio drills, and we can all draw the maps from memory. Yesterday, a large number of us, in our full "battle-rattle," gathered around a terrain table (a map made on the ground with marker tape, water bottles, and rocks) the size of a volleyball court. It was Iraq, complete with route markers, rock cities, sand pile mountains and canyons, and our final destination. We went through this briefing, one of our last in Iraq, like children preparing for a visit from Santa.

While information was being put out and NCOs were pointing to

roads and cities with a stick, a Marine Cobra attack helicopter continually circled around. I really don't know what it is about that Cobra. We
have the more technically advanced Apache, with it's big shark mouth
too, but that Cobra, boy; it just says, "I'm coming to kill you." It made
large sweeping circles, low and close enough to see the pilots giving us
the thumbs up sign. The deep "thump, thump, thump" of the old bird
of prey, and the sand blowing across our large earthy map really added
to the experience. I swear, sometimes I don't feel like I am in Iraq, but
instead a character in a movie.

The game faces are on. Everyone knows the plan. We are ready. I have
loaded up extra ammo (other than my 210 standard combat load) in
places I can get to it quick. I will be the vehicle commander, which is the
right seat, but I will also take shifts driving and riding turret. It's a big
turret in a huge truck. It will make for an interesting adventure. I pray
this will be a boring convoy. If you have a minute, say a little prayer for
RHHT, 3d Armored Cavalry.

I will try to e-mail from Kuwait. Hope to see you soon!

Brave Rifles!

SSG Bryan D. Catherman

FROM: Catherman, Bryan D. SSG
SENT: Friday, April 2, 2004 9:10 AM
TO: Friends and Family
SUBJECT: The Other Side of the Sand Box

It is done! I am back in the USA. I finished all the tedious paperwork to
out process. Tomorrow, Lisa and I will drive back to Salt Lake City. Ruth's
Diner is calling my name and my motorcycle is screaming for attention.

What a great life experience. I wouldn't trade it for anything; although,
I don't think I would ever want to do it again. I can't tell you how scary
it is to watch the news. They make it out like all we do is drive around
and wait to get attacked. I have yet to see the positive angle that I know
exists. We were doing good things over there, trust me. Iraqis are print-

ing their own free press newspapers. They have satellite TV dishes now, and the Internet. Children are going to school and you don't have to be a member of the Ba'ath Party to go to college. The Iraqi court system is running cases through its halls. The police are working to keep the streets safe. They are all excited for a free election. There is more going on over there then I have seen on the news, really.

I have been doing some thinking about war and how my feelings about Iraq have changed throughout this deployment. When I first got to Fort Carson, the leadership wouldn't even say if the deployments were to Iraq. They would only say "Southwest Asia." We called it the Sandbox. Those getting deployed were going to "play in the sandbox." What a stupid phrase we used. Nobody played. It was a war; we worked. We weren't building sand castles; we were tearing down walls. We went to establish a place where freedom could grow, but nothing grows in a sandbox. Growth occurs in a garden, and we simply needed to pull some weeds. We did some gardening and planted some seeds on the other side of the sandbox – in the garden. Besides removing a few nasty plants, we dug up the shit from the neighbor's cat; but then removing the poop makes the sandbox a better place to play, just like pulling weeds makes the garden a better place to grow. I hope over the years, we see the children play and the people grow. Maybe one day, that place really will be a sandbox to play and enjoy life. Let freedom ring from the purple mountains' majesty and from the sandy plains of the sand box too!

Thanks for the support over the last 15 months; I couldn't have done it without you! Remember those who replaced us and pray for them. There is a still lot of work to be finished over in the sandbox, and I pray they can get the job done. As for me, I'm home!

SSG Bryan D. Catherman

4

A LINE IN THE SAND

Sgt Chris Missick
319 Sig Bn, C Co
US Army
Iraq
April 2004 – March 2005

APRIL 7, 2004

The launch of my first ever blog has finally taken place. Over the course of the last few months, it has been very difficult to communicate with many of you back home. Since October, when the activation orders came down and this arduous process began, my life has been the military 24 hours a day, 7 days a week. It is a situation I had never anticipated as a child. I was never one to have foreseen the military in my future, I was never the kid who emulated his action figures. With that said, the experiences offered have been invaluable in forging discipline and above all patience! The thing I have realized even more than I ever had before is that it is not so much the things back home that I miss, but the people, all of you, and the memories we have together. Hopefully this site will allow me to keep in touch with many more of you all at once and help me keep you informed of how things are going over here. For the time being, rest assured that my unit and I are fairly safe and secure in Kuwait, supporting the Army's Echelon Above Corps communication needs. We are providing data and voice communication for the war's architects and "brass," and as a result are placed in the rear of a lot of the urban warfare currently occurring just north of us. I am grateful for the security and peace of mind this offers me and my family. As a soldier, however, there is always the desire to do that much more, to be that much closer to the line and to help solve the problem. That is not my part at this time however, as we will be serving this mission for some time. I know my job, my specialty as a multi-channel systems transmissions operator/maintainer, and I will do my job with pride in the year ahead as I operate as a cog in the great machine known as the United States Army.

April 11, 2004

Holidays are always an extremely important time for my family. Growing up, I remember all sorts of mini-rituals that occurred within my household, which fell under the umbrella of the larger, macro-social rituals connected to holidays like Christmas, Thanksgiving, or Easter. Halloween for example, always witnessed my mother preparing a special family recipe of "Dodgers," a donut-like pastry that is fried and coated with sugar. Christmas morning could never begin without my father first entering the living room, turning on the Christmas lights and preparing the family for the first perfect moment when we would come out of our bedrooms to explore and enjoy the gifts that awaited us. Easter was no different, with the Easter Baskets, new clothes and a morning spent at church. These rituals are not forgotten when you wear the uniform, if anything, they are appreciated even more because you simply do not have them. Even though we may go to those moments in our minds, they are never lived in practice. The days all blend together, none more essential than the one that preceded it or the one that will follow. It doesn't matter what day of the week it is, because you will probably be working. For a military where time is absolutely crucial for soldiers, dates become a different story all together. This morning, on my way to chow, I passed the chapel. It wasn't until I reached the chow hall and saw the handbill advertising a special Easter service that I realized that this was a sacred day, not just another blur of hour hands walking in a sphere. The military has a way, they say, of making a man of you. I wonder if this is necessarily what it is to be a man however, to be so far removed and increasingly desensitized to life's landmark days and important moments. It is not that there are no longer important moments, it's just that those moments don't involve family and generally involve a relief that a mission was completed without any injuries. These are the moments that become important, the ones that pass and usher in a relief that the day has passed and that perhaps your daydreams are closer to the realities they once were. Fortunately, most days are not filled with fear for me here, but fear or at least an extreme sense of caution, does come when certain duties call. I thought today would be one of those days. Another convoy was planned, and I was nervous that the Christian holiday would make some over-zealous anti Americans more eager to act. If they are out there, they will not have the chance to act today with my unit however. The convoy has been postponed, and on yet another rare, cool, drizzly day in Kuwait, I will enjoy some time to myself, and celebrate Easter. Happy Easter Mom, Dad and Matt. I wish I could be there . . .

April 22, 2004

Our convoy arrived at our new base camp on the Iraqi border shortly before a major sandstorm rolled in like a morning fog that blocks the sun and leaves visibility so small that only a few feet in front of you it becomes hard to recognize the objects or the persons standing there. We knew it was coming, the sky looked similar to those familiar images of Southern California during the major fires of 2003. Everything was orange and brown and once the wind came to welcome us to our new location, the climatic metaphor for the chaos just meters away was all too appropriate. Like Camp Virginia, our new camp is relatively secure. We are able to go to the chow hall and use the recreation facilities with few worries of attacks, but the atmosphere of this base is much different. With rumors of the mortar attacks that frightened but did not injure anyone from the group we are replacing, and the eyewitness accounts of the gunfight that took place at the gates of the border several weeks ago, everything seems much more serious. At the same time, there is a much more relaxed atmosphere when it comes to the areas of garrison military life we are used to. Back home, uniformity is the crux of military appearance, but here in the desert, you make do with what you have. No two military vehicles look alike as each is a hodgepodge of lumber and steel used for vehicle reinforcements, and positioning for the crew serve weapons such as the M249 and M60 machine guns, and the beast of all gun truck crew serve weapons, the 50 caliber machine gun. Vehicles regularly pull into be serviced that have faced the improvised explosive devices (IEDs) that litter the highways, and other damage from small arms fire inflicted from the innumerable AK47s in Iraq. I am still very far away from the fury of the Baghdad streets, but much closer to the solemnity of this war.

April 27, 2004

The inclement weather has continued off and on the last few days, with a sudden sun shower occurring just an hour ago. The nights have been filled with crashes, I assume every time that it may be something I should be more concerned with, and yet it continues to be simply roars from the heavens, thunder. The thunder has not been the only substance of nature to startle me in the few days we have been here. Since arriving, we have found one scorpion in our tent, one desert viper just outside our tent, and several camel spiders around our living and working areas. Camel spiders, for those of you who have been fortunate enough to avoid even a brush with a picture of one, are the most hideous of all these creatures. They have been known to attack humans, can often outrun humans, can be as large as a medium size crab, and have a large face and eyes that peer up at you with a look in their eyes that makes them stunningly intelligent appearing and yet even more frightening. Their most potent ability out here however, is their known ability to play dead. The other evening, Tevino stepped from outside his shelter to find a rather small one walking across the sand. He stepped on it, and assuming it was dead, stepped back inside the shelter. Coming out of his shelter a short while later, he discovered that it was gone. Incidentally, the scorpions around here are considered the third deadliest in the world, and left untreated, a man can die from them in seven hours.

All this has not only reminded me of history lessons past, but ingrained upon me a personal realization of why so many cultures in this region developed the way they did. It has been long understood that primitive cultures viewed their gods based in large part on the environment around them. The early Mesopotamians, the culture that flowered from the Tigris and Euphrates Rivers (the Fertile Crescent) around 3,000 BC, saw their gods as vengeful and at times even cruel. This was developed by the harsh conditions that plague this region, from the drought to the floods, and in my opinion the beasts that bring seemingly nothing but terror to human beings, creatures 1,000 times their size. For approximately five millennia the souls in this region have lived within truly hostile conditions, and to experience them firsthand lends some personal understanding in a view of the world as a much more hostile place than we perhaps see it in America, where the coasts are rich with breathtaking beauty, the continent is scattered with natural wonders such as Niagara Falls and Yellowstone and where heartland's rich soil feeds the world. Aside from the natural discomforts, one thing has been ingrained upon me since setting up camp here, that is the amazing pains that many of us here have gone through.

Of course, as a signal unit, I have been relatively safe or secure. I was enjoying a cup of coffee the other day, when I overheard an 88 Mike, the MOS identification for a truck driver, on a phone call. The 88 Mikes here transport a great deal of equipment supplies, thus they are constantly on convoys. He was a reservist who had been extended four more months and was recounting a story from a few days back. As he described his experience, I listened intently and had some powerful thoughts. "We were on a convoy, going right through Baghdad. They completely shot up my truck' he said. 'Yeah, lucky I didn't get hit, but they were coming from both sides. There was a large crowd with AKs shooting from every direction. The crazy thing was, this guy was shooting right at me but had a woman in a firm headlock, holding her body right in front of his. He just kept shooting and I had no choice but to put a bullet through both of them. It was crazy to see (MFs/expletive deleted) dropping all around. They said we killed about 45 of 'em. Lucky they didn't get one of us." He spoke with such passivity about the event that it stunned me.

The thing I don't think most people at home understand is that Reservists are all around them. Silently bagging your groceries, serving you at the bank, working on your construction sites and doing just about every job you come in contact with every day. A year and a half ago, they were working beside you or going to school with you and yet here they are, here we are, in a war, fighting with weapons, acting on the most primal of human behaviors, survival. A year from now, they will be back at work, contributing to society with their jobs, and with their taxes. Once a month they will attend drill and prepare for the next time their country calls. Many of these men and women are above thirty, some in their fifties. These are America's new war fighters, these are the heroes who no one will ever really know, because to know them is to know what they've been through. As close as I am and have been, even I feel strange at times with these personal accounts because of the bravery these good Americans exhibit. I have never claimed to be a hero for what I have done, I merely allow these people to talk, enable their medivac calls to be made, their 15 minute discussions with their family to take place. I am a cog in the wheel that enables their job to get done, and yet I am more proud of my job than I have ever been about anything else. I just want you all to remember that being a veteran is no joke, it is not another title to add to a resume of life work. It is a sacred brotherhood of people who have witnessed the worst human nature has to offer, and yet have had a glimpse of what the best human nature can offer as well. The glimpse has come from the people we are surrounded by, the people who are the first line of defense for our own lives and our country's preservation. It is not to say that credit should not be given to our active duty Armed Forces. It is just that Reservists interact within the confines of our society on a vastly different level. The US Army Reserves is an imperfect system, but it is filled with some of the most perfect examples of freedom fighters you could ever envision. It is the same concept of the citizen soldier that ignited the Revolution and it is this concept that will carry us through this period of uncertainty.

May 14, 2004

I am posting much later today because of a recent change in my schedule. For the next couple days I will be working from midnight until noon. As a signal soldier, our mission never takes a rest, communications are needed 24 hours a day, and we need to be sure that the entire system runs smoothly. Changing shifts like this and suddenly going on a nightshift can be difficult, but it is nothing we aren't used to.

Tonight was actually a welcomed break from the normal routine. There was a special morale evening with a band composed of soldiers that played popular "top 40s" songs. The band was decent, but better than that was a chance to unwind, in civilian clothes, with other soldiers. It was a chance to meet a lot of other people who, because of the nature of my rather isolated job, I don't get to interact with a great deal. There was no talk of prisons, no talk of what missions lie ahead or any of the tragedies of the last week, it was simply music and friendship. For so many years growing up, you see documentaries on television of wars gone by, and you always see one of the morale building soldiers shows featured. It is a unique experience to be a part of, and it certainly does help raise morale and break the monotony. I must admit to a certain level of music snobbery back home, often shunning many popular main-stream music acts, for people I felt were qualified musicians in a variety of music genres. In those days, I would rather go to an intimate setting such as an art gallery of small venue to view a musical performance than view pop stars on a stage with gaudy sets and thousands of screaming teenagers. Tonight, it wasn't the music that was important, the music simply set a carefree mood that lasted until I had to head to work.

On a slightly political note, the war on terror, from day one, has been black and white. President Bush declared in those grave days after 9-11, that you were either with us, or with the terrorists. Before the war, a divided America was faced with a clear decision, to support or to protest the war. As fighting still rages on, we are at another point in which each citizen has the right to either support Iraqi reconstruction or demand withdrawal. Republicans are in near lockstep on the question of follow-ing through with the job before us in Iraq. Democrats however remain divided as Senator Kennedy bellows outrageous accusations against the Bush Administration and entertains propositions of complete with-drawal from the rebuilding process in Iraq thinking that such retreat will actually win over the hearts and minds of the Iraqi people since they "don't want us there to begin with," and Senator John Kerry has been supporting reconstruction and at points proposing increasing the troop strength in the region by 40,000.

The last two weeks has shown us how squeamish politicians can be when faced with dilemmas. The message I wish to send you tonight, is not one of spineless politicians, or of a misguided segment of public opinion (as I see it at least), it is rather a message many of you already know in your hearts.

There are soldiers here who were vehemently against the war itself, there are also soldiers here who do not support the reelection of President Bush, and want to see Secretary Rumsfeld resign. Although they tend to represent a minority of soldiers, they are entitled to their opinion. The important point however, is that regardless of their opinion, they wake up every day, or begin shift every night ready to do their job, and nearly every soldier I speak with supports reconstruction. It was one thing to be against the war, but opposition to reconstruction exhibits not just a political bias, but a disregard for the well being of a complex nation.

Perhaps we view things differently than those in Washington and on street corners still protesting our involvement here, but then again we have a reason to view things differently. It is us who are in the streets, it is us who support the mission day in and day out to ensure the goals of a free Iraq are met. It is not simply that men like Michael Moore live in a metaphorically different world than us, it is because men like Michael Moore do live in a different world than us. To be in any nation at its republican birth is an honor, even one that poses as many conflicts as Iraq. The road to freedom in America was paved with acts of atrocious disregard for humanity, on an even deeper level, the Civil War was a violent affront against an inhumanity taking place within our own republican system. Violence is not the end we have sought, but as a soldier, I do see it as a means to a very desirable end, an end which will hopefully make all the sufferings of the Iraqi people under the regime of Saddam an uneasy memory in every living Iraqi. Even more importantly, it is the American people who will ultimately have only an uneasy memory of the horrors of global terrorism in the decades that lie ahead. The job here in Iraq is one that should receive no opposition, the debate should lie only in the means to which we are seeking here. That is where the debate will be the most constructive and the point in which we can work to fulfill the dream of planes and boatloads of troops returning home from a victorious front and a truly free, republican Iraq.

May 15, 2004

I want to bring your attention now to two topics I discussed in the last few days. The first being Nick Berg and the slaughter that took place at the hands of one of America's Most Wanted. It appears as I was monitoring news reports from the States that the gravity of the event that took place simply has not sunk in. I gather this from the under-whelming coverage it has garnered as opposed to the prison abuse scandal. Those of you who read my blog regularly probably share a similar opinion as I do as to the symbolism of this travesty. It seems as though the actions of 7 Americans have now isolated the coverage of 135,000 of us soldiers who complete our mission daily with honor. We have chastised those individuals personally, publicly and very soon, judicially. However, still acting with evil incarnate are 5 individuals who brazenly acted without regard not only to human decency, but to humanity itself. These 5 do not stand out as misrepresentative of their respective ideologies nor did they act as a rogue element of an occupying force. They are in fact both. Before the media continues to focus on the misdeeds of a few Americans who do not represent America, should they not first focus on the atrocities of a few Islamo-Fascists who in fact do represent all Islamo-Fascists. We must not forget that they are indeed an occupying force in Iraq as well. Yet, they are a force of a much different nature. The majority of Iraqis do not want the presence of third country terrorists in their newly freed nation. They do not want the bloodshed to continually spill into their small communities and into their neighborhoods. They are aware of what happened in Fallujah that led to the death of 1,300 Iraqis and counting. They have witnessed and heard the pleas of Al-Sadr in Najaf and have rejected his ideology and want his militiamen of Iraqis and extremist Shias from around the Middle East to stand down. The forces of Al-Sadr, the Sunni terrorists in Fallujah, the terrorists that have flocked to Iraq from all expanses of the Muslim world, are not rebuilding schools, are not building better infrastructure for water, power and transportation and are not advocating human rights. These people are not tending to the dilapidated Iraqi hospitals and above all, are not respecting Islam. To those in Congress who have never fought for freedom and are not willing to stand for it now, for those on America's far left who want "the occupier" to leave, I agree, the occupiers should recognize they are not welcome. The Coalition is not the occupying force that must remove itself at this time from this land however, it is those who are a stain on their religion and on the hopes of a free Iraq that must leave.

Clearly this is not a call to cast all of the Muslim world in a bad light. Those historians among us may remember the 442 from World War II. They were the most decorated combat unit in the war, and every one of them was Japanese. I believe history can and will repeat itself here. Just as it is one element of Islam that poses the greatest threat to the entire world, it must be that it is those from within Islam will prove to be the greatest blessing to Iraq when it comes to guaranteeing a free Iraq.

Ultimately we can not nor will we as Americans tell the media what it should focus its coverage on. I do ask however, how long can the imbalance continue before their bias is either rejected or accepted? Their coverage appears to convey this simple message, "Yes, we know the terrorists are evil, they are outrageously violent, but look how bad America is as well." My plea to Americans reading this blog is not to forget the images you may have seen or perhaps only read about in regards to Nick Berg, but emblazon them upon your heart and do not lose the fortitude that it takes to continue this war. There are 135,000 of us on the line in Operation Iraqi Freedom. We are the ones who are willing to sacrifice all for our country and what we need most of all is encouragement from those on the home front, fortunate that they can enjoy their life of peace and prosperity. We fight so that the actions of Nick Berg do not translate into a metaphor for the terrorists of decapitating American support and its allegiance to a free Iraq and a world without terrorism. We are fighting not just for the heart of Iraqis, we are fighting for the life of America.

May 19, 2004

There are seminal moments in every career, a point where you look back with pride and recount stories about to your friends and family in the years to come. Today, I experienced a moment I will remember for the rest of my life, today I became a Sergeant in the United States Army. I have been honored to receive a number of military awards, and represent my battalion as Soldier of the Year, and yet, being pinned on my collar with the sergeant stripes by my Company Commander, Captain Hicks, was just about the most proud I have ever felt. I have always been a man who feels connected with history, and joining the non-commissioned officer corps initiates me into a group of men and women who are unrivaled in history as leaders of the world's greatest fighting force. The weight of responsibility is much greater, it is a moment of pride and humility to have earned this title, and yet I stand ready for the challenge, eager to make my family, and my country proud that I am a non-commissioned officer in the United States Army.

Despite my elation all day and the pride I felt wearing my rank for the first time, a story from a year ago came to mind as I began thinking about a situation that happened to me a year ago and how it relates to Abu Ghraib. It has been nearly three weeks since the Abu Ghraib story broke, and the treacheries of a handful of soldiers still make headlines daily as their knowledge of their abuses and cruelty reach ever new levels of inhumanity. Crawling on broken glass, a fist to the temple of a man who was rendered unconscious by the force, and humiliations that extend beyond those photos we have already viewed. In no way, and in no corners of American society, should such actions be defended. Interrogations may require a level of "truth or consequences" as they do in American prisons, but the cruelty exhibited is inexcusable. This small group truly are the dogs of this war.

The "dogs of war." I first heard this phrase used in a new light last year while visiting my girlfriend at the time in Oakland, California. She had always remained quiet about the subject of support for the war in our discussions, but was generally supportive of my service. She was involved in her student government and attended every school function. As I was in the Bay Area visiting her, the school function that I attended with her was in fact an anti-war rally. I felt it would be enlightening since I have generally only encountered support for the uniform and encouragement from those around me. Even attending a public university in California I rarely witnessed overt displays of anti-US troop behaviors. And yet, as I sat in the auditorium of a private religious college, I witnessed slander after slander, not just of the politics of this war, but of those who have chosen to serve in uniform to defend and protect America's constitution and her citizens. I sat in my seat, disconcerted, like a man on trial who knows a conviction is just moments away, and for the first time felt I could associate on the most basic levels with what our soldiers in Vietnam experienced on the arrival home. I knew in my gut that I would be in the Middle East by the end of the year and I sat there listening to each opinion they had about me and my battle buddies in every branch of the armed forces.

The most virulent words that evening came from a man of the cloth, a priest who stood up there referring openly to all American soldiers as the dogs of war, marching into Baghdad, murdering the innocent and participating in subjugating a nation to an American imperialistic lust. I am a considerate man, a patient man, and it took everything I had that afternoon not to stand in objection to the lies being perpetrated and applauded by Americans who have never struggled to earn their freedom, who have never experienced the fear of a dictator. I knew I would never convince this crowd to change their minds about us in uniform. They were and probably remain the zealots, the radicals among us.

My message today is one of appreciation to most Americans who already support their soldiers, regardless of whether or not they support this war. And yet, it is a plea to those who truly disdain the uniform not to miss the forest through the trees. We are here every day for you as well. We fight for the values of life, and liberty and the defense of our great nation. We are representative of the soldiers you have sent as ambassadors to a foreign land, we are the forest of hope that will inspire another generation to understand that freedom is not a right, but a gift purchased in the blood of those who came before you. The decaying trees that were a select group of guards at Abu Ghraib are dead now. They have been removed from among us, and can not longer hurt those whom we have come to free. We must struggle with their wrongs and continue with their prosecution, and yet we must halt all focus of the job before. Those of us in the field cannot afford to spend our time calculating the political expenses of their actions. We have a mission, and we accomplish it with pride every day. I wish to remind Americans that they too have a mission, one which will never be accomplished, because it is one that has no end. The mission for the home front is to stand by their soldiers, to understand that we are here, as an extension of you, with an intent to bring goodwill for a brighter future in Iraq. Believe what you may about the war, but believe me when I tell you to be proud of the job we are accomplishing here.

May 31, 2004

Before I begin, I must first wish you all a very warm and solemn greeting on this Memorial Day. Of course we will be working all day here, but it gives us even more meaning in the labor of the day, to think of those who have come before us. If you have a chance, please go by a military or national cemetery and reflect on the soldiers who gave their lives for you. There is more than a headstone in the ground for each service member laid to rest there. There were families, friends, dreams and hopes for the future that all lost a great champion when they died. I am no hero for simply being a soldier here contributing to the effort. I am simply doing what I felt needed to be done, the call to duty is something that many feel, and I am honored I was able to answer that call. It is my honor to be able to serve the US Army, to wear the tape that bears our nation's fighting force over my heart, to wear the flag on my sleeve. The men and women who died, who put their lives on the line for your sake; they are the heroes, and they deserve to have their names and their memories emblazoned upon every single one of your hearts.

June 28, 2004

Today is the big day, and it was a bit of a surprise. The handover has taken place and Iraqis are officially in place as the sovereign authority in Iraq. It is a day that numerous soldiers including myself have been thinking about, speculating over, and discussing for months. I must say, despite the difficult road ahead for the Iraqi people, I am as proud as I have ever been to be here at the birth of a republic. The weight of history is spread evenly across the shoulders of the soldiers and the Iraqi people, as we forge forward with a new path for Iraq and Middle East.

It is amazing when you think of this from the eyes of a soldier in a historical sense. In what was just over a year ago, the Iraqi people were liberated from the tyranny of Saddam Hussein by a nation many decried as imperialistic. And yet, today we as soldiers stand proud that we are here, despite a very difficult year, giving this nation back to its people. There is no desire to plunder and pillage, no campaign to abuse the people or establish an American protectorate that will last indefinitely. When these dark tendencies have crept into view, they have been dealt with severely and condemned by the American people. We are here, returning the government of Iraq to its rightful handlers, and all of us are applauding and hoping for the best. As a history fanatic, I am hard pressed to remember a time similar to this since the establishment of civilization. When has a military taken on a national army, dealt with insurgents and foreign nationals seeking to derail the process, and begun rebuilding infrastructure and emphasizing education? Even more importantly, when has such an effort been successful? I would argue that despite the problems currently plaguing Iraq, we will see a genuine improvement over the next few years as Iraq exercises its newfound democratic values, and the extremists realize they will not succeed. Indeed, despite the tragedies of the last few weeks, their efforts are beginning to seem like frantic attempts to regain ground in a battle where they have continually lost. I can't help but think that the fortitude the military and the Administration has shown is part of the reason for success.

Overall, between the civilians and military personnel I have spoken with today, there is such a great amount of hope for what lies ahead. I just hope that a glimmer of the hope that is brimming over here on this historic occasion will be captured in the States and over-shadow the darkness over the war that has been encapsulated by a recent film. To all Americans, you have great reasons to be proud of yourselves and your country today.

July 2, 2004

As many of you know, a common theme in my blog has been dedicated to what I feel has been the disservice of some major American outlets. Day after day, verbal mortars are launched in headlining stories throughout the world to discredit and disgrace the effort we are putting forth in Iraq. In the midst of this era of conflict, the hot war rages in the Middle East as a cold war has arisen among many of the elitists in the press. As the bullets fly and a very unconventional war is underway in Iraq, the war of words rages on in the press, where hyperbole and an excess of the negative have come to be the rule more than the exception. With an abundant amount of good news and optimism brewing in Iraq, I find it frustrating and difficult in my position here, to view what America's news sources have been turned into. It seems that the propagandizing of the war has been more important than being the purveyors of truth that I feel Americans crave in their news outlets. I have to tell you, a large portion of my absence recently has been due not just to our workload, but a frustration that had seemed to render me speechless for a few days. I feel I have found my voice yet again however, and am more inspired than ever to write.

I want to add that I am not one that shares an industry-wide disgust with the media. There are some wonderful reporters putting forward both the good and the bad that has come out of Iraq. I could never lie to you all and say that everything has worked out well here, just the way we had hoped. The bad news, the negatives of this conflict must be put forth so that we as Americans can learn from our mistakes, and have an even broader knowledge of this conflict, so that we can determine the course of our future foreign policy in the region and the world. What I truly disdain however, is the arrogance with which certain outlets, especially papers that boast the title of being the "Paper of Record," have ascribed to their articles, and the endless opposition and negativity they spew while claiming to be objective. I feel in politics we need a return to civility, and I plan to write more about that very soon, but an even more pressing matter for the soldier at this time is the return to civility, honesty and fairness in the media. It is not exaggeration to say that the lack of this in recent years has cost soldiers their lives.

This was the theme of Diana West today in a Washington Times editorial. In the editorial, she speaks of what she is referring to as the "Battle of the Humvee," a story very familiar to those of us in theater. It is a modern epic of American soldier fighting not just an unscrupulous enemy, one that hides in mosques and cemeteries and then accuses Americans of denigrating these shrines, but a press all too ready to turn a story of bravery and victory into a 15 second news clip that signifies defeat. It's the story of soldiers in the 32nd Armored Regiment, 2nd Battalion, fighting a battle to secure a destroyed Humvee, not for tactical purposes, but so the media would not have the image of gleeful insurgents dancing on top of a vehicle in a battle we won decisively. Although I am young, a baby of the eighties as I've said here many times, I can not imagine a member of the GI Generation facing similar concerns and worries that their own American press would have the ability, with a single destroyed vehicle, to turn victory into defeat in the minds of the American people.

July 4 2004

I write this far away from home, where the reminders of the USA this 4th of July are not the commercialism or the relative ease of life back in the states, but the dedication of the men and women around me and the American flags that they erect on their own, outside their tents. The wind blows hard every day now, the sand beats against our national colors and tatters the edges, but it is never long before a soldier erects a new one, and flies it again with conviction and pride. Being here, there are no views of amber waves of grain or sunsets seen from sea to shining sea, but just knowing that the same sun that shines on our great country is shining on me gives me hope and strength. Not a day passes when I don't feel that despite the discord at home, something is stirring in the spirit of America that will inspire an ever greater hope in our nation.

I can't help but smile when I think of the future. Perhaps it is because I see the future of America every day in the actions and the faces of young soldiers who sacrifice for the home front.

On this holiday, most of us here are working. "The freedom we have isn't free" as the saying goes, and another small example of this is the sacrifice soldiers are showing on this day that is traditionally filled with friends, family, parties, bar-b-ques and fireworks. I remarked to a friend the other day, that this may be the only Fourth of July I can remember that I really hope there are no fireworks, for out here, they have a much different connotation. Yet for me, I am honored to be serving this holiday, in the place of someone who has the chance to be home, in the place of most of you. Enjoy the day and thank God for our country, but say a prayer for those of us not with our families.

Happy 4th of July America.

July 11, 2004

As war in the 21st century has changed many aspects of the way soldiers fight, it has also changed the way soldiers entertain themselves in those moments of relaxation or time away from their duty station. Long elaborate letters have turned into group e-mails, pen-pals are now cultivated on internet chat sites and online communities, Gameboys fill the pockets of soldiers who want their video-games at their fingertips, and as evidenced by my most prominent pastime, some of us blog our experiences for the entire world to read. Just as poignantly as this war has shown us that the technology that has made waging war more advanced than it was ever dreamed of at the creation of our republic, we have also seen that there is still no substitute for "boots on the ground," and for soldiers slugging out long difficult days to achieve and maintain peace. It is true that in many areas, the more things change, the more some things stay the same. Despite the advancements of technology that provide us entertainment in the field, these things are still no substitute for the one thing that has carried soldiers through long hours of loneliness and been a constructive hobby that sharpens the mind. Books are as popular today among soldiers as they have been in many previous wars.

Every camp and small outpost usually has a tent that serves as a library, enabling soldiers to pick up their latest round of distractions whether it be a mystery, science fiction, memoir or history. These libraries are the center point for a burgeoning class of educated soldier who exercises his or her mind as intensely as they do their body. It is common to find soldiers who have read 20, 30 or even 40 books by the time their re-deployment date approaches.

I write this today in light of two things, first off being the kindness of folks back home who send us books. One person in particular deserves an immense amount of credit for her valiant efforts over the last few weeks. PJ Dahling, of Carson City Nevada, began what she termed her "Book Brigade for Soldiers" several weeks ago and accomplished a wonderful mission by providing us here with dozens and dozens of paperbacks to disperse among the soldiers, as well as a number of valuable toiletries and snacks that have helped us all be a little more comfortable. One of the great aspects about the books, especially because of the transient nature of the camp where I am currently serving, is that soldiers are able to go to the libraries throughout the theater and borrow these books. They are circulated throughout Iraq and Kuwait as they are finished and returned to the library where they may be staying at that time. I have written some of you in the past and stated that although we soldiers are the fists of American power, you remain our backbone for the immeasurable support you provide. I can honestly say that her hard work and contributions helped me stand a little straighter these last few days, more proud than ever before of the country and the citizens I am fighting for. The compassion and sheer determination to support those of us over here instills in me the spirit of greatness that is America and her citizens. In writing about the contribution of some wonderful books, I must also thank Alice Jonsson, who sent some very prescient selections for me and my battle buddies to share. As many of you who are regular readers know, books are a source of light and life for me, something that brings a great deal of joy and companionship, and I cannot thank you all enough for your support.

August 03, 2004

I've shared with all of you over the last several months the level of support I feel like I receive from home. I received a package a few weeks ago that was very unique and very special to me. It came from my own first grade teacher, Miss Anderson, an amazing woman who was my teacher from 1986-1987 at Liberty Christian School in Huntington Beach. She had always been a pivotal influence on me, and someone who I personally attribute as being someone who guided me intellectually and spiritually in some very important ways. Opening a package from Miss Anderson and several other teachers who also taught at Liberty Christian when I attended, and seeing a bunch of wonderful drawings and messages from these children immediately took me back to a moment almost a decade and a half earlier, to when I was a child in classes sending messages to soldiers of support. There was something extremely special about the fact that these letters were from children being taught by the same teacher as I was that made me feel immediately connected to these promising young Americans. Some of their words made me laugh, as they wrote out questions like, "I like to play tag. Do you get to play tag in the war?" Some of them made me feel extremely proud, like when they said, "I love our soldiers. I want to be a soldier when I grow up." Looking at their pictures and reading their carefully written words and questions, I have so much hope for the future of this country.

August 06, 2004

It's been very hard for me to write the last few days. We have been doing our best to work through a variety of difficulties in commo systems here, and blogging was the last thing I was thinking about. It's amazing how even out here, when things are going well and our system is green,

I feel great, I keep my optimism and each day is just another day down until we all go home. This last week has been the total opposite however, with each day feeling like it was an eternity, and the overwhelming sense that I will never get home. We joke around sometimes when we're in this mindset, that it's almost like we are in a work camp, spending long hours at tedious tasks feeling emotionally and mentally exhausted. I know better than to actually believe that though, after all I signed up, I am still proud to be here, and I know that things are not that bad in the grand scheme of things. I realize I am a small part of this war with my duties in the Signal Corps, and I touched on how I felt about all this in the last few weeks. It truly is amazing to me when I think about the scale of this war, and how many soldiers are involved, and all the different experiences we are having. I realize that I am at one end of the spectrum here, a soldier with a technical skill, assigned to a fairly safe location where I spend most days troubleshooting any problems with the phone and internet services.

At the recommendation of some of you out there, I visited http://cbftw. blogspot.com, and was absolutely blown away by the different lenses with which we are viewing the war before us. His stories truly are the stories of heroes, and he truly is the face of American courage that this war has shown to the world. I am sure most of you have read his site, but if you haven't, and missed the blog http://cbftw.blogspot.com/2004/08/men-in-black.html he took part in a few days ago, it is a must read.

I have to tell you, I am extremely humbled when I write from out here after reading what this soldier is going through. Of course we are all reliant on each other in some ways, but seeing how he faces life and death on a daily basis makes me see his contribution as so much greater. In a way, it causes me a bit of apprehension in writing about what I am experiencing. Rather than stifle my writing however, I still feel it is important that I have a chance to share the other experiences soldiers are having in theater. This war and the ability for soldiers to blog and send mass e-mails is showing Americans the individuality and humanity of each and every soldier. It is showing that behind my experiences there are tens of thousands of people, possibly family members of yours, doing the same things I am doing and probably feeling the same way. It is also showing us, even more crucially, the feats of bravery daily displayed by soldiers like "CB". Even serving here in uniform my contributions seem so small in this war effort, but I rest on the knowledge that we all have a role and we all serve a purpose. As the saying in the Signal Corps goes, "You can talk bad about us, but you can't talk without us."

September 09, 2004

I received a somber e-mail today from the wife of a First Sergeant in my battalion, Mrs. Barbara Blackmon. We have communicated from time to time, and I always enjoy reading her e-mails. This one was riddled with grief however, as she mourned the death of her friend SPC. Anthony J. Dixon, who was killed in action August 1, 2004, Samarra, Iraq. SPC. Dixon was assigned to the Army's 1st Squadron, 4th Cavalry, 1st Infantry Division, Schweinfurt, Germany.

I wanted to take this opportunity to ask you all to say a prayer for her and SPC Dixon's family, and for the families of all soldiers who have been lost. As Mrs. Blackmon wrote me, every soldier we lose leaves a ripple of grief that impacts hundreds of Americans and lasts a lifetime. Although I am in theater, I don't face the daily dangers that soldiers like SPC Dixon did. The infantry soldiers and the men and women who face the dangers

SGT CHRIS MISSICK AND FELLOW SOLDIERS FROM THE 319TH WITH A BANNER OF SUPPORT SIGNED BY HUNDREDS OF PEOPLE FROM CARSON CITY, NEVADA. *Photo courtesy Sgt. Chris Missick.*

of Operation Iraqi Freedom daily are the real heroes. Like SPC Dixon, they go where their country asks them to, do what their country asks of them, and risk their lives for the freedom of others. They pay the price for freedom and though they will never hear our thanks here on earth, we can never thank them enough. I can't help but think that God has a special place in heaven for those who have delivered freedom to the oppressed and spill their blood to defend life and liberty wherever it is threatened.

October 22, 2004

It's been far too long yet again since my last post, and I can't wait until I finally get settled in at my new camp and have access to the Internet as regularly as I had in the past. First of all, I want to apologize for not getting back to e-mails, I will hopefully have the chance to work through them in the coming days.

After being away for so long, I am overwhelmed by the continued support you all show. I am reminded that regardless of political persuasions, Americans are an amazing people who stand strongly behind their soldiers. Skimming just a few titles of the e-mails without much opportunity to read at the present time, I am more honored than ever to be wearing the flag of our nation over my right arm.

In short, the last few weeks have been filled with preparations for moving, including inventory of equipment, hand receipting equipment to the new contingent, and all the other details I will hopefully delve into deeper tomorrow when I'll have a chance to write some more. We arrived at our new location about three days ago to prepare for taking over the operations at this camp, and have been keeping busy ever since.

For me, the best part about coming down to this camp was the opportunity to meet up with friends who had been stationed throughout the region with other contingents on separate missions. Several of the soldiers I hadn't seen in nearly six months, and we all had a great time the first day swapping stories and talking about how things had been. It has felt like a lifetime since I saw many of them last, but at the same time, I know these soldiers are great friends because it's as if we never served a day apart.

As I mentioned, time is brief right now but hopefully tomorrow I'll be posting more.

October 24, 2004

Perhaps I acclimated too quickly here, because I received word today that I will no longer be working with this contingent. I am being moved to work with the Battalion Operations at the base camp for our battalion and our company. After only a few days here, I will be returning to the camp where I spent the first two weeks in theater. I wish I could add more about what I'll be doing, but honestly I just don't know. I am a little disappointed to be leaving here though. This contingent contained some of my best friends in the Army. Most of these men I have known for years and one of them I even went to AIT with back at Fort Gordon. It looks as though this may be my last assignment in theater and will spend the remainder of our time there, but if the last few days proves anything at all, it's that things in life and especially in the Army have a tendency to change at a moment's notice. Although I am disappointed to be leaving my battle buddies here, I still have a lot of great friends back at the other camp and I plan on making the best of it. The last year has taught me so much, and it has also reinforced a saying my dad used to tell me all the time growing up, "never make your master plan your master." I am also learning that flexibility is one of the most important keys to happiness.

December 08, 2004

Today was one of the days throughout this deployment that I will remember the rest of my life. It was an opportunity to meet one of the key architects in the War on Terror, and a man whom I personally admire. Secretary Donald Rumsfeld stood before about 2,300 soldiers today on what was a fairly cool and overcast morning, and spoke to us about our

SGT MISSICK WITH SECRETARY OF DEFENSE
DONALD RUMSFELD. *Photo courtesy Sgt.
Chris Missick.*

place in history, the difficult job we have before us, and the thankfulness that the American people hold in their hearts for everyone deployed in the Global War on Terror.

We found out last week that the Secretary of Defense would be coming to one of the area's camps, and that we might have the opportunity to attend the address he would make. Fortunately, my contingent took volunteers and five of us boarded a bus and headed to the location where we would have the opportunity to listen to and even meet Mr. Rumsfeld. It was indeed a great speech, and like Victorino Matus in the Wall Street Journal Opinion pages today, drew parallels to what occurred on December 8, 1941 as America entered WWII. The Secretary spoke about how the Germans and the Japanese underestimated the resolve of America's finest, but that the men and women in uniform performed magnificently.

Mr. Rumsfeld gave a very good speech to "Rally the Troops" and it was heartening to sit there in that aircraft hangar, only feet away from the man who holds the power of America's armed forces in his hand. After his formal speech, he opened the floor to questions. I was impressed once again with our nation, when a 20 year old Specialist has the opportunity to stand before the Secretary of Defense and ask him a direct and difficult question. Mr. Rumsfeld did receive such questions today, and handled them fairly well. Certainly, in areas such as stop loss, the answer was not one that some soldiers wanted to hear, but honestly, even that was slightly comforting. His answers were usually direct and blunt, telling the audience the realities of a situation rather than an overly sugar-coated prepared sound-byte. I will admit, I am partial to the Secretary and believe he puts America's and the military's best interests first, but even from the most un-biased position I could conjure up, I was impressed at both his speech and the fact that he visited today.

December 25, 2004

Merry Christmas. It is a strange feeling today, being Christmas and all. It is as if there is an internal calendar that is instilled in you as a child, a calendar that leads you to anticipate this day all year long and look forward to the relaxation and gifts exchanged in the company of friends and family. It is as if I know today is exceptional, and yet being here makes this Christmas the exception to everything I've ever known. For most of us, it is just another day in theater. I am working my normal shift, accomplishing all the standard duties. The only difference was the exceptional lunch in the chow hall, which was festively decorated and a delicious reminder of the sort of meal I would normally enjoy, and the Christmas music playing in the PX.

I ate an enormous amount of turkey. It made me think of my family with the same sense of nostalgia I wrote with the other day. My family is "turkey crazy," and as they read this today they'll probably laugh knowing how true that statement is. No matter what time of year it is, there is always at least one spare turkey in the freezer. It is kind of like an insurance policy, one that says just in case we have family from out of town; a great traditional dinner can be ready by the end of the day. The great thing about it as a meal is that it always promises to leave you with enough leftovers to have sandwiches late into the evening or the next day, when the talking of old times continues. In our family, there is a rich nostalgia for the era when my mom and all her siblings grew up in Rochester, NY. The same stories get told year after year, of the tree lined sidewalks with rich history on Augustine St., where for years my grandparents' house and most of the children's houses were just yards away from each other. There are the stories of the woods behind Aquinas High School, near their old home, and the bittersweet stories of what family life was like.

My mom, dad and brother flew to upstate New York for the holiday, to be with family there. From what they say it is five degrees below zero, an almost unimaginable temperature (about as unimaginable now as 145 degrees was before I spent a summer over here).

It is definitely a different Christmas for them as well. Usually, our California Christmas truly leaves us dreaming of a white Christmas, but knowing my dad (who in his single days used to go sailing every Christmas morning in Long Beach) that dream won't occur to him for several more years. He is a typical Californian in many ways, always donning his Reyn Spooner Hawaiian shirts and happy to be outside with a short sleeve shirt every day of the year. I think they may have gone to New York this year to help change their routine as well, perhaps using a change of scenery and step away from tradition to make the holiday a bit more palatable for them.

More than anything else, I want to wish everyone reading this a Merry Christmas. I want to thank you all for taking time out of your day to check in, and thank those of you who have sent e-mails, cards and packages. I do have more I want to write today, so hopefully later I'll have a chance to get back to the blog.

January 19, 2005

One of the things you have to be cognizant of at this point in the deployment is short-timer's thinking. It really does happen, you get into the mindset that home is finally on the horizon and begin to pay less attention to the crucial details. To counter that, our leadership has addressed the issue on an individual basis, taking aside NCOs and reminding them that we aren't home yet, and there is still a lot that lies before us. My First Sergeant did this a few weeks back and it really helped to keep me focused and in the right state of mind. I do find myself dreaming in my free time though, of what the year ahead may hold.

For many of you who have followed the blog for a while, you may also know about my goal of going to law school. Hopefully that dream is one step closer as I received confirmation the other day that two of the schools I am applying to received my application. Very few times in my life have been as daunting as the last few months, with so much on my plate and so many things to prepare for when I return, but after what has felt like endless months, everything seems to be coming together perfectly. Sometimes, you just feel the winds of personal destiny at your back, and all you can do is smile and thank God for your good fortunes.

January 25, 2005

Unfortunately, I was not able to watch the Second Inaugural address of President Bush. Throughout the election season, when I was carrying out a communications mission at a different camp, I was working nights and was afforded the opportunity to scrutinize for myself every word of both presidential candidates in their debates. In recent weeks, as we have been tending to all the required duties of preparing for redeployment, I have been working during the day, pretty much guaranteeing I would miss any major address by our nation's leaders while they were occurring live. Regardless of my lack of specific knowledge on the subject, I had one gut reaction after viewing the numerous editorials and commentaries that proliferated the web in the aftermath of the national event.

First and foremost, my thoughts in reading the criticisms of the president's speech, was that it was one that will have potentially generational impacts. Although the clichés of freedom may have become commonplace for many folks to hear from this president, it is his cries of freedom that resonate most with me. Each time he retorts that freedom is the only thing that can sustain peace, or that it is our duty to carry forward the torch of liberty to bring light to a world darkened by tyranny, I am reminded of the fact that my small role here in OIF is about something larger than myself, and that it has the potential to bring striking change to the world for the century that lies ahead of us. Dissenters may call me a sucker for idealism, but I will not recognize those criticisms. Rather, I am a sucker for the idea that Jefferson illuminated the most profound vision in the Declaration ever to be enunciated at the foundation of a new nation. I am a sucker not just for the rhetoric of freedom, but for the belief that freedom under republicanism is the only thing that has the potential to establish peace amongst nations.

I think we forget these days, when reading the Declaration, that when Jefferson wrote "We hold these truths to be self-evident ...," that such a statement was remarkable. The colonialists and patriots that demanded independence believed the concept that "all men are created equal" was a concept that was intrinsic in what is human nature, but it was not something that was self-evident to the world at large. Freedom, liberty and representative government was still a foreign concept to the world. In casting off the chains of British rule, the framers exclaimed their divorce from a government that did not hold such values to be self-evident. We have seen however, in the centuries that have passed, that governments not founded on such principles pass away as those which enunciate the ideals our framers laid at the conception of the world's most powerful nation, grow in strength and influence. The framers not only established the vision that was to be fulfilled for our own nation, they set in motion an agenda that the entire world would one day cherish. What was once self-evident only to radical colonials and political philosophers is becoming more so for the global masses everyday.

Lincoln's second inaugural address is heralded as the most important inaugural ever given by a president of the United States. Lincoln eloquently bridged the gap between a war torn country, he exclaimed the vision of the framers and believed that we were moving ever closer to the vision of freedom and equality in our nation. His speech was about building an enduring freedom, where there were no masters and there were no slaves. It has become the benchmark of presidential speeches and is a cornerstone in the rhetoric of what is the great American experiment.

Today, I believe that although the language of George W. Bush is not up to par with the wonderment that Lincoln's words invoke, his vision is set to become a new benchmark in our continued national experiment. I say this based partly on the immediate reaction of many of the prolific writers of our time. The reactions I read most quickly stated that his vision went too far, that it was frightening, that it was bound to fail. I imagine much the same was said after Jefferson had written the Declaration, and I am sure that there were newspapers around the country that disparaged Lincoln's address as too fanciful, too idealistic. I believe that the reactions in the days after President Bush's address are proof enough that this address will have a resounding impact on the direction America takes in the decades before us. It is the idealists and radicals that breathe life into decaying political corpses, and I believe the resuscitation that George W. Bush has given to the ideology of freedom will bring to life the decaying value of freedom that has afflicted the world in this post Cold War era. This is not to say I believe we should embark on a path of conquest in the name of freedom. Rather, I believe that the models we are establishing around the world as we speak will impact generations in every corner of the world.

In many ways, America has always been several bold steps ahead of the rest of Western civilization. At times, that leadership is comforting to our allies, and yet at other times it serves as a cause of trepidation for those following in our footsteps of freedom. We are in a transitory period right now, one in which we must possess the fortitude of the framers. I rest assured however knowing that in the years that follow, the spirit of our nation's fathers and mothers lives on, and has not left. President Bush is freedom's new radical, just as the great presidents before him articulated the radical ideology of freedom. Let us not forget that we Americans have always had a tempered fanaticism for obtaining the rights assured us by our Creator. President Bush's second address was nothing if it wasn't a reminder of where we came from and where we are going. If we were to be true to the intentions of why our nation was founded, such a speech had to happen in such a time as this. The vision has been laid before us, the direction illuminated once again for the American people. Now, it is time for us to continue in our role as Americans to elect leaders that will fulfill this mission in the spirit of the framers, not necessarily to jump into every war, but to protect Americans' safety and promote liberty throughout the world. The means of continuing the march of liberty are contingent upon the situations that present themselves, but let us never forget that as Americans, we were born with a duty and responsibility that we cannot shirk. Let us disagree on the means of achieving this president's vision, but let us never stray from that vision.

February 28, 2005

As I sit in my tent this afternoon, I'm writing to you realizing that this may be my last post while in theater. With our re-deployment impending, our access to regular internet usage has declined and there is still so much we have to finish before we leave. I never thought I would write this, but leaving will be bittersweet. Anyone who has been deployed can attest to the feeling you have when you are about to leave a place like this. The desire of a return to some semblance of normalcy runs deep, it consumes your thoughts every day. Time passes between you and your battle buddies by talking about all the things you wish you could be doing right that moment. Conversations turn to thinking about what your friends are enjoying on any given night. You realize after a 12 hour day that it's Saturday, and back home your friends are sleeping in, and doing whatever they feel like doing that day. You wish you could just get into your car and drive, anywhere.

I always say I'd go the local Starbucks and buy a nice venti latte, maybe even buy two or three if I want. My mind goes to afternoon drives down Pacific Coast Highway, pulling off in Hunting Beach or Seal Beach to go to my favorite Mexican food restaurants, or meeting up with friends in the evening to sit around and talk about politics, and life and dreams we have, all while practicing the Zen art of shooting darts. I think about sitting around with my friend Ian playing guitar and writing our own compositions for no one but ourselves, just to relieve stress. I think about walking around Barnes and Noble on a Sunday afternoon, browsing the titles and thumbing through my favorite magazines. If you want to know what you crave as a soldier who is deployed, think of all the routines you have, the routines you take for granted, and those are the things you want to do. Think about dropping the kids off for school, of watching television in your favorite armchair in the evening, or even walking through the grocery store. You can even think about the things you don't enjoy, like going to a normal day job or cleaning your house or apartment, and I guarantee that there is a soldier craving those activities right now. They are all things I know I've said I'll never take for granted again.

And yet, while vowing to never take things for granted, I am looking back on this year, even the lowest points, and realizing that these are things I may not experience again and that maybe there were times I even took this for granted. In a way, I'll miss the conversations I've had with my friends here, about all the things we're missing. I'll miss the sense of purpose you have when you wake up for a shift and know that you're part of something larger than yourself. I'll miss the solidarity you feel with men and women who are going through all the same feelings you are, but who are all enduring through them together, in good times and bad. I'll miss the sense of anticipation that there is finality to the hard times, that there is a definite end to this long and strange chapter in anyone's life. There is something to be said about knowing you can't be here forever, that no matter how you feel, things will get better, and they'll do so by the mere fact that soon, never soon enough, but soon you will be home.

I write to you all today knowing that even if we only exchanged a few e-mails, I feel as though I made a friend for life. I also write this entry today with regret that I was never able to write back to all of you. In fact, I can tell you now that throughout this year, the only regret I can say I will live with was not writing to more of you. When those glorious days off would come around, I always had such great expectations that I would sit down at a computer and knock out a couple hundred e-mails just to say thanks for the support. Unfortunately, on far too many of those days off I usually just went to chow and stayed in my tent reading a book or preparing a law school application. For those of you who read this, I want you to know I appreciate absolutely every word you have said. The support was overwhelming, and I am not ashamed to say that many of your letters brought tears to my eyes. Though my blog may have put a face and a name to what may seem like a faceless war for many of you, the e-mails, the care packages, the letters and the support put a name and sometimes a face as well to the heart of true American patriots. As I said to some of you, soldiers may be the fists of American might and goodwill, but you are all the heart and the backbone of America. You support us in our mission, you give us the strength to go on when the days seem so long you just want to throw up your hands and quit. It always seemed that letters of support came at the moments I needed them most, and they were always uplifting. Even the letters from folks who disagreed gave me strength, because I knew in those moments that what I was writing was being read and was having an impact. My mission was not to change hearts or even to change minds on the war, but merely to open minds as to what one soldier was experiencing, what he was thinking about, what was weighing particularly heavy on his heart.

The heart of America's patriots is one of the things I have discovered more than anything else on this deployment. Despite the rhetoric that seemed to go back and forth in the United States on the war, the one thing I am most proud of is the hope that the American people hold for those in Iraq. People from across the world may find it hard to believe that the world's greatest power would be willing to expend its treasure, and even more importantly some of its greatest citizens, just to help out another nation. Regardless of where we started with this war, I believe that this is where we currently stand. We are an incredible nation, I feel that in the depths of my bones, I can sense it in my spirit. Your support of us solidifies that sense, it shows me what being a patriot is, it encourages me to do the same when I return. I too plan on "Adopting a Platoon" once I am a civilian again, on writing letters of support to those soldiers currently away from friends and family.

March 05, 2005

Tonight, for the first time since my blog began in April of 2004, I am writing to you from the United States. In a way, the feelings are overwhelming and can only be defined with one word, surreal.

Arriving the other night, it felt as if even the air was welcoming us home. Is it possible that even the air in America is inviting? I can answer that tonight with absolute assurance. Stepping off the plane, we were greeted by an Army band playing in the background, and a line of Sergeant Majors, a General, and several Colonels welcoming us home and thanking us for our service. It felt like a dream, suddenly it seemed like the entire year momentarily disappeared from my mind and I had never left. I did feel somehow different though, somehow a lot older. I tried soaking every image and every feeling in, narrating the feelings and images in my mind as if I was writing them down that very moment. I didn't want to forget any aspect of it, and if it was a dream I wanted to be able to remember it the next day. I did have dreams like that over the year. In my dreams, I kept waking up in different locations, sometimes I was home, sometimes at different sites in theater, sometimes stepping off the plane like I did last night.

One of the more powerful images for me came as we marched in our company element from the plane to the hangar, passing a group of fire-fighters by their engine; its ladder extended what seemed like hundreds of feet in the air, with a large American flag gently waving in the night sky. The sight of that flag, the sounds of the band, looking around and seeing the men and women I served with taking physical and metaphorical steps closer to being home, combined to form moments of absolute perfection that I know I will remember the rest of my life.

There is now the process of de-mobilization to endure before I can be re-united with my family and have more time to write. I had to find a computer and internet access though, and let you all know that I couldn't be happier to be back in America and that me and my unit had made it home safely.

5

WHO'S YOUR BAGHDADDY?

Captain John Upperman
56th Brigade Combat Team
Texas National Guard
Talil, Iraq
January 2005 – December 2005

S ATURDAY, JANUARY 01, 2005
  In the beginning

Well, here is my first post on the first day of the new year. Welcome to my blog. If you have found your way here, then you are probably family or a friend since I don't know why anyone else would come across this web site.

This is my first attempt at publishing any type of web site so I'm a little nervous about doing it right. I'm not sure if there is some sort of "blog etiquette" that I should be abiding by in order for this to meet the approval of everyone who sees it. Ultimately, I am putting this together so I can communicate with all of you while I'm serving in Iraq, and give you a way to communicate with me as well. It would be difficult for me to consistently email everyone with the latest news … so I'm hoping this will help me get the word out on a regular basis. I plan to post entries regularly, but I'm not sure how often that will be. I'd like to keep it interesting so I don't plan to pepper this site with daily posts that have no value.

I also plan to publish pictures, once I can get the software installed. I'm currently using a military computer, and I can't even change the clock on the blasted thing without administrative access (which I obviously don't have).

I hope to chronicle the interesting events that occur with myself and my unit (56th Brigade Combat Team) over the next year, and hopefully publish some of the good things that are occurring in Iraq since they don't get published in the nightly news. Hopefully all of you will find it valuable, and we can keep it going. I'd hate for this to be one of those "projects" that starts out with a bang to only fizzle after a few weeks.

To quickly bring everyone up to date; I am currently at Ft Hood, TX and have been since my unit was activated last August. We have completed our training and I am scheduled to depart for Kuwait tonight. (I was supposed to depart on Dec 28th, but my name was not on the "list.") Once I get there it may be a while before my next post since I don't know what type of computer access I'm going to have. Once we get to our base camp, I'll have access on a daily basis.

Feel free to post and leave me some messages. I'll talk to you soon.
John

MONDAY, JANUARY 10, 2005
"Let's roll"

Well folks, it is finally game time. I leave in about 2.5 hours for Iraq. I'll be going ahead of my unit as part of the Advance Party in order to get things set up logistically for the main body to arrive. I'm actually kind of excited for a couple of different reasons. One, we are finally leaving "training" mode, and moving into "execution" mode, which means we can start making a difference. Secondly, it means we are beginning the next chapter in this saga, which means I am one step closer to coming back home to my family.

Keep praying for all of the soldiers in my unit. We are entering a crucial time with the elections coming up at the end of the month. Let's also pray that the elections go well, and with a large turnout, which will solidify its legitimacy.

Thanks again to all who have posted. I always enjoy your comments.

John G. – thanks for the offer on the bullet you found ... but ammo is one thing that is not in short supply around here. They hand it out like candy at Halloween. BTW ... was that post your last post to the last post, or is there another post to another post?

Still don't have an address, but I will in about two more weeks.

I have lots of pictures, but still no way to get them uploaded to the blog. I should be able to set something up once we get settled in.

Talk to ya soon.

J

FRIDAY, JANUARY 14, 2005
Ur of the Chaldeans

Well, I'm here and "here" is Talil Air Base which is also know as Camp Adder. You can read more about it at the following link: http://globalsecurity.org/military/world/iraq/tallil.htm

The reference to Ur in my title is due to the fact that the ancient city of Ur is located right outside of the base camp. Ur, of course, was home to the patriarch Abraham in the Old Testament. They run regular tours for soldiers to go and see the archeological sites. I heard it is worth the trip, and plan on going there sometime.

Right now the weather is quite pleasant. It gets pretty cold at night. Enough to require a coat and gloves in the morning. But by mid-afternoon the sun is bright and the temp rises into the mid to high 60s. I'll enjoy it while it lasts. Some of the guys that have been here a while have witnessed temps in the 130s during the summer.

I want to say "thank you" again for all the posts. It's great to see words of encouragement from all my friends at church, Dell, and of course, family. It motivates me to post more often knowing that all of you are reading regularly.

Amy, Alex, Jessica, Jennifer, Seth and Luke – I miss you all very much and think of you every day.

Mom – Megan and I are doing fine. We are emailing each other and trying to figure out when we can link up.

John G. – I adopted you as my brother about 20 years ago. I only wish we would have met sooner. Yes, I can definitely use some space to publish photos. Send me an email and let me know what I need to do.

All my friends at Dell – keep up the good work and get the stock price higher so I can get that boat when I get back. :-)

Gotta go. I'll be blogging again soon.

j

TUESDAY, JANUARY 18, 2005
Interesting day at the office . . .

I had an "interesting" day today. It was neither good nor bad, but it was an experience I wanted to share with all of you.

First, I need to put everything in perspective. As you may recall, when I entered Iraq last week I was flown in on a C-130 transport plane and landed directly in Talil where I am currently based. Therefore, I have never seen Iraq outside the confines of the base camp . . . until today.

As the battalion's logistics officer, I am responsible for the movement, tracking, and accountability of all the unit's equipment. Some of that equipment was mis-routed to a base north of our location, and I had to track it down. So I and my driver grabbed our gear, got into our HMMWV (pronounced "Humvee") and headed "outside the wire."

The surreal-ness of the day began as soon as we got to the gate, and had to "lock and load" our weapons. I've done this a thousand times before over the course of my military career and have fired my weapon many times, but this was the first time I did it with the intent of defending myself if necessary. I was a little on edge, but of course everything went fine and we made it to our destination without any incident.

We did, however, encounter some Iraqi citizens along the way. They were mainly Bedouins (nomadic sheep herders) who had set up their tents along the highway. The conditions they live in would make most of you cringe, and it really affected me emotionally. There were children along the route, some appearing to be as young as 4 years old, running up to the edge of the road as we passed by, holding their hands out and/ or motioning to their mouths indicating that they wanted something to eat. We can't do anything about it since giving them handouts only encourages them to run towards our vehicles. We are typically going about 60 mph and they could really get hurt. Not to mention that insurgents have used children in the past to get convoys to slow down in order to conduct an ambush. I thought about how protective I am of my kids, and these little tykes are running up to the edge of the highway.

I know it is an overused cliché, but we are truly blessed as Americans. We have wealth and privilege that these people can not even fathom. I ask that you take some time today and reflect on how blessed you really are. Regardless of your circumstances, I know you are better off than the people I saw today.

God bless,

j

FRIDAY, JANUARY 21, 2005
I'm going postal

It has finally arrived! I now have a mailing address!
Here it is:

John Upperman
HHC, 3-112 Armor
56th Brigade Combat Team, APOAE 09384

Now, there was an earlier address that I thought was the right address... and it was ... to the other unit's address ... but not to our address.

Make sense?

Bottom line: if I gave you an address before today (i.e. Dad and Amy) it had the wrong APO. So make sure you use this one.

I know a lot of you have been requesting this for quite some time, and have also asked what types of items guys would like to receive over here. I can tell you that between charities, school organizations, churches, and other generous groups there are enough toiletries over here to stock a Super Wal Mart. Here are some suggestions based on my own experience and observations:

Lip Balm – the good stuff . . . I picked some up the other day and when I put it on it tasted awful.

Foot powder – we're wearing boots all the time and our feet . . . well . . . 'nuff said about that.

DVDs – a lot of the Joes have a notebook, or a portable DVD player to pass the time when it's not busy. If you have some laying around that you don't want anymore someone here will appreciate it.

Music – Just send anything you don't listen to anymore. Regardless of the genre, someone here will appreciate it. I even found a guy listening to Barry Manilow the other day. Kinda diminishes the image of a steely-eyed killer . . . but each to his own.

Scooby Snacks – any kind of candy, or munchies. Keep in mind that it will be traveling half way around the world. You'll need to be even more selective once the weather starts to warm up.

Books & Magazines – again . . . anything you've got laying around that you don't want anymore (nothing inappropriate please).

Beyond the above, just use your imagination and send something you would like to have if you were in a desolate, third-world country for a year. :-)

Rick M. – I would have you send that boat over here, but quite frankly, there ain't a whole lot of water over here. So just put a cover on it and we'll take it for a spin when I get back.

TTFN

j

FRIDAY, JANUARY 28, 2005
The hardest thing I have ever done

I'm going to bare my soul for a moment. I just finished "chatting" with my wife via instant messenger, and the pain of being apart from her is really starting to hit me.

This deployment is by far the hardest thing I have ever had to do.

It's not being here that is so hard. I have endured far worse conditions during my military career. It is being away from my family that makes this so tough. There is so much I miss that if I ponder it for too long it really starts to get to me.

I miss my oldest son, Alex, and his incredible wit and sense of humor. I miss being amazed by his level of intelligence and maturity. I only wish that I had been as level-headed as he is when I was his age.

I miss my fourteen-year old daughter, Jessica, and the way she gives me a hug every single morning and puts her head on my chest . . . as if to remind me that no matter how big she gets she will always be my little girl.

I miss my thirteen-year old daughter, Jennifer, who has a smile as big as the sun and laughter that is contagious. I miss the joy I feel when I see her taking the time to play with her little brothers for hours at a time. She has something special inside of her that she does not even realize.

I miss my five-year old son, Seth, and his incredible grasp of the world around him at such a young age. I miss listening to him carefully enunciate every syllable as he speaks, and the mind-boggling statements he makes that are well beyond his years.

I miss my two-year old son, Luke, and the way he runs to me with arms wide open when I walk through the door. I miss hearing him say to me, "lets wessle daddy", and his incessant giggling as we "wessle".

I miss my beautiful wife, Amy who is my best friend in the entire world. I miss looking into her beautiful eyes and holding her close to me. I miss the feeling I have when I am with her and the fact that I am still infatuated with her after fifteen years of marriage. I miss her laugh-

ter and her impenetrable optimism that keeps my suspicious pragma-
tism in check. I miss going to the grocery store with her just so I have an
excuse to hang out with her. I miss feeling her next to me when I go to
sleep at night.

I miss home.

J

SATURDAY, JANUARY 29, 2005
Making History

Our unit took part in a historic moment yesterday. We had the distinct privilege of escorting and delivering the ballots that will be used
in Sunday's election.

I talked to one of the guys who was about to go on the mission, and he
was really pumped about what he was about to do. The insurgents would
love to get their hands on those ballots and cause havoc in the election
process, and we are here to make sure they don't even get the chance.

Make no mistake, they will continue to use terror and intimidation to
keep people from the polls. I only pray that the Iraqi citizens will have
the courage and conviction to stand against them and begin the process
of taking their country back.

I'm proud that we have the opportunity to contribute and make a difference.

"Above all, we must realize that no arsenal, or no weapon in the arse-
nals of the world, is so formidable as the will and moral courage of free
men and women."

—Ronald Reagan

J

FEBRUARY 1st

I really appreciate all the encouraging notes. I know a lot of you are
checking the blog regularly, and I want all of you to know that I do the

same. Your words of encouragement are a real morale booster, and they are the first thing I look at when I boot up my computer in the morning (most of you post as I'm sleeping since we're 9 hours ahead of Central).

This has become my hobby while I'm here and I really look forward to putting more effort into it. Just know that all of your comments are deeply appreciated and are sustaining me while I'm here.

I am determined to "thrive" and not just "survive" during this deployment and become a better person in the process.

Thanks again to all of you.
John

Captain Orlando Bonilla

Late yesterday I received an email from a friend of mine currently stationed in Baghdad. The subject line was titled "CPT Orlando Bonilla", who is a mutual friend of ours and a helicopter pilot deployed with the 1st Cavalry Division.

I had a bad feeling when I saw the subject line, and unfortunately my fears were proven true. My friend was writing to inform me that Orlando had been killed in a helicopter crash on January 29th. The crash is still under investigation, but people close to the situation are confident it was an accident that occurred when Orlando's helicopter hit some electrical wires. Orlando and I were not close. It had been years since we last spoke, but events like this really hit home when it's someone you know.

What makes this story even more tragic is the fact that Orlando's wife just lost her father in the Iraq conflict last March. I can not fathom what she must be going through, but was amazed at her response to the situation. Here is a quote from the CNN article:

"I stand behind my daddy and my husband, and I stand behind the job they had to do, and that's my take on it," she said. "I just support them, regardless of who sent them over there and why they sent them over there, no matter whether it's for right or wrong reasons."

No one would have blamed her if she had responded in bitterness or anger, but instead she responded with grace and courage.

I'm sure she will have difficult days ahead, and I ask that you keep her and the rest of Orlando's family in your prayers.

John

THURSDAY, FEBRUARY 03, 2005
Nu Shooz

Here is some good news from the front. This is the kind of stuff you'll never see on the evening news, but is more indicative of what is really going on over here on a day-to-day basis.

Our medical platoon went on a mission the other day to provide basic medical care for the local Bedouin community. Additionally, they brought some donated shoes for the children, which for these kids is a rarity. Most of the time you see them running around in bare feet, and contrary to popular belief it does get pretty cool here in the winter (lows in the 40s). So you know their little tootsies have to get cold.

I realize that some of my recent posts have been kind of "heavy" so I wanted to share something on the lighter side. I didn't intend to bring everyone down, but I do want this blog to be an honest depiction of my life while I'm here . . . both good and bad.

I sincerely appreciate the continual words of support and prayer from all of you. It truly is a morale booster, and I can feel God's sustainment.

Things are going well here and the days are passing quickly. The quicker the better since with each passing day I am one step closer to home.

John

SATURDAY, FEBRUARY 12, 2005
Contact

Our unit had its first contact with the enemy two days ago. One of our convoys was hit by an improvised explosive device (IED) on its way to

Baghdad.

Everyone is okay.

IED is just a fancy name for a homemade bomb. This has been the insurgents' modus operandi for quite some time. They place the bombs on the side of a road that has a lot of military traffic, and then wait for just the right moment to blow it. They are usually about 300 meters away hiding like cowards when they detonate it. They know if they fight us toe-to-toe they will get to meet Allah sooner than they hoped.

Two of the guys in the convoy suffered minor injuries. One caught some shrapnel in the face, and the other suffered a mild concussion. I saw them both today, and they both look and act fine. They are very fortunate since it could have been a lot worse.

I know this is news that a lot of people don't want to hear (i.e. my parents, wife, kids ... etc), but I want to keep everything in perspective. Yes, the elections were a huge success, and a true testament to what we have accomplished here, but the insurgents are still active and they will not stop until we have eliminated every last one of them.
That won't be anytime soon.

God Bless,
John

TUESDAY, FEBRUARY 15, 2005
Road Trip

I went on my first significant road trip the other day. I know one of my previous posts talked about a trip I took "outside of the wire", but that one was only about twenty minutes from our current location, whereas this one kept us on the road for about six hours each way. We went through some areas where we are not real popular, which was a little nerve racking. Fortunately, however, the trip ended without any incidents.

... children who come running up when they see American vehicles. I'd like to say its because they love us so much, but the truth is that they just want us to throw them some MREs (meals ready to eat). Trust me, you have to be really hungry to want an MRE.

... during the entire ride all I saw was land that is as flat as West Texas, and then we suddenly ran into this huge escarpment.... the next morning when we were about to push out again ... I remember his briefing going something like this, "Alright guys, if you see someone with an AK-47 and they are pointing it at you ... shoot 'em."

I enjoyed his brevity.

Relatively speaking, the trip was not a big deal. My little sister, Megan, is in a transportation unit and she and her fellow soldiers are on the road, and putting themselves in harm's way for days at a time. As my mom pointed out in a previous post, they suffered their first loss last week. There is a 23 year old girl who will not be going home now. Please keep Megan and her unit in your prayers as well.

More to come.

j

TUESDAY, MARCH 08, 2005
Hope

I apologize it has been so long since my last post, but things have been really busy. Nothing out of the ordinary, just a lot of nitnoid stuff that keeps me running around all day.

(For those of you wondering what the heck "nitnoid" means, you won't find it in the dictionary. However, it is used frequently in America as slang to indicate a "small matter of no consequence, or something that's nit-pickingly frustrating.")

Anyway, enough of that and on to more interesting things.

Last week our Battalion Chaplain had the opportunity to visit the city of Babylon (yes ... that Babylon; Tower of Babel, King Nebuchadnezzar, etc.) He returned with some really interesting photos of the of the ancient sites, but what I found most interesting was the story he told about a conversation he had with one of the Iraqis escorting him through the sites. They broached the subject of the recent elections, and the chaplain asked him if he felt things were getting better in his country. To which the man replied, "Yes . . . before we had nothing to look forward to, but now we have hope."

There is no medicine like hope, no incentive so great, and no tonic so powerful as expectation of something better tomorrow.

—Orison Marden

John

THURSDAY, MARCH 10, 2005
Thank You!!!!

I have received so much support from so many people, I wanted to take a moment to show my appreciation to the following (in no certain order):

Ginny Rollie and all my coworkers at Dell

All of you have been incredibly supportive from the beginning. I'll never forget when I first found out that I was being activated for deployment. I was truly blown away by all the words of support and encouragement. Your recent packages have been a real morale booster to me and a lot of other troops. I look forward to getting back to the "real world" and working with all of you again. Ginny – you are the hub that keeps that wagon wheel rolling.

Jim Dunmire and his fellow coworkers at J.C. Penny

I received your care packages yesterday, and all I can say is "Wow!" Nine packages in one day made me really popular with the mail handler (he had to haul them all from the post office). I made it worth his while by opening them up and letting him take what he needed. You have blessed more soldiers than I can list, and we all appreciate it greatly. Please pass on our gratitude to everyone who was involved in such a large effort.

Aunt Maidi and Uncle Ivan

Aunt Maidi, your emails of encouragement always arrive at the perfect time and I want you to know what a morale booster they are.

I appreciate your unwavering support, and your care packages. You are truly a class act.

Mom & Dad

I know having two of your kids deployed has been tough for both of you. Your packages have been great . . . especially since they are just for me. :-) I am the man I am today because of both of you. I love you both, and I look forward to our next reunion.

Gary Moore

Your friendship has been a real blessing, and I always get a lift from your emails. It is always great to hear from you, and if there has ever been a time I haven't written back it is not due to lack of appreciation. You are a true friend and I look forward to my next flying lesson.

Justus and Joan

Justus, I appreciate your posts . . . especially the funny ones. I can use all the laughter I can get over here. I just received your package, and I really appreciate you both making the effort to show your support. On a final note . . . Justus, this is just for you . . . yeah, you little brother . . . lean in real close, and listen to your older, wiser brother . . . Propose to the girl for the love of Pete!!" I expect to come home to a wedding.

John Geyerman

14 pounds of coffee and several hundred MP3s will go a long way in making this year more bearable. Thank you for the longest lasting friendship of my life.

Charles and Carol

Thank you for your thoughtful posts, emails, and the recent goodies. I know you have a true appreciation for all of this since you have "been there, done that, and got the t-shirt." It's always good to hear from you.

Donn and Sue

I am truly blessed to have such great in-laws. You both have been extremely supportive, and I know you are checking on Amy on a regular basis. Thanks for your packages and words of encouragement and support.

Amy, Alex, Jessica, Jennifer, Seth, and Luke

Each of you gives me the motivation that keeps me going over here.

While this is extremely difficult, I want to learn all I can from the experience so I can be a better husband and father when I get back. I constantly day dream of when we are all together again, and I can hold each of you in my arms. I am truly amazed at how much God has blessed me with such a beautiful family. You are my passion.

There are so many others that I could thank for their posts, emails, prayers, and lending a helping hand to Amy while I'm gone. I appreciate each and every one of you, and I want you to know that your support makes all the difference over here.

You are all awesome people.

j

MONDAY, MARCH 14, 2005
On the road again

Well, it looks like I'm moving again. I got the word a few days ago that our command post will be moving to a base located a few hours north of here. Our mission is going to change a bit, and we will pick up some additional responsibilities. During the move I will have very limited access and it could be a while before I can post again. I just wanted to let everyone know so you don't think I'm being a slacker. Continue to post and send emails, and I will check on them as soon as I can.

I'm sure you have noticed that I have not been posting any pictures recently. I have run into some technical difficulties that currently prevent me from doing so. The "long and short" of it is that I can no longer connect my personal computer to the military network (I wasn't really supposed to be doing it to begin with, but as usual I was trying to "buck the system"). My personal computer has the software that allows me to upload photos, and obviously my military computer does not, nor am I allowed to install it.

In order to remedy this situation about 30 of us have gotten together to purchase our own satellite internet system so we can have unrestricted access at any time. It's a bit pricey at $7,000, but we've raised about half the funds and it will be well worth it. Once we have it set up I will be able to publish all the photos I want.

That's all for now. I would tell you more about the move and the new mission . . . but then I'd have to kill you. ;-)

TTFN

j

SUNDAY, MARCH 27, 2005
Soldiers

Well, I'm finally back up and running with my computer equipment so I will be able to blog more often and post pictures again (and there was much clapping and rejoicing).

I've posted a lot of pictures of the local Iraqi people, and I will continue to do so in the future. However, I wanted to pay tribute to some real heroes . . . the American soldier. The pictures that follow are all of guys in my unit. You will probably never read about them in the paper, but they put their necks on the line every day. They obviously don't do it for the money, glory, or fame since they will receive little or none of those during their deployment here. They do it because that's just what soldiers do, and at the end of the day all that matters is the guy on your left and your right and making sure everyone gets back home safe . . .

. . . All of these photos reflect every day occurrences here. Nothing too exciting, but as my Father-n-Law aptly puts it, " . . . no excitement in a combat zone is a good thing."

I agree.

Let's save all of the excitement for when we all come home.

j

MONDAY, APRIL 04, 2005
Fallen

I attended my first memorial service today. I hope it was my last.

The fallen soldier was not a member of my unit, nor did I know him.

He belonged to an Artillery unit that is right next to us and conducts the same type of missions we do, so I felt an obligation to attend. On March 30th his squad was running a convoy north of here when a vehicle packed with explosives pulled up next to them and detonated. Two other soldiers in the squad were wounded.

I'm not sharing this story for the shock value, but rather I wanted to quickly record the memory I have of attending the service. One that will be forever etched in my mind. I will always remember the display. At the foot of an M16 rifle standing on its barrel end was a pair of desert combat boots filled only by the memory of the soldier who once wore them. Mounted on the butt stock of the weapon was the soldier's combat helmet with his name still affixed; a tradition that stems from how the location of a fallen soldier was marked on the battlefield. Hanging from the M16 were the deceased's dog tags blowing in the wind like a wind chime singing the hopes and aspirations of a 21 year old man that will never come to pass. I'll never forget the haunting sound of a single bugle playing Taps, or the jolting report of a 21 gun salute. All of this was like a kick in the gut reality check of the price that is being paid here.

I find myself somewhat conflicted after an experience like this. I firmly believe in what we are doing here, and I know we will succeed. On the other hand, however, I question the cost and whether it is worth it.

Don't get me wrong, I'm not here to question or debate the war in Iraq. I just know this guy wanted to go home some day just as much as I do . . . but he won't.

"The soldier above all others prays for peace, for it is the soldier who must suffer and bear the deepest wounds and scars of war."

—General Douglas Macarthur

posted by John at 3:23 AM

THURSDAY, APRIL 07, 2005
Hail to the Chief

Today was a momentous day in the history of Iraq. Today, the first freely elected President in 50 years was sworn in and a new Prime Minister was appointed. The newly elected President is the Kurdish Jalal Talabani and the PM is Ibrahim al-Jaafari, who is a Shiite.

As I write this I can hear what you're thinking, "Shiite . . . Kurd . . . Sunni, what the heck does all that mean?" Trust me, I follow this stuff pretty closely and I still find it confusing. So in an effort to expand your geo-political knowledge from the perspective of someone on the ground I'll give you a quick lesson. (I promise to keep it simple so I don't lose your attention. Especially you, Amy. Don't go surf'n over to eBay before you read all the way through.)

Shiite (also referred to as Shia): Are the largest ethnic group in Iraq. They tend to live in more rural areas and practice a more conservative form of Islam. When I'm on the road and see sheep and camel herders outside of small villages, they are most likely Shiites.

Kurds: The second largest ethnic group in Iraq, and the hardest to categorize. They are considered Sunni Muslim, but because of their nomadic, non-Arab past they have a completely different heritage and dialect. They have been oppressed for centuries, and with the fall of the Ottoman Empire after WWI they were promised an independent state, which was never fulfilled. They have been striving for their independence ever since, and this strife contributed to Saddam's murderous chemical attack on the city of Halabja in 1988.

Sunnis: The ethnic minority in Iraq, but the ruling power under Saddam. Saddam was a Sunni, so they have had all the power for the last 30 years. They have a minority of seats in the National Assembly largely due to the fact that most of them boycotted the elections.

Now that all of this is as clear as mud, maybe some of the news will make a little more sense to you.

I'm sure the news of the newly elected officials taking office may not be very exciting to everyone back home, and the story was probably buried beneath coverage of the Pope's funeral, and the Michael Jackson trial. To those of us here, however, it means we are one step closer to handing this country back to the Iraqi people, which means we are that much closer to getting everyone home.

Oh…one other thing that was pretty cool about today's proceedings… Sadaam watched the whole thing from his prison cell.

I love it when a good plan comes together.

John

FRIDAY, APRIL 22, 2005
A daughter's poem
This poem was written by my daughter, Jessica.

The Soldier

You are my hero
Doing what you are doing.
Leaving our family and
fighting for another
so that we may keep our freedom.
We live in the land of the free
because of the brave.
You are the brave.
You are my hero.
You are my father.

> Thanks, sweetie.
> I'm walking a little taller today.

SUNDAY, MAY 22, 2005
More pics you won't see on the news

I seem to have found my blog niche. There are a lot of military blogs being published from the front lines and they all have the unique perspective of the individuals writing them. Some are simply day-to-day journals, others like Alexander the Average contemplate the impact of American foreign policy and the ideological war we are waging, and others like Michael Yon give gripping accounts of toe-to-toe slug fests with the insurgents that are both inspiring and painful.

My blog is none of these. I want to show you the real people of this country. Not the radicals and the criminals, but the every day people that are trying to live their lives and figure out how this is all going to pan out. The people of Iraq are no more like the cowardly insurgents you see on the news than you and I are like the people in Hollywood movies. I still have not reached a point where I easily trust any of them, but I occasionally see glimpses of their lives that remind me that they are ordinary people . . . just like you and I. You cannot allow your judgment of this nation and its people be shaped by what you see on the evening news. The main stream media (MSM) is only going to show you profitable news. News that shocks, grabs your attention, and drives ratings. They will never report the subtle victories that occur here everyday.

They won't show you people putting aside old prejudices and forging new friendships . . . Nor will they show you people working to make a better future . . . or contemplating life just like you and I do. They won't show you the laughter . . . nor the playfulness. But I will.

John

MONDAY, MAY 30, 2005
Memorial Day

Today is the day we remember the dead. In particular we remember those who have died in our nation's service. This day has become one mainly marked by a day off from work and outdoor barbeques. It has become more of an annual tribute to the opening days of summer than an actual day of reflection. I don't think any of these things are wrong. I just think that while we celebrate we should take time to remember why we celebrate. For 1,647 families this and future Memorial days will take on new meaning since this is the number of soldiers who have paid the ultimate sacrifice since the war in Iraq began.

Obviously, we will not have the day off nor will there be any parades or festivities. So in order to observe and remember I took time today to visit a few of the Memorials we have here that are dedicated to soldiers from our base camp that have fallen. I took pictures as I went along. They didn't turn out very well, but at least a few more people will remember their names today.

Specialist Daniel Paul Unger

A Company, 1-185 Armor

March 21, 1985 – May 25, 2004

"SPC Unger, 19, of Exeter, California, was fatally wounded on May 25th, 2004 at Forward Operating Base Kalsu when FOB Kalsu came under a heavy volley of 100MM Mortar Fire. In total disregard for his own safety, SPC Unger directed local nationals that he was escorting to safety while executing the battle drill for indirect fire. His actions saved two lives."

Corporal Darrell L. Smith

D Company, 1-152 Infantry

February 22, 1975 – November 23, 2003

"CPL Smith of Otwell, Indiana, was part of an Infantry Squad assigned to provide security around Convoy Support Center Scania, Forward Operating Base Kalsu, Camp Nakamura, and MSR Tampa. CPL Smith gave his life on 23 November, while conducting a combat patrol on the northern sector of MSR Tampa."

Sergeant Heath A. McMillin

105th Military Police Company

May 24, 1974 – July 27, 2003

Specialist Michael L. Williams

105th Military Police Company

September 11, 1957 – October 17, 2003

"SGT McMillin of Canandaigua, New York, and SPC Williams of Buffalo, New York were part of MSR Patrols patrolling their AOR when their vehicles were engaged by Improvised Explosive Devices (IEDs)."

Specialist Paul T. Nakamura

437th Medical Company

October 17, 1981 – June 19, 2003

"SPC Nakamura of Santa Fe Springs, California, was part of an Ambulance Crew transporting an injured soldier from CSC Scania to LSA Dogwood for further treatment when his FLA was struck by an RPG and small arms fire."

Sergeant Eric Toth

A Battery, 1-623 Field Artillery Battalion

April 16, 1983 – March 30, 2005

"SGT Toth of Edmonton, KY, was part of a convoy escort that was returning to CSC Scania after escorting a convoy north when his vehicle was struck by a Vehicle Borne Improvised Explosive Device (VBIED)."

I attended SGT Toth's memorial service and wrote about it in a previous post titled Fallen.

I sincerely hope you have a wonderful Memorial Day full of good food and laughter. Just take time to remember.

John

MONDAY, JUNE 06, 2005

Road Warriors

I just returned from a short trip. My destination was six hours round trip, and the three hours each way just about sucked the life out of me. The ride is monotonous and the barely-working air conditioner was struggling to make a difference in the 115 degree temperature outside. Combine all of this with an extra 40 pounds of body armor and gear, and you have a sweat-drenched uniform at the end of the trip.

Yet I only do this a few times a month. The troops in our unit are doing this daily and sometimes they are traveling ten or twelve hours round trip. They are either providing security for re-supply convoys, or they are performing patrols along the road looking for IED's or any other signs of bad guys. As they repeatedly drive along these routes they are watching and waiting for the next ambush. I'm sure they feel like moving targets as they wonder when the next IED, RPG, and/or the next round of gunfire goes off in a less than desirable direction. A vast majority of the time nothing happens, but sometimes there is that "brief moment of chaos" that I have referred to previously. So far we have been fortunate with no serious injuries. But there have been some very close calls.

I guess my point in all of this (and yes, I do have one) is that I see these guys doing this day in and day out, and it makes me proud. It reminds me of why we have the greatest Army in the world. Because men like these (some are barely old enough to be called "men") are willing to do a job that no one else will do. Do they gripe and complain? You betcha! Griping is practically an art form in the Army. If Joe isn't complaining about something, then he's probably sleeping. But despite all the moaning and groaning, he crawls out of the rack every morning and does his job in a manner that should make you proud. Every day he puts his neck on the line for a place he doesn't call home and for a people that he doesn't know . . . and he does it with honor and integrity.

Let no one convince you of anything less.
John

TUESDAY, JULY 05, 2005
Trouble sleeping . . .

We received some intel last night that our base was going to be mortared (a mortar is an indirect fire weapon which has a range of approximately 3 to 7 kilometers depending on the size). Our area has been relatively quiet for a while now. We've had a few incidents outside the wire, but there has not been a direct attack on this base for about 10 months. However, we have seen increased activity since the commencement of some of the major operations in the Baghdad area to crack down on enemy activity. The insurgents are just like cockroaches that scatter when you turn on the lights and come looking for them and it appears some of them may have scattered into our area. We immediately launched our Quick Reaction Force (QRF) and some combat patrols who were out all night looking for suspicious activity.

I'm happy to report that nothing happened. This was our first interaction with this particular informant, but when linked to some other activity his story seemed credible. Given that nothing occurred there are only a few possibilities:

1. He concocted the story in order to make himself look like a good guy and will later try to get something in return (job, money ... etc).

2. He was telling the truth, but our QRF and combat patrols scared the bad guys (i.e. cockroaches) away.

3. The cockroaches intentionally fed this informant bad information just to see how we would react and thus gain insight into our tactics and procedures.

Only time will tell which of these is right.

Needless to say, it's a bit difficult to sleep when you have this kind of info looming over your head. I stayed up until about 12:30 a.m. and then realized there was little I could do (too many cooks spoil the broth). I tried to lie down and get some shut-eye but found myself bolting upright every time I heard a HMMWV roll by or any other strange noise. I felt like such a wuss since I know there are soldiers in other parts of Iraq that get mortared on a regular basis.

As I was lying there I began to reflect on all the times I had restless nights back home over such insignificant things.

"Please God, let me get that promotion."

"Man, I wish I made more money."

"What am I going to do about these bills?"

"How can I afford to get that new home ... new car ... or some new 'thing'?"

"Man, am I ticked off right now ... ummm ... what were we fighting about?"

All of those restless nights seem so trivial now that I almost start to laugh. I look at how most Iraqis live and realize that once I'm back home I should sleep like a baby. I am blessed with the love of a wonderful woman. My children are all healthy, beautiful, and smart. I have great friends, a good job, and I live in a country that offers freedom and safety like none other in the world. What do I have to lose sleep over?

God is teaching me so much while I'm over here and I have promised myself that I will not forget it after I get back home.

Later,

j

SUNDAY, JULY 17, 2005
Scum

Early yesterday morning there was an insurgent attack to the north of our base camp. This in and of itself is not unusual but the nature of the attack serves to illustrate the level of depravity of these scumbags.

In the morning hours there was a funeral procession traveling along the main highway that eventually leads into Baghdad. As the procession was moving it came under insurgent attack, which resulted in a few dead and several wounded civilians.

Subsequently, an Army Military Police unit was notified of the attack and moved into the area to provide support. Once they arrived and secured the area it appeared the insurgents had left the scene so the MP unit began treating the civilian wounded. Unbeknownst to them, however, the insurgents left behind a Trojan horse in the form of a car bomb. It was remotely detonated, which resulted in several more civilian and U.S. casualties.

In other words, the insurgents attacked innocent civilians knowing that we would arrive to offer medical aid and then left a car bomb to attack the U.S. forces as they were treating the wounded.

This is the bile we are dealing with on a daily basis. I have a hard time referring to them as "men" because they are human in form only. They have no soul, no conscience, or anything else that permits them to be associated with the human race. They are an evil cancer and they need to be extracted from the body of earth.

We are here to conduct the surgery.

John

FRIDAY, AUGUST 26, 2005
Wake up call

My alarm clock went off this morning, and as usual I habitually hit the snooze button. About three minutes later we all woke to the sound of mortar rounds impacting. Needless to say, I got up without hitting the snooze button anymore and headed straight for the bunker. Everyone is okay.

This was a real wake up call. After coming back from leave one tends to be complacent as your mind is filled with thoughts of home and a renewed sense of anticipation of returning. The stark reality is that we have a way to go before we return home, and there are people out there who want to bring us harm. It doesn't really matter whether their motive is political, criminal, vengeance, or anything else. All that matters is that they want to kill us. The reverse is true as well . . . we don't really care about their motive. All we care about is ensuring that they fail . . . and they will.

j

MONDAY, AUGUST 29, 2005
Gotcha!

We caught some of the scumbags that were responsible for Saturday's mortar attack. A raid was organized and conducted in the early morning hours yesterday and we netted several bad guys. Out of this group of thieves we have identified at least four of them as suspected members of Muqtada al-Sadr's militia. The troops are all pumped from the results of a successful mission, but we are not done yet. We are continuing to tighten the noose in order to flush more of these rodents out of their hiding places. Obviously I can't provide a lot of detail, but I will post updates as I can.

"If you are going to yank the tiger's tail, you had better have a plan for dealing with his teeth."

John

TUESDAY, SEPTEMBER 13, 2005
Brrrrr

I stepped out of my tent this morning and was surprised by a very cool breeze. I looked at a thermometer and it was 76 degrees. I can't remember the last time it was that cool. It's currently 9:30 am and the temp is only 90 degrees and usually it has broken 100 by now. The forecast for today is 110 which will seem like a cool autumn day compared to the consistent 130 degree plus temps we have had for so long.

The season is changing.

posted by John at 10:15 PM

THURSDAY, SEPTEMBER 15, 2005
Babylon

For the past fifteen years, any discussion about Iraq has been negative. I know most people my age knew nothing about the country until the first Gulf War. Now my teenage daughters have grown their entire lives knowing it only as a place ruled by an evil dictator and now as a place where their Dad has to go serve for a year.

During that same time period the only news about Iraq has referenced war, Saddam Hussein, U.N. sanctions and now the insurgency. Because of all of this "bad press" people no longer recognize this region for the incredibly rich history it contains. This area is the Cradle of Civilization and is the birthplace of some of the most ancient cities known to man. I had the unique privilege of touring one of those ancient sites and the experience was pretty amazing.

Many people know of the city of Babylon from the Bible stories found in the Old Testament which tell of the reign of King Nebuchadnezzar, and the stories of The Tower of Babel and Daniel in the Lion's Den. This city was considered the mightiest of its time and contained the famous Hanging Gardens, which is one of the seven wonders of the ancient world.

The city was eventually conquered and laid to ruin and due to the kilned mud and clay bricks used in the construction, the remaining structures have significantly decayed over time. In the early 1980's Saddam began reconstructing certain portions of the city. He did this not because of his love of history but because of his own delusions of grandeur and because he saw himself as the next King Nebuchadnezzar. Archeologists cringe at what he did since he built over the actual sites thus destroying many of the artifacts. The original bricks, which rise two or three feet from the ground, contain ancient inscriptions praising Nebuchadnezzar. Above these, Saddam Hussein's workers laid more than 60-million sand colored bricks with the words, "In the era of Saddam Hussein, protector of Iraq, who rebuilt civilization and rebuilt Babylon." The new bricks began to crack after only ten years and based on what I've seen during my travels his "rebuilt civilization" didn't fare too well either.

Saddam's megalomania is further demonstrated here by the home he built for himself. First he built a hill so the structure would sit higher then any other in the area and then built a four story palace complete with marble floors and golden fixtures. Local villagers say that he had over a thousand people displaced during its construction, but then never really used it. Since the fall of his regime it has been looted and sits empty, looking over villages of mud huts and stands as yet another symbol of his selfishness and greed.

... the area is very lush with vegetation, which is why this particular region is referred to as the Fertile Crescent.

As we were leaving, I overheard my brigade commander telling someone that people will one day pay thousands of dollars to visit this area and see what we had just seen. Obviously that can only happen once the country is stable and secure and I believe he is right.

I stood in the place where civilization was born and branched out into the rest of the world. Now it is time for us to bring civilization back.

John

MONDAY, SEPTEMBER 26, 2005
Milestones

I apologize for the sparse blogging of late, but I have found myself busier than usual. The good news is that the busyness is being driven by our quickly approaching redeployment date (i.e. we're getting ready to go home). We still have a couple of months to go here, but we are definitely within the window that necessitates planning.

One particular milestone that brings me much relief and joy is seeing my little sister over here for the last time. (She has been serving in Iraq for the past year as part of Transportation Company from the Illinois National Guard). Although it has been a great pleasure having the ability to occasionally spend time with family while I have been here, I will not miss worrying about her as she takes another trip on what are very dangerous roads. She has done her time, served with distinction, and now it is time for her to go and let someone else take their turn.

Sis – if you are reading this, please know that I am very proud of you… but I am also glad you are leaving. :-)

I'll see you when I get back.

Big bro'
John

MONDAY, OCTOBER 10, 2005
Shadow Run

A soldier came in tonight needing to borrow some equipment so he could get ready for a mission. It was about 2100 hrs (about 9:00 pm) and I was curious what they were getting ready to do.

"Where ya'll going?," I asked.

"Shadow run," he replied.

A "shadow run" is when a gun team runs behind a convoy as extra security. The extra combat power gives the entire convoy added flexibility to maneuver against the enemy in the event of an attack. The practice itself is not unusual, but takes on new meaning when they are going north (north bad) and we are in the middle of Ramadan, which brings an increase in insurgent activity.

"Be safe," I demanded.

"God, I hope so," he replied as he walked out the door.

We are down to the last couple months of our deployment, and I am anxious for the day when I don't have to worry about stuff like this anymore. I look forward to having a normal conversation with my coworkers, and I imagine it going something like this:

"Hey, Gary . . . where you going?"

"To a meeting."

"Okay . . . be safe."

"Uhhhh . . . okay." (as I get a strange look).

Yeah . . . I can picture it now.

That will be a good day.

John

TUESDAY, OCTOBER 25, 2005
On the Edge of History

I apologize for my long absence, but I have been on the road a lot lately with very limited internet access. I left my base two weeks ago for a two day meeting, and I just got back. In fact, I just returned from Kuwait, which was never in my travel plans to begin with. Much has happened since my last post; the most notable of which was the election ratifying the Iraqi Constitution on October 15th. I think it is important to revisit the fact that the weekend of the vote was one of the most peaceful since the beginning of the war. Despite the looming threat of car bombs and suicide bombers, 66% of registered voters cast their vote and thus took a significant step towards giving ownership of the governance of Iraq back to the Iraqi people.

During the day of the elections, our battalion chaplain had the opportunity to capture some photos of some local villagers at the market

HAPPY IRAQIS SHOW OFF THEIR INK-STAINED FINGERS
AFTER VOTING IN CONSTITUTIONAL ELECTIONS IN 2005.
Photo courtesy Captain John Upperman

after they had voted. As he relayed the story he shared with me that when he noticed their dye-stained fingers he motioned for them to raise them so he could take their photos. He said at first they gave him a puzzled look and it was apparent they didn't understand why he was so interested in seeing the proof of their ballot casting. He continued by saying, "Sitting on the outside looking in we understand the significance, but they don't see it yet. They don't even realize they are on the edge of history."

Maybe not now ... but one day they will.

John

MONDAY, OCTOBER 31, 2005
False Alarm

Late last night as I was sleeping, I was jolted back to consciousness by the screeching sound of the camp siren. The siren is referred to as the "big voice" and it is used to sound the alarm in the event of enemy attack.

So here I am sound asleep and I hear the unmistakable sound of the sirens blasting in the dead of night. My immediate thought was, "mortar attack!" and I quickly jumped out of bed and started heading for the bunker. Despite my sleep induced grogginess, I quickly realized there was another noise that was noticeably missing ... the sound of mortar rounds exploding. (This is an important point since no one would know to sound the alarm until after the first mortar round had impacted).

At about that moment, the siren fell silent and was quickly followed by the "all clear" which indicates the danger has passed. As I stood there in nothing but my shorts and flip-flops, I was completely befuddled by what had just occurred. "Surely that wasn't a drill" I thought to myself as I made my way back to bed. It took me a few minutes to get my heart rate back down but I soon drifted back to sleep.

The next morning I found out the truth. Some klutz in the TOC had bumped into the siren control panel and set it off.

Not cool. Not cool at all.

John

WEDNESDAY, NOVEMBER 09, 2005

This was probably the last time I will interact with the local Iraqi people. My unit will be going back home soon, and I need to focus all of my efforts on redeployment activities.

Regardless of how many times I go on these types of missions, their impact is always the same. I am continually impressed and frustrated with the local populace and I am always a sucker for the kids. If there is anything that will be forever impressed upon my memory from my time here it is a profound hope for the future of the Iraqi children.

This particular trip was to a school at a local village not too far from our base camp. We were able to sit down with the headmaster and the village sheik for a brief visit. As usual, the conversation quickly turned to the topic of what the Americans can do for them and poignant questions about particular projects they would like to have done in their village. Our Civil Affairs officer, CPT Sean Walton, tried to explain to them that we do not have the liberty to randomly choose what projects are done and which village receives them. He also encouraged them to utilize their newly elected local leaders to lobby for the help they need. The concept is so foreign to them, they just don't seem to get it and before Sean could finish explaining what they need to do they were repeating their plea for American help. I could tell he was getting frustrated but he handled it very professionally but I'm not confident they got the point.

Afterwards, it was outside to hand out some goodies to the kids. I've

CAPTAIN UPPERMAN WITH CURIOUS KIDS IN IRAQ. *Photo courtesy Captain John Upperman*

expressed before about how they can be extremely forward and demanding. I tried to instill some order and at one point shut the vehicle cargo hatch and tried to explain to them I wasn't giving anything else out until they got in line and waited their turn. That lasted all of about a nanosecond and they were back at it again. At the end of it all, however, I'm just a softie and a sucker for kids in general. Besides, how do you say "no" to a kid who has no shoes, rags for clothes, no running water, and intermittent electricity?

You don't ... you just give.

John

MONDAY, NOVEMBER 21, 2005
On the way!

This will be my last post from inside the borders of Iraq. Just typing that sentence and reading it back in my mind seems surreal. This place, these people and this war have been the major part of my existence for the past year of my life. Reaching the end of this journey has been a daily obsession since I set foot into this desert land and now that the time has finally arrived it is almost catching me by surprise.

I took a final walk through my area today and was amazed at the well of emotions that rose to the surface. It's hard to believe, but I have actually become attached to this place. I can only think that it is some sort of "Stockholm Syndrome," which refers to the emotional attachment hostages grow towards their captors. For the past year this place has held me hostage from everything I previously knew and now by the grace of God I am about to be set free.

I have learned much about myself during this time and though this experience has been difficult, I have no regrets. Being here has changed me and I know that ultimately it will be for the better. I once read somewhere that "going into a combat zone is a one way door since the person that leaves is not the same person that returns." This new person returning is committed to being a better husband, father and friend. I have felt the pain of leaving all that I hold dear and I will not take it for granted again.

This is not my final post. I will continue to write once I return home and share the experience of my homecoming. But it will take a while to make my way from here to finally being back in the states.

Until then.

j

MONDAY, DECEMBER 12, 2005
Home

Our plane finally touched down at Ft Hood, Texas, at approximately 3:30 in the morning on December 4th. This was a full twelve hours later than we were originally scheduled to arrive. The major part of our tardiness was due to the plane out of Kuwait being delayed by nine hours. By the time we actually landed, all 250 soldiers on the plane had been traveling by either bus or plane for over 43 hours. Needless to say, we were all a little travel weary by the time we touched down, but it wasn't enough to quell the elated cheers of every man on the plane as soon as we felt the Texas terra firma beneath the landing gear.

Once we unboarded the plane, we processed in, turned in our weapons and boarded a bus where we waited for what seemed an eternity before being shuttled to the gymnasium where our families were waiting. We formed up and ran in to the sound of loud, patriotic music playing and the ironically appropriate haze of a fog machine. We all stood there in formation and my eyes darted back and forth across the stands as I tried to locate my family. Once I spotted them, an uncontrollable smile broke across my weary face, and I locked eyes with my best friend and my wife, Amy. There was an appropriately short speech from our commanding general, and after the command of "Dismissed!" was given, every man burst from the ranks and found their objective as quickly as possible.

HOMECOMING IS THE BEST PART OF EVERY TOUR OF DUTY. CAPTAIN JOHN UPPERMAN IS RE-UNITED WITH HIS FAMILY. *Photo courtesy Captain John Upperman*

6

DEVIL DOG

Sgt. David S. Bateman
RCT 2 3/6 USMC
Western Iraq
September 2005 – December 2005

Sept 1, 2005
Hello Dear,

Greetings from Iraq! Things are not as bad as they seem. I have a great living space, all of the comforts of home. I shower almost everyday. The air is so dry here, it's great for my oily skin. My spots are pretty much gone. SSgt and I are going to the gym together. I'm learning so much so fast. It's a good feeling to know I chose the right career.

I think about you and Ethan a lot. I miss you guys. Now I know what it's like having someone behind waiting. Every day I think about how hard it must be. Sometimes I feel so awful for getting you involved in this, but I guess if you weren't willing you wouldn't have agreed to it. I love you so much and can't tell you enough how much your support means to me. I'm so excited that you're proud to be a part of this. It helps me more than you know.

So, congrats, you are the recipient of my first war letter. Sure I've done this a lot, but I have never written home from a hot zone. Interesting, it doesn't feel different yet.

Anyways, I love you.

Tell Ethan what's going on over here and that I love him.

David

SEPTEMBER 1 (via email)
Hey Sweetheart,

I hope everything is ok at home. I wish I could talk to you. We should be getting our wireless satellite set up soon. Until then, it's Staff Sergeant Smith's E-mail. I wanted to let you know that it is ok to reply here; also, that our incentive pay won't start until the 15th. So that should be a big check. That thing about combat pay going up to $750 is not approved yet, it is in the budget for 2006. But, enough bad news. This place isn't bad. It's not too hot, the food is great, my platoon is well under my command, and my boss loves me. Everything a guy could want in a job except that I am a million miles away from the two most precious things in the world to me. Tell me what Ethan has been up to. I hope he hasn't been too hard on you. Hate that I had to go away so soon. I am putting my package in to go Officer as soon as I get back. I have to go now, but please write back as soon as you get this, just so I can hear from you. I love you.

David

SEPTEMBER 3 (via email)

Hey Baby, Tell Ethan that I got his E-card. I loved it. I love him too. I can check the Yahoo obviously so you can e-mail me here if you want but I can get Staff Sergeant's e-mail right in our room so I would just keep sending stuff there. I hope to hear from you soon. Tonight I will write all about the trip over here. It was very long and exhausting. I love you.

David

SEPTEMBER 3 (via email)

OK, one more mass e-mail to include everyone now. I have arrived in Al Qa' im, Iraq. All is well, we have already started operations and raids, so far with complete success. Our unit is very good at what they do. It is exciting to watch. I have been apart from harm's way to this point. I will soon have an official e-mail account that you can reach me at directly at my work station. I will get that out as soon as possible. Thank you all for your support. I love you guys.

David

SEPTEMBER 3, 2005
My Dearest Robin,

So here I am. Its 3 am and it's my last chance to write before we leave. I still remember the night I left. I guess it seems like a short time ago but also like an eternity. It really sucked. Just after you guys left, it started to rain. So of course, I got wet. Then, when I started to dry off, I had to lead a group of Marines to get all of the bags on the plane. After that, with dried rain and sweating from moving bags, I had to ride in an airplane all the way to Kuwait where it would be another three days before I could shower. Needless to say my trip over was less desirable that I had imagined. I did, however, get to know my guys a bit better. Not to mention having a true pint of Guinness in Ireland. I wished every moment that you could have been there for that. I still do which means our second honeymoon *will* be in Ireland. In the country of course, but near enough to Dublin to do some quality shopping. I wish that I could marry you every month. I'm just glad that our wedding won't be the happiest day of our marriage. I see many more happy days in our future. The first of which will be the day I hop off that bus and into your arms.

I think of it often. I can't wait until this is over. No doubt you have seen the destruction and carnage on the news. They say this is supposed to be bigger than Fallujah. I guess by now you know if that is true or not. We will be working with the 82nd Airborne Unit. That is the Army's most famous and historic unit. So it will be nice to be a part of that. There shouldn't be any shortage of coverage. We have CNN, C-span, Fox news and one other crew here that are going in with us. I hope they can find a way to tell at least part of the truth this time.

These men out here deserve to be publicly recognized for their accomplishments. Day in, day out its amazing but you get these guys together at a party and you would swear they are all 15 or 16 years old but you let these kids loose on the enemy and you will see combat efficiency at its finest. These young guys don't even require the slightest direction...They know their roles inside and out.

Please believe that I will be safe. I trust them as should you. I will write again soon. I love you.

Yours truly, David
Tell our son he is loved, missed and protected.

SEPTEMBER 6 (via email)

Sup? How is everything going? Sorry I haven't been able to get a hold of you sooner. We lost a man last night in an accident, so they shut down communications to the outside until his family is notified. Same old thing here, work work work. Will you find out if my mother or father got their e-mails? They haven't responded to SSgt Smith's e-mail and I haven't had a chance to check my Yahoo. Tell Ethan that Daddy loves him. I love you and miss you. Bye Bye.

David

SEPTEMBER 7 (via email)
Hello, Sweetheart,

The guy we lost was one of our own Navy Docs. He was a good kid, just took a sharp turn and flipped the Hummer over a ridge. Bummer. Just a note, but that guy at the Army Navy place we stopped at that day is full of shit. Our MREs have heaters in them!!! I'll save some for you. I can't believe how big our boy is. That is incredible how tall he is. I miss you guys a lot. Talk to you soon.

David

SEPTEMBER 11

Hey Babe,

Tell this to everyone. I don't need anything to eat over here. I have all the food and Gatorade I can eat or drink at the chow hall. I grab an extra Gatorade every time I leave. We have everything we need as far as food and drink. I really don't need anything else besides baby wipes. All I want is letters and support. I will take care of the rest. I promise I will let you know if I need anything else. I know everyone wants to send me things to make life easier, but unfortunately for you guys I have more than I need. I am very well taken care of over here. I love you very much. I am sending you a letter today. I hope you get it before I get home. Take Care and hug Ethan for me, if you can get your arms around him still.

David

OCTOBER 4

Hey Baby,

I just got back I'll call you in a little while. I'm beat. My arms are about to fall off. Anyways, I can't say much, but I'm sure you saw CNN. I'll talk to you soon. I love you.

David

FROM: Robin Bateman
SENT: Wednesday, October 05, 2005 12:55 AM
TO: Bateman Sgt David S (GCE RCT2 3/6 RADIO NCO)
SUBJECT: RE: check this out

Oh I am so happy to hear from you!!!! I of course have been watching the news. And up until today they kept saying no casualties. Today they said 5 and I just about flipped. I know the chances of those being you is slim, but with all the great luck we've had lately . . . you just never know. I guess we are a lot alike in that way. We both expect the worst then when things turn out OK then it's that much better! :-) Love you lots!

Robin

SUBJECT: RE: check this out
DATE: Wed, 5 Oct 2005 23:07:39 +0300
FROM: Bateman Sgt David S (GCE RCT2 3/6 RADIO NCO)
TO: Robin Bateman

Hey Baby,

Of course I am ok. Try not to worry so much. It could be so much worse. I was talking to the guys tonight. It looks like I may be getting back a lot of my ribbons and stuff. I hope that is true. Those awards are a great source of pride for me. It really doesn't make much difference though. I know what I've done, you know what I've done. That's what matters to me. Anyways, I probably won't be going out for a little bit now. Things are going to get back to normal for a few weeks. We'll be getting ready for a much bigger thing here in a little while. I know I'm supposed to keep my head down, but Marines were invented so everyone else could keep their heads down.

Hey, do you think you could download Yahoo messenger so maybe we could catch each other online sometime? SSgt Smith talks to his wife quite a bit on it, it works really well for them. This is assuming you would have a moment to do it. I know it will be hard. Just a thought, my computer is all ready to go just in case you find a good time to do it.

My sister emailed me and she was a little upset that I hadn't emailed her, so I had to tell her that I was busy and figured everyone else would pass the word. So if she asks, just let her know it was nothing but an accident.

I love you more every day, I couldn't have married a more wonderful woman.

David

FROM: Robin Bateman
SENT: Saturday, October 8 2005 2.44 PM
TO: Bateman Sgt David (GCE RCT2 3/6 RADIO NCO)
SUBJECT: I hope you're ok

Hey honey, I'm so worried about you right now. I really hate all of this, all I keep hearing on the news is that 6 guys died in western Iraq, but no one says where or anything else. And all of the sudden you just stopped all communication. It's enough to give a girl a heart attack. I keep expecting a Marine to show up on my door step, but not the one I want to see. I really hate this. I'm not used to feeling so out of control of everything. It's horrible. Every day is lived just hoping that today isn't your last. I have no idea what Ethan and I would do without you. I guess he'd probably adapt pretty fast, but he'd grow up having an overprotective, nut case of a mother. He probably wouldn't like me very much. Me, I'd just be depressed all the time. I'd probably get fat and ugly and stuff. I can't write anymore of this . . . I'm already crying too much. . . and Ethan just pooped.

I love you so much and I hope that I get to hear from you today.
Robin

SUBJECT: Re: I hope you're ok
DATE: Sun, 9 Oct 2005 23:09:30 +0300
FROM: "Bateman Sgt David (GCE RCT2 3/6 RADIO NCO)
TO: "Robin Bateman"

Hey Honey,

Just wanted to let you know I'm going out for the day tomorrow. It will be an all day affair, so I will try to call early in the morning I hope you guys had fun at Epcot. I bet Ethan is so cute rolling around Disney. I wonder if he will be interested in the animals yet. I look so much forward to seeing you two when I get back. I can't wait to share all of the new things he can do. I sure miss you a lot. I'll think of you all day tomorrow. I'm just going up to fix some radios and move them from one point to another so try not to worry too much. I'll talk to you soon.

I love you,
David

SUBJECT: Re: I hope you're ok
DATE: Sun, 9 Oct 2005 23:09:30 +0300
FROM: "Bateman Sgt David (GCE RCT2 3/6 RADIO NCO)
TO: "Robin Bateman

Hey Baby

I am OK. We lost a few guys and when that happens they cut all communications here until their families are notified. Everything is just fine, I promise I won't say "I'll talk to you in an hour" anymore. I am so sorry you had to go through that just now. I haven't stopped thinking of you since we talked last. Things will be back to normal by the end of the day and hopefully we can chat or talk later. I just got your last two letters. They kind of put me in a really bad mood. I feel so awful that things worked out the way they did. You know the reason I am here is that they were looking for a Sergeant in Radio with some experience. I guess I am the victim of my own success again. Anyways, I'll keep trying to get a hold of you. I love you so much, everything is gonna be OK. Bye.

Ethan, Daddy loves you, too.

David

FROM: Robin Bateman
SENT: Saturday, October 09, 2005 2.15 PM
TO: Bateman Sgt David (GCE RCT2 3/6 RADIO NCO)
SUBJECT: RE I hope you're ok

Oh thank god!!!! I was about to lose it after the first 24 hrs. When it passed 48, I was still worried, but kinda figured someone would have come by already if something had happened to you. Anyways, I'm sooo happy that you're OK!! Ethan is too. We're going to Disney today to Animal Kingdom and Epcot. I'm going to take lots of pictures to send to you. Hey, when you get back we can take him to the Magic Kingdom! He'll be standing good by then, so maybe we can get him to pull Tigger's tail too! Well, I have to go jump in the shower so we can get a move on. I, as always will have my phone with me. So if you want to call, please do. I can always get Yahoo messenger on my phone now and check my email. I subscribed to the web on phone for $5 a month. Not bad!! I love you sooooo much!!

Love
Me

FROM: Robin Bateman
SENT: Friday, October 21, 2005 4.29 PM
TO: Bateman Sgt David (GCE RCT2 3/6 RADIO NCO)
SUBJECT: RE hey

Come on honey...you've gotta give me more than that! This "delayed" crap isn't cutting it with just one liners coming from ya! I need more than just a quick thing. We ordered an entire package this time. So when they come in we'll have a copy of the one in the gator outfit (the one without the ball), one in the dog outfit when he's just sitting on the rock smiling, the close up of the dog outfit one where he looks like he's 'such a perfect little gentleman', a black and white one of the duckeys where he's leaning over holding on to the side, and a bronzed one of the dog outfit where he's looking at the leaves. Then we'll also have a proof sheet that has all 3 duckeys in color, the scarecrow one and two of the dog ones. The scarecrow was the last one we did at Sears; we only managed to get those 2 shots off before he started crying. He was so soooo tired and hungry!!
   Tell me about LCpl Roberts; I ask again, I met his mother online. She said his 21st bday is on Nov 2nd and that she was organizing a huge card

thing, so he should be getting something like 100 birthday cards!! She even asked me to send one, so I'll have one in the mail for him today, and just so you know ... it says for him to tell you that you'll buy him a beer in the airport on the way home – assuming you're on the same flight and all ... Just so you know!! :-) Love you lots..

Ethan's Mommy

SUBJECT: Re: hey
DATE: Fri, 21 Oct 2005 10:34:56 +0300
FROM: "Bateman Sgt David (GCE RCT2 3/6 RADIO NCO)
TO: "Robin Bateman"

OK. You're right. I'm sorry for not being more detailed, so here are the details. LCpl Roberts got promoted, so Cpl Roberts will be here with me. I think that's great about his birthday. He is a really good kid. Tell his mother he is doing a great job out here for me. He and Cpl Murrillo are my best guys. I gotta have his and my picture in the dog outfit. I love it. I love all of them. He is truly the best looking baby I have ever seen. All thanks to his wonderful gene pool. If this was WWII I would probably not talk to you the whole time. I would be in some distant hole of an area where we couldn't even send mail or something. But since I am not there and it's not WWII, I encourage you to be thankful for technology. It wasn't even this good last time I was in. We are very lucky to have what we have here. I am writing a short letter to a little kid who wrote me. He is in 3rd grade. He is from NC and likes football. Whatever, I gotta write back I guess. Not much going on here really, just juicing up for the next push. It will be very soon. I can't wait. It's starting to get cold here. I walked outside this morning and it was in the 50s BRRRRR!!! How is the weather there? Did you get my letter yet? I mailed it a while ago. I hope you get it soon. I miss you so much and love you even more than you know.

David

SENT: Friday, October 28, 2005 8.33PM
TO: Bateman Sgt (GCE RCT2 3/6 RADIO NCO)
FROM: Robin Bateman
SUBJECT: RE book

Hey honey. Some Navy dude is writing a book. See the email below . . . I think it's pretty interesting. We can submit some of your letters to me if you don't mind. Let me know. I love you lots!

Robin

SUBJECT: Re: book
DATE: Fri, 28 Oct 2005 22:51:27+0300
FROM: "Bateman Sgt David (GCE RCT2 3/6 RADIO NCO)
TO: "Robin Bateman"

Hey baby,

That sounds good. I guess I have to write more now, huh? I got my glasses and stuff! I was so excited. I got Kiff's stuff and a box from my Dad. What a night! Thanks for the stuff; it will come in handy on this operation. It is still very bright outside. Kiff sent three boxes of shit for us. Swell guy. I really enjoyed talking to Ethan yesterday. It made me feel really good all day long. I had a good day yesterday. It sounds like the op will be a bit shorter than anticipated, but don't hold your breath. SSgt Smith, Cpl Murillo and I are going out tomorrow to check some things out. It should be cool! Nothing serious, just putting some things in place to be ready for the push. I tried all day to call but things kept coming up, I will continue to try, but more importantly I will write you a letter. I love you with all my heart.

David Scott

SUBJECT: Re: hi
DATE: Wed, 9 Nov 2005 09:03:19+0300

FROM: "Bateman Sgt David (GCE RCT2 3/6 RADIO NCO)
TO: "Robin Bateman"

Hey honey,

I'm back. It didn't take too long. We just had to go get medical supplies from a hospital we blew up. I'll try to keep up the dreamless nights. I'm not going to be "messed up" when I came home. I may need to adjust for a little while, but I will be fine. Only time will tell about those things. We are leaving tomorrow sometime and we are not coming back to camp until this thing is over. It will be several days, like we talked about last night. I will, however, be able to call you soon. I love you with all my heart. I will write often.

David Scott Bateman

SUBJECT: Re: Back in AQ
DATE: Wed, 16 Nov 2005 19:13:09+0300
FROM: "Bateman Sgt David (GCE RCT2 3/6 RADIO NCO)
TO: "Victoria Bateman"
CC: "Robin Bateman"

Just wanted to let you know I am back in Al Qa'im and safe. Everything went just fine and we are settled. I am very tired. I got the sheets and lights. I have already put the lights up. We really enjoyed them. They make the room very cozy. Thank you. I want to get the word out through you about Christmas. I want nothing. I don't want candy, presents, cookies or stockings. Nothing. Robin and I only wish that anyone who simply cannot go without getting us something simply contribute to our cruise fund. That is our Christmas present to each other. So we decided we would like everyone to share in the thing we so very much look forward to. We have booked it for the first week of April, so there will be plenty of time to prepare. I am very serious about this. I want nothing to come here. I will take part in the group offerings with the platoon, but will not personally celebrate Christmas this year. Please, please do your best to understand? The more I get the worse I will feel about being here. It's bad enough to be away from all of you this holiday season, but I am missing my son's only first Halloween, Thanksgiving, Christmas, New Years and Birthday. I really can't stand it. Just help me get the word out. If they insist on doing something nice for us, help us with something we can enjoy after I get back home ... I love you all and miss you awfully.

David Scott

DATE: Wed, 16 NOV 2005 16:37:32 0500
FROM: mymanleftme4usmc
SUBJECT: RE Hey
TO: Robin Bateman

Hey, sorry to be so to the point, but do you know if Ryan came back to Al Qa'im with your husband? I have not heard from him at all, and he told me that he was going to be gone at least another 2 weeks after he got back from Camp Gannon. I am a little freaked out, and then today I woke up, and it says that 5 Marines were killed in Western Iraq providing security for Operation Steel Curtain, which the boys were a part of. I just wanted to know if your husband has any idea of where mine is. I hate to ask you, but I have been so freaked out, pregnant or not, I MISS MY HUSBAND and I want to know that he is okay. Let me know ...
Thanks, sorry again for being so spastic.

Dede

SENT: Thursday, November 17, 2005 3.14 AM
TO: Bateman Sgt David (GCE RCT2 3/6 RADIO NCO)
FROM: Robin Bateman
SUBJECT: RE Hey

Hi honey ... I'm forwarding you an email I just got from Dede, Ryan's wife. She's pretty freaked out. So, I don't know if you can, but if you can, have Ryan send her something back. She's wiggin pretty bad! Anyways, I wrote her back and told her not to worry, that if anything had happened to Ryan she probably knows by now. And that she doesn't have to apologize to me for worrying or going spastic, cause I do it too! I love you so much honey!! I hope to talk to you soon!

Always, Robin

SUBJECT: Re: Hey
DATE: Thu, 17 Nov, 2005 07:01:10 +0300
FROM: "Bateman Sgt David (GCE RCT2 3/6 RADIO NCO)
TO: "Robin Bateman"

Hey Baby,

I emailed Dede and let her know that Ryan is at our retransmission site and he would be back in four or five days. Everything else is fine. I have a meeting this morning for my officer stuff so I am excited. I can't wait to start making this happen. I hope to hear from you soon I miss your voice so much and I can't wait to hear Ethan. I love you dearly.

David Scott Bateman

SUBJECT: FOR ETHAN
DATE: 11/20/2005 3:52:59 a.m. Eastern Standard
FROM: "Bateman Sgt David (GCE RCT2 3/6 RADIO NCO)
TO: "Robin Bateman"

Hey Pal,

Today you are 9 months old. In three months you will be a toddler (your Mum told me that). I am so proud of you. You have grown big and strong and healthy. That is all I wanted for you. Your mother is incredible. She has taken such good care of you. She is to be thanked for the little gentleman you are becoming. You are the world to us both. I wish so much that I could be there with you today, but I will be home soon.

SGT DAVID BATEMAN WITH ROBIN AND NEW SON ETHAN. *Photo courtesy Robin Bateman*

I have so many stories to tell you when I get home. We can have story time every night if you want. You know we get our very own entire day together when I get home. You and I are going to get to know one another again while your mommy sleeps and takes care of herself. She gets so tired sometimes because she wants to make sure you have everything you need to grow into a healthy young man. We can watch TV or go to the park or just hang out on Mommy and Daddy's bed and play together.

I want you to know that just because I have to be away from you now; it doesn't mean I don't think about you everyday. I wonder what you are up to, how heavy you've gotten, how tall you are. I wonder if you have said any words. I hear you are standing on your own a bit now. That makes me so happy. I love you so much, Ethan. I will see you soon.

Happy Nine Month Birthday!!
Daddy

Sweetheart,

There is so much I want to say to you but don't know how. So, I guess I'll just start blabbering. First, thank you so much for supporting me the way you do. Seeing how much pride you have in me and the things I do makes me feel so much better about myself. It's like I have my own little cheering section at home. I want you to feel appreciated for everything you do. It doesn't go unnoticed.

He's getting so big. I don't know how you do it. You are amazing. I wish I could make you understand how completely wonderful you are. You are to me, what every man dreams of in a woman. You are beautiful, intelligent, sarcastic, funny, cute, fun to be around. Did I mention beautiful? You're an amazing mom too. Don't let anyone or anything ever make you feel otherwise. I miss you so much. I've never wanted to leave a deployment before. I just want to be near you. I want to hold our son. I can't wait to see him when I get off that bus. Its going to be nuts. After all of this shit, I'll be so ready to be home.

I can't even tell you how difficult it can be. Things are so different now. It's a new kind of war. Its so . . . Empty. Every time I go out I have internal struggles. Is killing again REALLY the answer to my problems? Not only that, but should I be enjoying it? Every time I pull my trigger or even sight in, I feel that familiar old smirk, like its some kind of fucking video game and I'm about to break the high score. Like I say, I am what I am so why deny it. I am still alive because of what I am. I tried to put it on the back burner in lieu of

ANOTHER DAY IN IRAQ FOR SGT BATEMAN. *Photo courtesy Sgt David Bateman*

a quiet, calm lifestyle, but it doesn't work. I didn't even last a year. I want you to know that I am alright. I'm even happy. I just came to realize that there is no denying that this is where I should be. I may not be the biggest or strongest but I am the one of the best at what I do.

So, anyways, now that's over with, I'll tell you what I've been up to. You know by now that we swept several towns in the area. We basically went on a frontal assault through every building, one end to the other. I even got to employ some of my special skills. Don't worry, no one really saw me or found out until I was done. It was cool. We took sniper fire from about 800m out. I found him in a three story building. We sent a team to the base and I set up on the roof of the building. I was near and waited. My team forced "the guy" to the second floor that's when we realized there were three "guys." I got the first and took off to my next spot. I closed in pretty quick, took another shot and actually missed. The next two shots found their mark and it was off to the races again. Shortly thereafter, another team was struck by a roadside bomb. That was where we lost our man. 1 KIA and 3 wounded. I was so disappointed. They never saw it coming.

I had another one of my dreams last night. I don't think anybody noticed they sleep pretty heavy here. I guess all of this letting out got my head spinning. I've been wondering if it would happen. Oh, well, I'll be fine.

I've been reading those "Making of a Marine Officer" articles in the Marine Times. They're pretty good. I'm going to try to start preparing for that while I'm out here. I need to find out how many credits I have between the Academy and the JC's I went to in California. I think I'll be pretty close to 75. I should have it, actually. Once I get those 75 credits I'll be eligible.

Kevin and I wrote Cpl Murillo (Joe) up for a meritorious promotion to Sgt. I hope he gets it. He deserves it.

So . . . seven days on the ocean just you and me. How much fun that will be. I'm going to soak up every moment of you . . . I hope you don't get sick of me hanging all over you every second. By then I will have missed you so much, I won't want to sleep because I won't be able to see you. But at least I can touch you. That is what I want most. I'll be writing more soon. Until then, I love you and Ethan with all my heart.

Yours in love and life.
David

NOVEMBER 22, 2005
Hi Honey,

I miss you something awful, too. I am so excited he can face the front now. That rules. 20 pounds . . . that is crazy. I have a hard enough time just lifting 20 lbs. much less when it is kicking and screaming. I guess I gotta get after it in the gym now. Oh well, it is what it is. I can't wait either way. In the morning it will have been three months. That is a long time to be away from the two most precious things in the world to me. I miss you so much. I have so many ideas about the things I want to do. I keep realizing that it is going to take a lot of work, more time apart, more frustration, but when it is all said and done, I am going to be a

Marine Officer. I know it will be worth it. Thanks for believing in me and supporting me. I love you so much, every hour of every day I love you.

Your Devoted Husband,
David Scott Bateman

NOTE FROM ROBIN:

This next email is partly in reference to a necklace that David managed to find the time to buy for my birthday in December. It's a shamrock made of heart shaped emeralds!

NOVEMBER 23, 2005
Well my Dear,

You are certainly very welcome. I had no clue what to get you and I was looking around and I thought that it would be nice if we BOTH had clovers around our neck for luck. I hope yours works as well as mine.

Things are still good here. I think I will be calling tonight. I hope so at least. I will be using the Sat Phone. I bet the money on the calling card will last the rest of the deployment at this rate, which is a good thing. Ryan is coming back today if you want to tell Dede. Have you guys been talking? I e-mailed her and told her that Ryan was fine and she said it made her feel a ton better. Anyways, he is pissed at me because he had to stay out there that long. I told him I would try to make it a week and MSgt said I had to wait to switch them out so it's not my fault really, but I think it's funny because he has still been out there for less time than my regular guys do. But, at least they can't say "Ha, Radio, what do you guys do? All you do is go to Retrans!" Now they know how shitty it is.

So, he's got three teeth now? He is going to bite everything. I can see it now. He is going to be like that girl from Lemony Snickett, hanging off the table by his teeth. Is he starting to be a good boy now? Does he play nice yet? Is he trying to walk? I just want to catch up on some of the things I haven't been asking about lately. I can't wait to grab him up. I bet he will weigh 25 pounds by then. He is such a big boy. Good job on him.

I miss you so much. I think about you constantly. I keep wondering what it will be like that first night. What will we talk about? Will it be weird? What will you be like? I guess I am just worried about an awkward situation. I keep thinking you will somehow be distant. I hope it is not true. I know I worry about stupid things, but I keep hearing stories about how they had to start all over again. I don't want to start over, I love you just the way you are. Either way I will be happy to be home with you and Ethan. I just hope we can lie in each others arms and enjoy the night. I love you so much, sweetheart and I would give the world for you.

David Scott Bateman

NOVEMBER 24, 2005
Hey Baby,

Happy Thanksgiving to me! I just got my 20 pull-ups. It's the first time in 7 years! I hope the holiday is going well. I know you worked hard on dinner. I'm sure it is great! I miss you so much. The phone is pretty tied up, but I will try for you. Tell Ethan Happy Turkey Day from Daddy. Also, give my love to all the family and tell them thank you for their thoughts. Thanks for getting the flags. I was worried about getting them on time. They have been sold out here and I don't trust them to get any in on time for me and I KNOW I can always count on you. You're the best. I love you to death. Have a great day and I'll talk to you soon.

David

NOVEMBER 27, 2005
OK,

Whew!! What a day. We accomplished so much today. We are getting started with our retrograde with the incoming unit. We are taking inventory of all of our gear and ordering all the missing parts, labeling the equipment and generally organizing everything in a way that when they get here we can just say "Here is your stuff, we are going to sleep. Call us if you need us." I think it is going really well. I am considering us halfway done now, because the next little while is all going to run together. Everything is so random and unplanned that we just wake up in the morning and wait to see what happens. It is kind of nice because we are just in cruise mode now.

I have been working on my officer stuff lately. I am getting more and more excited. I can't wait to get home and finish this thing up. I just want to get it over with and find out if I can go or not.

So what have you been up to? What has Ethan been up to? I can't wait until the day I don't have to ask you that anymore. I can just look next to me and say, "Sup, wife? I love you." Then I can grab Ethan and swing him around. It is going to be great. I love you endlessly and unconditionally. Always loving and thinking about you,

David Scott Bateman

DECEMBER 3, 2005

Yes, that coffee maker sounds cool. I will tell you I am drinking quite a bit more coffee than I used to. So if you want it go for it. I think you are right, it might save on coffee, even though we get it for free. I love you.

David

NOTE FROM ROBIN:

A few hours after getting the email above, I get a phone call, in the middle of the day, which is highly unusual, since it's the middle of the night in Iraq. Anyhow, David had apparently been trying to reach me to no avail. When I answered the phone his first response was "Oh my God! Thank God you answered!!! I've been trying to get hold of you all day!!" Naturally, I get a bit worried now! David's next line is "Don't worry, I'll be OK" So now I'm thinking . . . Dear Lord, he's hurt. I'm thinking he got shot or something. He then tells me that he broke his finger. Whew! What a relief for me!! The catch is, he not only broke, he broke it in 3 places and rotated the bone at the same time. These last emails are in reference to him being flown out to the hospital in Baghdad to be evaluated and eventually operated on and sent home, via Germany with a pin in his hand and a big cast.

DECEMBER 4, 2005

I haven't left yet. It's almost 12 noon. I am supposed to leave in an hour or so, now. I hope to be able to call you from Al Asad. I miss you even more now. I feel useless. I don't know how long I'll have to be like this. I hope it isn't long. I guess this could be something that will affect me the rest of my life. So, are you happy now? I know I am not unbreakable. Maybe that is the point of this. I guess we will see. I'll talk to you about it soon. I love you so much!!!!

David

DECEMBER 7, 2005

Hey love,

I am leaving here in about 20 minutes. I will be in Germany within 8 hours. I love you and will call as soon as I can.

David

BOOK TWO

Edited Compilations

7

CITIZEN SOLDIERS

Lt Col Dan Hokanson
National Security Fellow
Harvard University

NOT SINCE WORLD WAR II have the citizen-soldiers of our Nation been so integral to our military forces. In the almost five years since September 11, 2001, the citizen-soldiers of the National Guard have played an increasing role in our nation's defense and in fighting our nation's wars. It was National Guard F-16s that provided air cover over New York City in the immediate aftermath of the attack on the World Trade Centers, and since that time, National Guard soldiers, airmen and airwomen have answered their nation's call in unprecedented numbers.

National Guard citizen-soldiers are just that: they are citizens in our communities who when called upon, provide critical, timely and effective support to our nation. As this book is being written, National Guard forces represent twenty-seven percent of U.S. Military forces deployed

★ AUTHOR'S NOTE: This compilation of letters and commentary is from Lt. Col. Hokanson and they remind us of the debt we owe to the citizen-soldiers of our nation.

in support of Operation Enduring Freedom (Afghanistan) and Operation Iraqi Freedom (Iraq and Kuwait), down from a high of over fifty percent in early 2005. (Statistics provided by CPT Michael Braibish, Public Affairs Officer, Oregon Army National Guard on 26 Jan 2006). Citizen-soldiers, like their active duty counterparts, are also making the ultimate sacrifice for their country. Their performance in both theaters of operation has been nothing less than expected, and equal to their active duty counterparts. The challenges faced by our citizen-soldiers, however, are in some ways very different from those faced by the active component peers they live and serve with every day.

The National Guard, in addition to its predominantly Federal mission, performs numerous critical missions in the fifty-four states and territories of the United States. In peacetime the National Guard trains for its war fighting, or Federal mission; and at the same time provides states with important capabilities they might not otherwise have. These capabilities include a trained and equipped force to perform disaster relief, search and rescue, fire-fighting, law enforcement, water purification, engineering, and many other essential tasks on a moment's notice twenty-four hours a day, every day of the year.

In most cases, members of the National Guard leave not only their families and friends like their active duty counterparts when they deploy; they also leave their employers, their careers and the communities they are an integral part of. This in itself adds a different dimension to the issues citizen-soldiers face when they return home. In addition to reintegrating with their family and community, they must also reintegrate into a work environment that in many cases has changed significantly over the twelve to twenty-four months they were deployed.

These challenges, however, give National Guard soldiers a unique and often advantageous perspective on the battlefield. In addition to their military skills, citizen-soldiers bring with them their unique civilian skills. In many cases, especially as nations such as Iraq and Afghanistan rebuild, they can provide expertise and capabilities not normally found in active duty military organizations. In addition to having a military occupation specialty (MOS), National Guard soldiers are also schoolteachers, small business owners, construction workers, auto mechanics, police officers, firemen and women, or any number of other occupations. This citizen-soldier perspective gives them the ability to transition from a military mindset to one of trying to help a community rebuild when the situation calls for such action.

After returning from deployment, the reintegration of Guard "soldiers" to their "citizen" lives adds a dimension all its own and is often quite different from what active duty soldiers face. Guard soldiers return from the same hostile environment as their active duty counterparts, but instead of returning as a cohesive unit to their duty station where all services are available to them, Guard soldiers return to their community. Once home, Guard soldiers go back to their hometowns, their jobs, and only meet again as a unit on weekends during training. The camaraderie shared daily within their unit during the deployment does not continue daily like it does in active duty units. In addition, services such as counseling, medical care, and support groups found on military installations are rarely present in the communities where National Guard units are based. Services such as these must be a priority to the Nation to ensure the continued availability and exemplary service of our National Guard in the future.

Any historical record of the war in Iraq or Afghanistan would be incomplete without considering the efforts of the men and women of the National Guard. Their perspective of the conflict and of life in these war zones may be even more interesting to future generations and historians than that of their active duty counterparts. With their unique "citizen-soldier" background, they bring a unique perspective on their experiences.

Staff Sergeant Travis Powell sent the following five letters to family and friends. Travis is a Flight Medic with one of the U.S. Army's best Air Ambulance companies, which also happens to be an Oregon National Guard unit based in Salem. In his civilian occupation, Travis is a firefighter with the Portland (Oregon) Fire Department. Travis' first letter highlights one of the ironic yet thought-provoking events that happen during war. In December of 2005, he wrote:

Hello All,

We have visitors again to Bagram and this time directly in front of our hangar. The World Wrestling Entertainment show will be recorded and broadcast from our front door. Even though I'm not a wrestling fan, it will be cool to have an event here that gets everyone together for a moment to just let go, laugh and enjoy hanging out.

On another note I have another extraordinary mission we went on to share with ya'll. Some time ago I actually pondered this type of thing happening and wondered how I might deal with it. Just know once again we acted once again so that others might live. I don't say this to brag but others this time was the enemy. You see, beyond the so called "top stories" that make the news of aggressive attacks on enemy forces, fighting and more fighting the USA is doing, is the rest of the team which was quite the ironic Medivac mission. So, as you may know our mission is to provide evacuation and medical treatment to American and Coalition forces, to the civilian population and even to the enemy. It's actually part of the Geneva Convention that we treat all the same. I hope I can paint the picture enough for you so it hits you like it did me.

Outside of FOB ABAD (Forward Operating Base, Asadabad province) a young man (enemy) was attempting to plant an IED (improvised explosive device). These IEDs are responsible for so many lives taken here. The intent obviously was to plant the IED hoping troops would pass by and many fatalities and injuries would result. Well, this man failed in his attempt as the IED detonated near him. It caused tissue damage to his chest, face and one eye. It completely amputated one hand and all but three fingers of the other. I tell you this not to gross you out but to understand the extent of his injuries. This man had a task to kill/maim American troops. The hate for us must have been there too. Imagine though this man's next actions. He knew that if he came running to the front gate of the FOB unarmed that US troops would accept him as a casualty and treat his life-threatening injuries; which is exactly what happened. Even though the enemy hates us they also trust us to be obedient to the laws that govern us.

I received the patient which the on scene medical folks did a great job of packaging, along with two armed guards. He was now a prisoner under control of the U.S. Army and for me, my patient. It was something how there were no hateful feelings bursting out of me, not even an impulse to yell at him for what he did. It was just time to go to work and stabilize him for transport to our hospital in Bagram where he went to immediate surgery. En route to the hospital this man felt enough peace to gesture to me he was thirsty, so I cleaned his lips that were stuck together from the blast. I put a moistened 4X4 bandage over his mouth to at least wet the inside for him and bring some comfort. The look in his eyes I won't ever forget. Thankfulness I saw in him. I then sedated him somewhat to relieve the pain he was in and to help ensure an uneventful transport.

I wonder later as the man recovers from surgery, is fed hot meals daily, is bathed, and is given water to drink how overwhelming it would have to be. For the hands that cared for him came from the same people he tried to kill. These hands belong to the people which are the heart of our country. I sure would like to find this man 5-10 years later to see if his story is one of a changed heart, hopefully one that passes onto others the character of the American people.

Well my family and friends, God has again amazed me at what He let me be a part of. I'm thankful He guided me through this event and hopeful this injured patient of mine saw the one true loving God through me.

Take care of each other.

Travis

And now these three remain: faith, hope and love. But the greatest of these is love.

In addition to the daily challenges our citizen-soldiers face, they also deal with the mundane day-to-day events that occur during their deployment. Mail, as it has always been, is one of the greatest morale-builders to soldiers. As they read and re-read letters and emails, it gives them a few moments to drift back into the lives they left and hear about the things they are missing and the lives and experiences they will one day return to.

The efforts of organizations to show support for our soldiers, sailors, airmen and marines, has had a significant impact on their morale. In addition to sending reminders of and a taste of home, they also show perhaps the most important element to our fighting forces, that those at home have not forgotten them and they appreciate their sacrifices.

Travis wrote the following letter to thank one of the many organizations that provided support to his unit while deployed:

From: Travis Powell
To: Coalition of Troop Support

20 November 2005
Dear folks that brought this soldier joy,

I hope this note makes it back to those who poured out a labor of love to us in Afghanistan. I don't know how you got my address and I only have a return address on the box to respond to. In addition I hope that thanks would go out to the VFW Ladies Auxiliary of Tualatin, OR, who made the individual handbags that our care packages were in. Also the Oregon Coast Avid Stamper's group who were thoughtful to send us many cards and envelopes so that we may use them to send to our loved ones back home. It was almost like having a Hallmark aisle in a box to choose from. Please also extend our thanks to the students of Milwaukee High School that took time to drop each of us a note of encouragement. It's a bit of hope felt here when the younger generation also recognizes what we do here is very much for them too.

I'm so thankful for the good people that made it be known to us serving throughout this world that we are supported, loved, thought of and lifted up in prayer daily. It was a touching day for me to receive a box, which I did not expect to be coming or recognize the return address on it. I was happy as I was opening the box and wondering which loved one of mine had sent another care package to me. I soon found out the senders of the big ole box were many friends whom I have not yet met. My heart is truly touched by all those who cared.

I am the flight platoon sergeant in our group, so as I saw each handbag filled with love, immediately names of my fellow troops started coming to mind. Specifically I'm speaking of those who are single and who don't have an immediate family outside of us brothers and sisters here. I was so thrilled to go soldier-to-soldier telling them to "come to the medic office now, for I need to meet with you." I want you to know the look in their eyes and appreciation felt as each soldier took a handbag just for them was just as if a loved one had come by to visit and given them a big hug or something.

Some may call what you people did as "nothing to make a big deal about" or "nothing at all for it was simple to do." Well, I agree with the latter of the two. It's quite simple to show love to others. It is simple to encourage a soldier. It also makes it easier for us here doing our job while away from home.

So you know a bit more about us; we are stationed at the Salem, OR, airport. We provide the search and rescue support day in and out for Oregon as well as some of Washington. We also assist with aerial firefighting support come that season of the year. You can easily pick us out as a UH-60 "Blackhawk" helicopter with the red cross on it. If it's a red cross flying in Oregon it's us for sure. It seems to be us flying elsewhere more and more lately. Feel free to come by and visit us sometime.

Feel free also to visit this web page that I have photos on from our tour here at http://groups.msn.com/OperationEnduringFreedom6

As I close, I just hope this note can reach all those involved in the care packages ya'll sent. Oh yeah, I got my part of it. I'm wearing the t-shirt right now that everyone signed. May God bless each of you for showing us just a little of His love.

Serving our country proudly,
SSG Travis Powell/ Flight Medic
1042 Medical Company (Air Ambulance)
Operation Enduring Freedom
Bagram Airbase, Afghanistan
And now these three remain: faith, hope and love. But the greatest of these is love.

As evidenced in this letter, the efforts of those at "home" and the time they sacrifice to show their appreciation can have a profound effect on our military forces. Their effort has an even greater impact when you consider that the happiness enjoyed by one soldier is shared with others and can often spread throughout an organization.

For all soldiers, the holidays seem to take on an even greater meaning when they are away from home and unable to enjoy the company of their family and friends. Often it is a time of reflection. The following letters sent on Thanksgiving, New Year's Eve and New Year's Day capture Travis' thoughts as he reflected on his many blessings:

Happy Thanksgiving to all,

I just returned from our Thanksgiving meal. Let me assure ya'll of something; many of you that were concerned of us having a traditional meal, of having a remembrance day, of how hard it is being away from home on the holidays. Well the latter is still a bit hard but the effort put in to have the troops a Thanksgiving Meal was amazing. We had the choice of every single main course, fixing and dessert I remember having at any Thanksgiving get-together. Turkey, ham, beef, prime rib, crab legs, cocktails, several stuffings, tators and gravy, veggies, every cake and pie to think of, actual Breyer's ice cream, and well that's the half of it. Oh and a bottle of sparkling cider/grape juice at each table to have a little family toast with whomever sat down with you. I was so thankful to have a day filled with happiness in just joining together, walking to the mess hall in numbers to all eat together. It actually felt good being part of this day so far. The only thing missing was a wheelbarrow to get back to the hangar. So, I don't tell you the above to rub it in but to let you know your prayers are answered. We were truly loved, protected and encouraged on this day of thanks even far away from home. We were not forgotten by any means. God smiled on our gathering on this side of the world too. Here, fall is definitely set in but no colorful leaves on the kinds of trees here to welcome the season. There is much snow on the mountain tops surrounding our base which is beautiful in itself. Missions have slowed down tremendously which slows the days down, but I'll take a slow day over action in this zone happily. Today we have had two MEDEVAC mis-

sions out of all our bases we cover though. Hopefully that's it. A few days ago I received a massive box that had many handmade handbags filled with comfort items from Oregon. Just wanted ya'll to know (especially whoever submitted my name) that it was quite a surprise. I was so happy as I opened the box and immediately names of all the single soldiers came to mind and I was able to give each one a gift from a friend we've never met. Just in time for the holiday season. Everyone was appreciative of knowing some good folks from our state organized this labor of love. I want to share with ya'll who all it was that was part of this. Between cards, snacks, personal items, books, handbags, notes, and t-shirts the following folks are the ones that did this. I tell you so in case you ever run into one of these groups you could help tell them thank you for supporting us. Milwaukee High School students, Coalition of Troop Support out of West Linn, Oregon Coast Avid Stampers out of Newport/ Depoe Bay and the VFW Ladies Auxiliary out of Tualatin. I may have missed some but that's the ones I could verify from what the box contained. What a gift that was. Attached to this is the final draft of an article written by John Tillman, the embedded journalist that was with us up until the Chinook crash. He went back to Oregon right after, for they were dear friends of his too. I'll send another email later with the rest of our Thanksgiving pictures. I sure miss my family and all you great friends. Just know the good Lord gave us a beautiful day, provided a welcoming and family atmosphere meal and allowed me to say hello now to those I love. I hope your Thanksgiving moments give Him recognition for all we have. I hope you cherish this day and hopefully create time to just rest and give thanks. I think of all of you this day and thank God for ya'll are a blessing in my life.

Travis
And now these three remain: faith, hope and love. But the greatest of these is love.

Happy New Year Everyone,

It's New Year's Eve and not a lot of hootin' and hollerin'. It is totally dark

*outside except for the occasional colored flashlight of someone walking by.
Our pastime is putting an object in the beaten path and watching someone
bite it bad. No – just kidding. We don't pull too many jokes with everyone
carrying loaded weapons. I'm at FOB Salerno now and will be until the middle of Jan. It's 8pm and we haven't had a MEDEVAC mission yet today here.
Nice for a change for until yesterday we were on a 10 day stretch of having
MEDEVAC missions everyday. In that stretch I had another tough to swal-
low call which drives home the reality of this combat zone. I know within
hours of the mission the word travels back in the states each time the news
says another tough day for the troops as we mourn . . . I am reminded of how
blessed we are in the USA and just hope we never let ourselves become insen-
sitive to life as many have in this country. I'm just so thankful I have God to
turn to in all times and situations. It's zero illumination out tonight so we
may not get approved anyway for a mission here unless it's a critical situation. I don't mind sleeping into the New Year for once if it works out that way.
I just wanted to wish ya'll a wonderful time welcoming in the New Year.
Thank you again for all you are in my life. There's no question I'm blessed to
have each of you. I hope the New Year brings our relationships closer and a
memory or two that will last a lifetime. I love ya'll.*

Travis
*And now these three remain: faith, hope and love. But the greatest of these
is love.*

Its 2006 here,

*My New Years was eventful after all. On this base where I'm at now there
was a New Years Eve service at the chapel. I had fun trying to find it in the
dark and when I did there were just a few of us gathered. It was cool. I didn't
know or recognize a single soldier there but for that moment us brothers and
sisters were all gathered together for the same purpose. Don't know a much
better way to close out 2005 and start the New Year. Ya'll know I think of you
often. It's hard to be away from home but it's still good to be here. Thank you
so much for your encouragement and keeping us lifted up in prayer. Oh, I*

can't believe I didn't mention it earlier. Ya'll over did it on care packages. Our goodies and gifts in the operations room in Bagram is overwhelming to look at. The folks to relieve us will still have leftovers from us. Thanks so much again. WOW. Create some great times together heading into the New Year.

Travis
And now these three remain: faith, hope and love. But the greatest of these is love.

For some soldiers, deployments are their first experience outside the United States. In many cases it is also the first time they have been away from home and loved ones for an extended period of time. It can be a very emotional experience: for the first time, soldiers have time to reflect on their lives, what is important to them, and the blessings they have. Each person reacts differently to the separation and stress of fighting in a foreign land. Some take the opportunity to take a step back, re-evaluate their life, and make course adjustments. The following letters were sent by a young female soldier in the Oregon National Guard and reflect her innermost thoughts and feelings during her deployment to Operation Enduring Freedom. They begin with her first letter home and follow with four other letters over the course of her deployment.

SEPTEMBER 3RD, 2005. "LIFE"
Stephan,

Oh my Gosh!! It feels so incredibly surreal to be here! I couldn't believe it when I walked on to the C-17. It was actually happening, I am actually going. I didn't know what to expect and when I climbed aboard the biggest plane I've ever seen with our helicopters on there and the rest of the gear in the back I lost my breath. We were seated on the outside edges in jumpseats with no spare room. I looked at Mr. W with tears in my eyes and said "just tell me everything is going to be ok." I had made myself so sick with anticipation, my stomach was in knots, I took Benadryl and Dramamine, I was out like a light, I slept on the floor with a sleeping bag for 10 hours, when we landed in

Frankfurt, Germany, I still felt really sick so I didn't drink beer like everyone else, I slept there and I slept again on the second leg to Afghanistan.

We left on the first and I am here on the 3rd, this feels so weird. Afghanistan is so dusty, there are 360 views of mountains, but the dust is clouding the view. It is pretty hot here, cat 3. Our MEDEVAC unit is housed in the hangar. Its a big building, we have separate rooms, (I hope) there are showers, latrines, washer dryer, and a little weight room, so we really have no reason to leave this place. The main road is called Disney Drive. North and south of us are the PX, Burger King, Dairy Queen, and the chow hall. The food isn't bad. It is so amazing how much money the military has. There is so much stuff here. So much. I will take pictures so that you can see.

I can't even put in words what this feels like. It blows me away that I am actually in Afghanistan!! Please tell my Mom that I am o.k. I made it here safe. This place is going to be fine. We are safe and everyone so far has been really nice.

Don't go overboard on my care package. I have a lot of stuff here that I need to use. Believe me this place is a little America on base. There is so much shit here!!! But if you could throw in some good smelly stuff for my room that would be cool. This place has quite a unique smell.

Thank you, miss you!! Take care of yourself!!
JE

25 October, 2005 "Miss you"
Hi Stephan,

I am so glad to hear from you! You look good in your costume! I am glad you had a good time and that you hooked up with the National Guard tent. I posted your picture on the wall of my room. Thank you!!! I still think about the fact that I replaced the unit your grandfather was with. Coincidence . . . I think not. Oh, I feel so good right now, I just got done talking with my momma. I love her so much and am so grateful for her and my family.

I will pray for you. Keep your spirits up though! I know its tough, but it's essential. You have so much to offer this world Stephan! Really, I mean that, and the best way you can do that some days is through a smile! Same for me, so I will try my best to heed my own advice. You have been very supportive of me lately, and we are getting closer connected as friends even though I am half way around the world. I look back at our disagreements and chuckle. Everything from Denny's Bar, to the ride home from Boise! We're growing up you know that!

Keep keeping on, the best is yet to come my friend!

Talk with you later!

Have a good day!

JE

06 November 2005 "GRATEFUL"

Mr. Stephan,

How are you today? I wanted to share this quote with you. Just to let you know that I am very grateful for the support I have received. Without the strength of family and friends I would not be this far. I am doing a lot of personal growth while I am over here. Every night I pray, but I find myself silently holding a personal conversation with the Lord, and I realize how much he is there for me. As a friend and a family for me. Purpose Driven Life *has given me many great insights! Life is to be shared, Life is all about Love!*

I haven't been reading it everyday, even a couple pages of that book every other day are a lot to handle. It's some good stuff. I am a little anxious about the holiday season coming up, but I will get by just like I am doing today. I talked with Mom yesterday, man she is being so insightful and supportive. I am very blessed, she is a lot different than when I was first here. She seems to have more peace and understanding about me being over here.

Well I am at work, it's pretty busy today. You take care of yourself, talk with ya later.

Today's Quote

In ordinary life we hardly realize that we receive a great deal more than we give, and that it is only with gratitude that life becomes rich.

—Dietrich Bonhoeffer

JE

18 December 2005 "My latest"
Stephan,

Hey there, I was gonna send you a text message but I have more to say than that.
First things, my foot is feeling a lot better. I do need to be better about stretching it though. It's funny how fast it came on! My insoles the Doc gave me help a lot.

So we just got letters from grade-schoolers. Apparently LT M's friend (who is also a pilot in the ORARNG) is a school teacher and had all of the kids write us letters. They are so sweet. I have to write them back, they are personalized notes and pictures. One girl asked how it feels to be a soldier and how it feels to fight. Brings a smile to my face.

I picked up Purpose Driven Life *today and today's reading was exactly what I needed to hear . . . Grow in Christ. Allow him to transform you from the inside out . . . my earthly ways want me to change from the outside in. It is the devil who wants me to obsess about guys, my weight, my feelings of inadequacy . . . those thoughts actually draw me away from God. So I need to ask the Lord to change my thoughts. Redirect my energy to a way that is more beneficial to Christ. I know I'm rambling about this. I have a ton of emotions swirled up in my body right now.*

I had to share this with you . . . read on myspace M's Blog . . . here's my response

Here goes my dip in the water . . . how deep I go who knows? Nothing shapes your life more than the commitments you choose to make. They can develop you or destroy you, but either way they define you! Here's a quote: the quality of a man's life is in direct proportion to his commitment to excellence. What does all this mean? That we have the power to choose, in that power lies the capacity for Joy, Happiness, Fulfillment, and LOVE! In relationships, when sparks fly we choose to commit . . . well when those sparks die we choose to leave . . . right? Oh but we blame it on "feelings." I don't feel the fire anymore . . . blah, blah blah. See I think you don't fall in love with a person, you fall in love with the anticipation of feeling that same way again. Makes you think then of what feelings you are addicted to. Love is more than a feeling . . . it's a commitment. and that commitment requires constant, careful, and thoughtful CHOICE! So go out and live your best life! It's your Choice!

Here's some more philosophy from Me:

I am in a state of reclaiming my Life. Reclaiming my strength, and my inner beauty so that I may Grow into the woman that God intended me to be. I have been given so much from His love and Grace that I have enough to Give. I am whole when I am happy. And that's not just a surface fix or feeling. It is a state of being that ignites my soul, the Joy of living, and aligning myself with God's will. In this state things happen naturally, weight control, relationships, careers and opportunities. It is in the state of Truth that I make the right decisions; Also because I have a guiding light directing my steps, making it easier to see. By allowing this new found energy to flourish I am making a transformation from the inside out, the best thing we can do for ourselves is not what we do to our bodies but what we do to our minds. Changing the way we think changes the way we feel thus changing our actions! I am committed to living my Best life! I am committed to live in Truth! I am committed to making those choices everyday!

Stephan I know I am on a roll. Thank you for hearing me out. I have so much inside of me that I need to get out. My connections are via internet, and I use them heavily. As always thank you for your support and faith in me. I hope you are doing well!!

Talk with you later!!

JE

04 January 2006 "OMG"
Stephan,

I had such a nice email written for you, when I accidentally closed out of it and lost it. So I will recap. I was writing it as I was opening your presents, it went something like this:

OH MY GOSH, I CAN'T BELIEVE YOU! HOW ARE YOU SO FREAKIN' GOOD TO ME, I FEEL LIKE A LITTLE KID IN A CANDY STORE! I CAN'T BELIEVE THIS!

quick side blurb: I feel so lucky right now, I have to say that this experience is truly God's divine timing, intervention and purpose in my life! I know I am right where I need to be! I have grown so much spiritually, emotionally and physically. I feel more blessed and loved than ever before. I am committed to achieving my full potential, and giving back to the world. I feel Magic

in my soul. I am happy and joy-filled, because I choose it, and I have time to
grow. There is so much stemming and pour over from me (as you can guess
by my email) that I am a bubble of magic.
    YOU DESERVE A GOLD STAR... A MEDAL FROM ME. JUST KNOW
HOW MUCH YOU MEAN TO ME.

    JE

Letters such as these reflect the emotions, thoughts, dreams and ambitions of their authors. They give the reader a rare glimpse into the mind of one of thousands of our soldiers who are in a foreign land fighting our nation's wars. Each one has their own life, own dreams, and own reasons for volunteering to be where they are. We are fortunate to know them and have them as soldiers and citizens in our communities.

In addition to the National Guard soldiers serving overseas, those who remain behind, either having just completed a deployment, or waiting their turn, strive to do all they can to support their fellow soldiers. The following story is just one of many events that National Guard citizen-soldiers continue to perform in support of their brothers in arms.

COMING HOME

As a National Guard officer, I have grown accustomed to a very close
relationship with the community I work in and have become a part of. The
Medical Evacuation Battalion I commanded conducts numerous search and
rescue operations in the community and much of the unit has already served
in Afghanistan, Iraq, Kuwait, Saudi Arabia and North Carolina. The com-
munity where we are based consists of smaller metropolitan areas, but pri-
marily small towns – towns that are very closely knit and ones where the
entire town mourns the loss of any of her sons or daughters.

    I grew up in one of these small communities, and feel a bond with the
small towns and those who come from them. It was this bond that commit-
ted me to help when representatives from the U.S. Marine Corps asked for
assistance in transporting and storing the remains of two Marines killed

in Iraq who were on their way home. One of the Marines was from Yreka, California, the town closest to my home town; the other was from a town I had flown to numerous times, Roseburg, Oregon. The trip from Portland to both destinations would be 4 and 7 hours in a Hearse and was scheduled to take place in the middle of the night.

The flight bringing them to Oregon came faster than anticipated however and was going to arrive hours ahead of schedule. After discussing our options, we decided the best course of action was to fly the remains to Salem for the night after they arrived, then fly them to their hometowns the next day. Each one of us knew these two Marines had made the ultimate sacrifice for their country and deserved no less than to arrive at their final resting places in the middle of a beautiful day, not in the middle of the night.

When we landed at Portland International Airport, airport officials had closed a taxiway and were waiting for our helicopters. Soon after we shut down a commercial airliner taxied in and a Marine contingent surrounded the aircraft as its precious cargo was unloaded. Six Marines surrounded each casket and slowly escorted them down the darkened taxiway to our helicopters. As they made their trip in the dark, security officers, policemen, firemen, and airport officials lined the way to pay their respects. The crew of each helicopter came to attention and saluted as the remains arrived and were carefully loaded. The helicopters departed together with a special clearance and flew directly to Salem. When they arrived, the remains were carefully unloaded and escorted to our briefing room where a guard remained with them overnight.

The next day we departed under an overcast sky, but as our flight climbed through 5000 feet the skies opened up to a beautiful day. A few minutes north of Roseburg our two helicopters formed up and circled the town before landing at the airport which was located in the middle of Roseburg. When we landed there were many people from the town waiting as we taxied up to the designated parking spot and shut down.

We could clearly see the family of the young Marine separated from the others. One of the most heart wrenching moments I have experienced occurred when the doors of the helicopter were opened and the family saw *before them the physical manifestation of the news of their son, husband, and father for the first time. The news of their loved one up to this point had been words from a Marine, but now, before them, they could clearly see the casket draped in an American Flag that held the remains of their Marine. The price of freedom sounded clearly that day in the sobs and tears of his family as they welcomed their son, husband, and father home for the last time.*

The trip to Yreka was in many ways similar, except this was the community closest to my hometown, Happy Camp. I would know people when we arrived, and the pain of the community would come to my family as well. In Yreka the airport was several miles from town so we asked to use the hospital pad in the middle of town. Once again we circled the town before landing and could clearly see the crowd gathering near the landing pad.

After we landed, the Marine's family was once again distinguishable from the others. In them, it seemed their hope that this was all a dream was fading away as the truth of all they had heard up to this point was coming to fruition before them. The fact we had just delivered one angel to his family earlier that day did not make this any easier. As the helicopter's doors slid open, we were once again reminded in a way none of us will ever forget, of the pain and anguish associated with the cost of freedom. A young bride's tears and loss of control will forever be etched in my mind.

As the casket was taken away, the mayor came up to thank us and said he heard one of us was from the area. As I shook his hand I could see in his eyes, and perhaps he in mine, that we had lost one of our own and the pain of the Marine's family would echo throughout the community who welcomed home one of their own for the last time.

As we departed and returned to our base, each of us realized that although we had only played a small role in returning these Marines home – they had touched our hearts forever. The price of freedom now had a clearer meaning to each of us, a meaning we would not forget, and one we would live through again in our own ranks a few months later.

Lieutenant Colonel Dan Hokanson

8

DEVIL DOGMA

Karey Keel-Stidham
Marine Mother
Orcas Island,
Washington, USA

T HE FOLLOWING LETTERS are from my son's first deployment, at the end of January, 2003, before combat operations in Iraq actually had begun. Most of the time was spent in Kuwait. Tim was an airframes mechanic with HMM-365, a CH-46 helicopter squadron. I have transcribed the letters and edited them only to protect issues and identities.

★ AUTHOR'S NOTE: Karey Keel-Stidham not only provided us with access to the many letters and emails she received from both her son and her many adopted troops, she also provided us with interesting footnotes to much of the material and we felt it was an integral part of the story she is telling. In many ways, she is the story of this chapter! Her flair for writing was evident in her emails to us during the writing of the book and so we chose to let her speak for herself and her adopted troops. Karey is a true patriot and we salute her.

Feb 1st, 2003

Hi, well we have been doing alright. Arrived safely, blah, blah, blah. Can't tell you much else. However, if you have any Q's, I can probably answer them. So, I love you and if you could get me a calling card and send me some granola bars if possible. Thanx Much.

T.W. Stidham
PS – Shitty handwriting is a sign of intelligence.

February 13th, 2003

Well, been here for 12 days now. Still like a big camping trip with higher risk level but still the same old. We're able to take showers, but usually they're full and also a half an hour away so two showers in twelve days is alright for me. I don't stink cause of the baby wipes and such. So how's things back home? Talk to Nick lately? Well can't tell you really anything I know because of security reasons. Happy birthday Dad and to Josh. Well not much to report. Love you both.

Oh, I need an address book again and envelopes please.
Bye

February 18th 2003
Dear Parents,

We moved tents today to supposedly a permanent place. Our birds are going to arrive some time today. Other than that not much is going on, we're just going. I miss you guys, can't wait to come home again, but for now just saving money. I should have tons of pictures when I return. I don't have much else to say, so take care. I love you both and I'll try to get a phone call to you soon as the phone center opens up.

Bye for now, Love Tim.

February 23rd, 2003

CPL. STIDHAM DURING HIS FIRST TOUR IN IRAQ. *Photo courtesy Karey Keel-Stidham*

Dear Ma & Pa,

Hey not much to report except I got two pen pals from the single Marine program. They are older moms. They send me letters and sent me a care package. We've been working for a while. Can't tell you what the plants are cause I don't know. Just watch FOX news or CNN so you can find out as it happens. HAPPY B-DAY DAD!!!

This should show up around then. Got a package from Maryland Meghan yesterday. It made my day. She's written to me as well so she's ruining me. She just treats me good.

Anyways, take care. Love Tim

March 8th, 2003
Dear Mom & Dad,

I received your package and letter saying you got my letter yesterday. For a look at our squadron go to blazingbluenights.com. Where I am at is 39 miles south of the border (Iraq). There are 4 camps between us and them. The camps you listed are south of us. We have been flagged out to do recon inspections. Anyways, I'm good. We're supposed to have a general come speak to us today. What a thrill!! (Sense the sarcasm). And I don't have much else to say except I'm not doing anything most of the time. I could really use a beer, just one. Well, love you both, talk to you in a day or two.

Love Tim

March 23rd, 2003
Dear Mom & Dad

The scuds have stopped for about 12 hours now. Most of night crew strayed cool, we had a couple who just wanted to stay in the bunkers. Not me, I knew that nothing was going to happen. We had them launched at us but our Patriots (missiles) took them out.

Well they say I'm a war hero. Feels about the same as turning 18 in boot camp, just another day in the life.

I hopefully will be home sometime in June. We're actually moving a lot faster than planned due to the fact that they keep surrendering. Well, I'll write again soon. By the way, I won't be calling for a while.

Love T.W. Stidham

March 31st, 2003
Dear Ma & Pa,

Well not much to report. I'm still on nights and everyday is a desert Marine Ground Hog's Day. I work 12 on and 12 off and basically sleep 8 hours of it and do nothing the rest. I have received all mail up till now. And Yeah. So I'm real bored and I hope I'll be home for Jerry's wedding, but we'll see.

Love you both, Timmer
PS – found out our reporter worked for FOX news. He was fired for

CPL. STIDHAM ON PATROL IN A HUMVEE. *Photo courtesy Karey Keel-Stidham*

telling secrets to the Iraqis. He's in Baghdad and I hope he's _!

April 3rd & 4th, 2003
Dear Mom & Dad

Today will probably be the last time I write until I don't know when. We're leaving for Iraq Saturday morning, so that's that. I'm excited that now we're going to get a piece, finally. Never Mind, I am going on Saturday and I'll not be writing anymore because we probably won't have mail. Rather I know we won't.

I love you both very much.
Tim.

We didn't hear from Tim for about 25 days, and then he called us, and told us what he'd been doing (dodging land mines in his Humvee), and that he'd be on a ship for home within the next 10 days. It was a month and a half before he returned to the US. His ship detoured to Liberia for a week.

LETTERS FROM TIM — OIF II

My son Tim returned to Iraq in August 2004 for his second tour. He was stationed at the airbase at Al-Asad, and had good email access. The following are a selection of the communications we had with Tim during this time.

August 15th, 2004
Hi!

I finally got the internet set up out here. I had to get your email address, so I love you. I will email my shop address.

Sept 2, 2004

Hi mom, I just wanted to say I love you before the email goes down again.

–Tim

Sept 3, 2004

Hey, I know all about living in two places. My working 14-16 hour days everyday for seven months and sleeping and showering 1.5 miles away. Well, I love you guys. Hi to dad, I love you.

–Tim

Sept 6, 2004
Hi Mom,

I assume you're back, so I decided to say "hi" and I love you. You and dad hug each other for me.

–Tim

Sept 10th, 2004

Hi, I don't have much to say except thanks for everything and I don't do anything except work and lift weights. So, yeah, just thought I'd drop you a line.

Love Tim.

Sept 13, 2004
Hi—

The computers are up and running. As of the time you get this I will be an official CDI (Collateral Duty Inspector), so that's cool. I'm saving money pretty well, not much to buy. I might even have enough to pay off my car and then some when I return. Not having unnecessary insurance on the car will save me money and I'll be able to pay off the truck early too. We'll see. So happy birthday to all. Thanks for all the people who are supporting us and f∗∗∗ off to all who don't and tell John Kerry automatic rifles are to get into the hand of terrorists, and criminals whether or not they are banned. Tell dad thanks for the email and I love you guys.

Tim

Sept 29, 2004
Hi

Well, I got the message, but is Sid KIA or MIA? (Sid was Tim's beloved little rat, and I had to tell him he was gone – KIA). Other than that I don't think he would have fared well on Orcas anyway, but it's about this time of year when he goes out and doesn't come back for weeks at a time. Anyways, I try not to think about it and keep plugging along. In a week, it'll be two months so only about 4 to go. Advanced party is supposed to leave the 3rd week of January, so we'll be about three weeks behind. I got a package from you and then I got a package from my girl today too, so I feel extra special.

I love you

–Tim

October 17, 2004
Hi

I figured you'd be home pretty soon, so I decided to write you a little note. We are busy, of course, but I don't really care. I'm ready to come home. I really hate this base. We work our asses off and half the base doesn't do sh*t except make up dumb ass rules. But anyway, Meg got a new job, so that's cool and that's all I have to report. I love you

Tim.

November 17, 2004
Hi

Well here's the scoop, I can't get into anything specific, but we are flying. I work still the same schedule, and then usually lift afterward. Oh, just so you know, I probably won't come home right away. I want to go someplace warm like maybe Cancun, when I get back but we'll see. My girlfriend is good; she's been working a lot and going to the gym. I'm trying to figure out what to get her for Christmas; I have Grandpa's present already in motion, in fact Bryan is flying with it as we speak. It's a US flag, and Bryan is going to take it with him to Baghdad and fly it out the window. It will come with a certificate telling where when and who. Plus I'll add some to it. Well, sounds like the house is coming along. I'm sorry certain things aren't working out, like dad's boss and the whole mortgage thing. Let me know if you need anything, I'll try and help. Well, I have a count down on the board in the shop, I have 98 days till we're leaving, which some think is depressing but I like it because I get to see the progress on a daily basis.

Well, mom, I'll let you go. I have to get back to it.
Love, Tim.

November 25, 2004
Hi,

Well, Thanksgiving isn't the same out here, but I can't complain. I don't know if I'll be able to call Brad's due to the time difference, but I'll call you and dad probably. I hope you have a good time. I get to stay at work all day. Fun, fun. Well, hi to all and thanks for the pictures. Tell Grandma I got her package and the cookies were eaten by the people in the shop, just like the last time.

Love, Tim

December 13, 2004
Hi mom,

Thank you for helping me out. Hopefully I'll be able to get your package in the mail soon. It probably won't make it till after Xmas so it will be on the way though. So do you have phone and internet from the house yet? I would like to try to call and I'm always disinclined to because of the cell phone reception. Other than that, I'm ready to come home. We're getting to the point where we are preparing for the advanced parties to be coming and going. HMM-264 should be here in about 30 days, and our advanced party should be leaving in that amount of time. Then, after that it's going to be hectic, but we'll be in the process of coming home. So after a few months out here, we're doing well. I can't wait to drive my car and truck. I hope I can come home during a time where I can still take my truck up to Mt Baker and play in the snow.
Well, I have to get back to it.

Love, Tim

December 27, 2004
Mom,

Christmas was just another day out here. I didn't get to call because the phones went down after I made a five minute call to my girlfriend. I would have tried calling you but I didn't want to call grandma and grandpa at 5 am and you weren't there anyway. Food sucked as usual and everyone told me to tell you thank you for their Christmas presents.

I had an idea for you and dad coming out, like maybe you could drive my truck out and fly back? Then my mattress and dad's old chair and my welder could come with you., Just a thought at this point, but I do want to bring my truck out because if I'm not living in the brick I'll need to move and I'm not buying a new mattress. Too expensive.

Love you, Tim

January 1, 2005

Happy New Year's Mom. Drink one or two extra for me.

Love, Tim

January 3, 2005
Hi mom,

I wanted to let you know I won NCO of the Quarter. I was tested on a board and beat out three other Marines. Here's a picture.

January 24, 2005
Hi

I'm glad you're looking at my statement because I haven't seen it in 6 months. What's the damage now? I need to figure that into my bills. I need the total please. You'll just have to wait and see what I have for you and dad when I see you. I'm glad you are having a good time with everything involved with the move to Orcas. I can't wait to see everything.

So, you got a woodstove, huh? That's great because you have plenty of it on the property (wood). Plus it smells good. It rained for like two days straight out here and I wish I had my truck so bad to play in the mud. I've been working out as well. The other day, on the flat bench I did my warm up of 185 ten times, then did 5 reps with 245, 4 with 255, 3 with 265 then I did 1 with 275, 1 with 280, 1 with 285 and then my chest failed on 290. It's the easiest workout for me to do, or the one I like the best, because I can lift a decent amount. I'm still trying for 300. My goals have changed though. I'm trying to get a six-pack (abs) before I get back so I've been doing abs and running with Bryan. I wish my biceps would grow and perform the way my chest and triceps do, but they're stubborn. I haven't taken any supplements since I've been out here because I want to hit 300 all natural.

Well, thanks for the note. Tell dad "hi" and I love you both.

Tim
PS I GOT 300 TODAY

January 27, 2005

That's pretty good (re: a letter from another Marine in response to anti-war protestors) but I like to take a more direct approach. Let me hear some protesters when I come home to WA or hear someone talk negatively about my fellow military when I get back . . . I might go to jail on assault charges but I'll be released on self-defense.

NO, I'm just mad because I haven't got much sleep and the bleeping maids were in my room today and I found out my birthday present for mom and things for my girlfriend were all in the same box as my other souvenirs which were burned about a week ago. So that's over three hundred dollars worth that was burned up. It was nice stuff, too. Okay, I'm tired of being pissed off, and no, I don't want to be pissed on either. I'll talk to you later, oh and I got my package today. Thank you.

Love Tim

February 4, 2005

Hi, I just wanted to say I should be on my way home in two weeks. Is that not cool or what? Don't worry about being there for the homecoming. I'm only going to be getting off a bus nothing special. I'll probably just want a bath and beer anyway. I'm all about some relaxation. I don't have much to report except I'm ready to come home as usual. WTI still up in the air, so I haven't bought a ticket to come home yet. I should know soon.

Okay, that's my bit. I love you both.
Love, Tim

Tim returned to his base in North Carolina about 20 days later, and we took a trip out to see him there the following weekend. I needed to hug him! In the fall of 2003, after Tim had been home for a while, I wanted to try and make a difference in the life of a deployed soldier or Marine. The way my friend Nancy and the DAR had for my son and I. Got in touch with Adopt-A-Platoon and asked to "adopt" a soldier. This collection of letters is the result of my ongoing campaign to help our troops through their deployments. Again, these have been edited only to protect identities and personal issues.

20 December 2003
Dear Karey,

How's it going? Not too bad over here. I'm doing good as a matter of fact. We had just received word that we should be back in the states by March 30 or around that date. Thank you so much for your gifts and care packages. They mean so much to me (especially the hot drink mixes). Thank you for spelling my name right, that means a lot to me also. I'm 21 Y/O, so a year older than Tim, lived in Minnesota all my life way up north in a little town. I have a brother and a sister who are both younger than me. As for my job in the Army, I am an infantry man. Anti-Armor is my specialty. That means I'm qualified to shoot any shoulder fired missile system or employ anti-tank mines, and recovery of the mines if need be.

Weather in Washington is much like here except for the snow part. Just cold and it rains like every other day. Personally, I like it cold. Its way better than 140 degrees F like it was in the summer. I have never seen a candle turn to liquid by just sitting outside till I came here. If you want me to take some pictures for you, I would be more than happy to. If you have email, you can email me at_____

I can send you pictures via the internet. I will be sending you a gift package from over here. My way of saying thanks for your support. If you have anymore questions feel free to ask. Well, got a big mission tomorrow. I'll write again after I get back from that. Thanks again for all your support. It means A LOT.

Sincerely
SPC Panovic
Iraq

I never heard from SPC Panovic again.

23 December 2003
Dear Karey,

This will be short as we are very busy. My return address is my rede-ployment address. I will write something more substantial after I rede-ploy to Fort Campbell, which will be relatively soon. Thank you so much for your kindness. God bless you.

Chaplain Chuck
Let not your heart be troubled ye believe in God, believe also in Me (John 14.1)

I never heard from Chaplain Chuck again, either.

29 December 2003
Dear Karey,

Thank you for adopting me. It felt really good to know that someone cares enough to drop me a letter. I was born and raised in the streets of Hartford, Connecticut. I'm 21 years old and went to boot camp 1 year ago in March at Parris Island, I don't have any family besides my beloved Marines, and my younger brother and sister that I haven't seen in about a year. None of my friends or family have called or written to me since I got to Afghanistan. This is my first deployment so I am very lonely and homesick. I joined the Corps for many reasons, but mainly to protect you and your family. I am an infantry rifleman aka Grunt. What's Co Stidham's MOS? I'm so glad you told me about your family, it makes me part of it. I'm stationed at Camp LeJuene, NC. I hope your son makes it home for Christmas. I got your letter on Christmas Eve. What unit is Cpl Stidham with? I love music; it keeps my sanity in check while abroad. Please send anything you can, it's all greatly appreciated, and write to me as often as possible. I'm already expecting your next letter. Continue to pray for me. God bless you and your family.

PFC Copeland USMC
Afghanistan.

That's the one and only letter I got from PFC Copeland, but my packages continued to go to his deployment address until late July of 2004.

3 March 2004
Dear Mrs. Stidham,

Well I want to thank you for the box and the letter. They came at a time I really needed it. First, some of the information that was given to you about me was wrong. I was born 1 July 1976, and I'm a female (Adopt a Platoon told me she was a he). I am the mother of 3 kids. My eldest son is 10, next is my daughter who will be 6, and my baby boy is 3. Both of my parents were in the Navy, I joined the Army when I was 20. I've been in the Army for 7 years now. My job in the Army is a Medic. I assist doctors and nurses, and my goal is to become a nurse practitioner. I'm presently stationed in Wiesbaden, Germany. I don't like Germany, though.

My job here in Iraq is to go to different sites and pull medical coverage. The site I'm presently at is near a river. The wind was blowing so hard every time I looked at the water I felt seasick. I guess it's a good thing I didn't join the Navy. I'm really not in need of anything. Letters are what I really like. That lets me know you took time out of your day to write to me. That's why I appreciate those the most.

Sincerely
Spc. Jamie
Tikrit. Iraq

1 April 2004

All I can say is thank you. I wish there were more people like you. Taking the time to do things for other people. I know that adopt-a-platoon is probably big, and I hope that a lot of other soldiers get stuff from nice families. I'm in the Army reserve out of South Bend, IN. I have a wife who is 29, a daughter who's 5 and a son that is 2 1/2. I've been married for 8 years. I was sent to Fort Hood, TX just one month after Sept 11, 2001. My son was just 3 months old at the time. That was a lot better year than this year has been. Hopefully I'll be home around the first week of December.

Things I need, it's hard to say. There's a lot of stuff that I have my wife send to me and some of my friends. I like cookies, homemade or from the store, but please no raisins. Hopefully when I get home, I'll be taking my family on a Mexican cruise. We've been on one before, after I got home from Texas and we had the best time. My dad is very happy with my military life; most of it has been reserves. He spent 3 years in the Navy, and then got out. I've been in since '90 and will be getting promoted next month. I'll also be signing a contract for 6 more years, and then I'll probably be done. So, I'll say one more time thank you. Tell your son I said "Hi" and be safe. I must go now. Thank you again. And I hope to hear from you again soon.

Spc. Jason – Baghdad. Iraq.

12 April 2004
Dear Mrs. Karey,

Well how are you doing? I'm sorry it took so long to write back. Every time I receive a package, I try to send a letter back.

For the most part I'm doing fine. The hospital that I'm at hasn't been too busy with patients which are a good thing. To answer some of your questions, yes I am married, but I'm getting ready to go through a divorce, it had nothing to do with me being deployed. My marriage was breaking up way before then. Yes, my parents are very proud of me. I'm the only one out of three kids that joined the military.

My kids understand that I have to go off somewhere to work. The oldest one is the only one of the three that knows I'm in Iraq, mainly because he's in a school that's run by the military and they talk about deployments.

I want to thank you for the packages. The majority of the stuff that you are sending to me I am not able to get at the PX here. I do a lot of missions that required me to leave the post. That's usually when I eat the food. Thank you, so much for the Pop Tarts and the tea. I think one of my room mates ate a pack of them, so naturally I've hid the rest.

I hope you have enjoyed this letter. I will write again soon.
Sincerely
SPC Jamie
Tikrit. Iraq

Late May 2004

Well I want to start out by saying thank you for everything. There are a lot of good people in the world; it would be nice if everyone was like you. We are all doing well. It's been very quiet here. I went home April 20th – May 5th to spend some time with my mom. She has had cancer for about a year and it doesn't look good for her. The doctor said she doesn't have much time. By the end of the month, I'll probably be going home to see her for the last time, but hopefully she can hang on a little longer. I'm doing okay about it. I have an older brother who is much closer to her than I am. He will probably take it harder than me. I really want to thank you for everything. Our unit will be moving to a new location, we don't have a date yet, but it will be soon so mail will slow down for a little bit.

Hope to hear from you soon.
Sgt Jason
Baghdad. Iraq.

20 June 2004

Well it's nice to hear from you as always. I have gotten behind on my letter writing. The reason why is because I got into a little accident with my hand. What happened was my water bottle rolled underneath some barbed wire. I went to grab it, and cut my thumb. Well, they had to give me two stitches. The cut was over my right thumb knuckle, so after I was stitched, they put a splint on my finger. You never know how important a thumb is. Well now I do. I had to have people help me button up my uniform, plus, I'm right handed. The stitches are out now, it still hurts when I bend my thumb, but at least I can write. I'm glad you finished your college class. I'm taking college classes myself. The post that I'm at is offering classes. Right now I'm taking US History, Algebra and Microeconomics. The only one that's giving me trouble is Algebra. I had to have other people take notes for me when I had the stitches. I'm glad you are settled in your new house. I hope your cat is used to his new home.

It's very hot here. It gets so hot here that my pen exploded in my pocket. That's hot.

I know it's a little late, but tell your husband I said Happy Father's Day. By the time you get this letter, I should be promoted to Sergeant. My promotion date is July 1st. It's been long overdue which also means I'm going to get more responsibilities. In the Army when you get promoted

to Sgt. you are now a considered a Non-commissioned officer or NCO.
Well, Mrs. Karey, I will write again soon.

Your friend Jamie
Tikrit. Iraq.

July 2004

Just a short note to say thank you for everything and for taking the
time out to write to soldiers around the world. I'm okay on boxed food; a
note a few times per month is fine. We are all doing fine. Hopefully we'll
be home soon.

Take care and thank you.
Sgt Jason
Baghdad Iraq

*Before I received the following letter, my dear adopted Sgt Jamie sent me a
dozen roses and a whole assortment of goodies, with a card attached that said,
"just wanted to brighten your day" and "just something to say thank you for
all that you do for me."*

19 August 2004
Dear Karey,

I'm glad that you liked the gifts. Your letters have been sounding pretty down. That and the fact that you always take time out to mail me all
the packages; I just wanted you to know that I really appreciated it.

My kids are doing fine. Yes, they are getting ready to start back at
school. By the time you get this letter, I should be with them. I'm going
on my R & R in a couple of days. So while I'm at home, I'm going to take
them shopping for school clothes. The surprise is my kids don't even
know that I'm coming home. Each month I've been sending them a box
of toys and gifts. This month its going to be me!

The days are starting to get cooler now, which is good. But the minute you start working or walking around too much you start sweating. I'm sorry it took me so long to write back, but my squad leader left so I had to step up to the plate. I'm still working on getting that picture to you. Well as always, thank you for taking the time to send me packages and especially the letters. I enjoy those the most.

Your friend, Jamie
Tikrit. Iraq

That was the last I heard from my dear little Sgt Jamie, I still think of her often, and wonder where she is, and how her little kids are doing. I know in my heart she will succeed in whatever she chooses.

September 2004

Had some time to write a letter. I'm doing fine. Work is going all right. 12 hour days. There are going to be a lot of changes coming up in the next 4 months. Less than _ of our unit will be coming home in or around November, but that could change. The rest will have to stay; they are not 100% sure when they will go home. The reason for that is a lot of us did a year in Texas right after Sept 11, 2001 and we're only deployable for up to 24 months in a 5 year period. On the other hand, the Army can send us to 2 other places in the world (I think), so we can be home for 6 months and be sent out again. Life over here is not too bad. It's mostly Groundhog Day; you wake up and do the same work day after day. The money is kind of alright. My wife and I are looking to go to Mexico on vacation for about 8 days, just us, no kids. After I got home from Texas, I took my wife and daughter to the Bahamas on a cruise. One of the best vacations I've been on.

My son turned 3 in July; he can be a handful sometimes. My daughter is almost perfect. I like to play golf and she likes to go. When I was home in June, I took her shopping for golf clubs. I'm not going to turn her into the next Tiger Woods, but as long as she wants to I will teach her to play and to have fun. My wife and I would like to have another child in 2007, but it depends on if I'm home. I'll be done in 2010, and will have 20 years in. In April I signed up for another 6 years, depends on those 6 more years, I'm looking at maybe 2 more deployments, unless everybody wakes up the next day and there's no more war. I don't think I can get that lucky.

I want to thank you for everything. If you want to drop a letter by my house, you are more than welcome to. You can probably stop writing here late October, so that the unit won't have to mail letters back to the states. Tell your son to hang in there and take care of himself. Tell him I said "hi." For now, take care and thank you. I hope this money will come in handy and don't spend it all in one place.

> Thanks for everything
> Sgt Jason
> Baghdad, Iraq.

This was my last letter from Sgt Jason, whom I grew very fond of. If only I had his home address. He sent us two Iraqi dinar bills with ousted Saddam's picture on them: they have no monetary value, but are nice collector's items.

In September of 2004, the following email letter from LCpl Jarod was forwarded to me from my friend Nancy Daniels. I wanted to include it here, because the young Marine, in my opinion, is a gifted writer, and his description of what he was seeing while in Kuwait is very good. I wrote to him soon after and about 4 months later, I received a letter back from him from Iraq, also included here. He later emailed me some pictures of himself with the Iraqi Freedom Guard he was training and working with.

Freda, 3 Sept 2004

We spent a long evening, night and morning out in the desert; was interesting. Saw some sheepherders, and we wonder what the heck the sheep eat. Then we see dead ones all over the sides of the roads, and think that maybe they don't. Lots of dead camels and an occasional donkey too. The ground is the flattest I've ever been on; it reminds me almost of the inland lakes when they're frozen over in the winter. The completely smooth and flat desert, however, stretches as far as we can see in all directions. Through the night we could see the lights of Highway 80 off in the distance to the south; they light their highways like we light our city streets. Looking at it at first, I thought of back in Michigan when standing on Pier Marquette, Muskegon, at night and the Grand Haven Pier is visible jutting out into the water to the south. The rows of lights are similar, except the highway too, stretches across the horizon as far as the eye can see.

The air cools at night to like 80 – 90, but it feels cold like 60s back in California. Since 60s seem to be the summer temp for you guys back in MI, I think I've forgotten what to compare it to.

In the morning there was a herd of wild camels about five+ miles out. They actually follow each other in lines we saw and the tracks prove it.

While we took turns practicing our IA drills, we watched each other and commented on how weird things look, like a Mars movie or something; nothing breaks the horizon, the ground is just tan sand and flat forever, and though it was light out, the sky was not yet blue. A huge machine on eight big tires rolls and glides across the distance and stops; a few people open up big doors on the back and jump out with their weapons, all in tan clothes with big, bulky jackets, helmets and goggles, and trot across the space to go investigate something. It can be seen clearly, but not heard, either because of the distance or of the noise of our own vehicle. It is funny to watch. At least Iraq will not be so hot and barren!

I had this great article about France and their two journalists held hostage in Iraq, but I keep forgetting the paper in my tent so it'll have to wait. Maybe I shouldn't say "great."

Uncle Keith: No sandstorms yet. We get wind from the Persian Gulf, which adds humidity to the heat, but no flying mud yet.

– Jarod

Sunday, 5 Sept 2004

Well it has been nice talking to you all while I've been here in Kuwait.

I have to type a quick message here then its back to work for me. Hopefully once we get to KV we will have internet capabilities. Don't worry about replying now, as I might not get it; if I can I'll email you all from Iraq. Wish us all luck on this road march; it is not going to be pretty! "But I will fear not tomorrow, because I have lived today. I will be strong and courageous! I will not tremble or be discouraged, for the LORD my God is with me wherever I go!" – From Joshua 1:9

Talk to you later!

12 October 2004
Karey,

Last week out in the field, I received your letter. What a surprise! Thank you for writing – with so much negative war media it is that much nicer to hear from a stranger taking time out of her life to give & wish us, other strangers, support. Thank you.

I'm trying to think who would have passed my emails on. Nancy Daniels – hmm, don't know but she sounds like a great person. My mom sometimes reads and posts with Marine Moms Online, but my family lives in Michigan. I think it probably must have been Sandy Jackson, a friend that lives in Burbank, CA very close to Hollywood. Actually, Sandy & I met under similar terms. Some friends and I often leave 29 Palms MCB on the weekends and come back to Burbank, where one of the Marines is from. His mom, Diane, who is very active with Marine Moms, was driving home a different way one day and happened to see this gigantic quilt hanging in front of someone's house. Being who she is, she stopped, pulled in and introduced herself. The quilter's name was Sandy. She and her husband Wayne, (in their forties) have no kids and didn't know anybody in the military, but they wanted to show their support for the troops. The quilt Sandy had sewn was a huge patriotic banner. At the top she had sewn, "Honor the American Soldiers Sacrifice" and in the middle she had printed the name of every serviceman and woman from all the branches of the military who had died in Iraq since the war started last March. It was amazing.

Diane has become a good friend to us – every weekend we had off since her son & I graduated SOI and entered the fleet early last April, Diane has had Marines at her house. She gives us a place to sleep, she feeds us, and we all spend time together. The next weekend, when we were 'home' again, she brought us over to meet Sandy. She and I have talked ever since, and we have become great friends.

Here in Iraq things are going well. Our unit is stationed at the Korean Village, an outpost in north-western Iraq. We are near the Syrian and Jordanian borders, and are mainly involved in a city called Ar Rutbah. For the most part the people are pretty friendly. Back in the states I was sent through an Arabic course, and I try to act as our platoon's translator and interpreter. It's definitely not easy, but I've been studying, and I learn more every time I use it. It makes things more exciting for me, because I am always where the action is. Thank you again for writing, and I hope you hear from you again. Best wishes to your son, Cpl Stidham, as well.

Orcas Island sounds interesting; you must tell me about it!
–Jarod

10 March 2005 (email)

Good to hear you finally got my letter! I was wondering about that. Here is an update I sent out to family and friends, thought maybe you might be interested. Hope the pictures work, too.

Hello All—

Sometimes I wonder if it's all really worth it. I mean, find something great and hold onto it. Meet some good people, have some awesome times, and stay there for the rest of your life. Screw everything else and what could've been and stay where you know you'll always be happy. Why go?

Comanche and Taskforce Wolfpack left Ar Ramadi in mid February for Camp Al Asad. We rejoined RCT-7 and stepped off for the heated cities of Hit and Haditha and what promised to be our last big mission in OIF-II. We were to go out with a bang.

First we picked up a team of the Freedom Guard from FOB Hit, and we made our way into the desert outside Haditha. We set up a screen line there for couple of days and supported a Force Recon unit and the British Special Forces before heading to the dam at Haditha, where we met up with soldiers from Azerbaijan. From there we crossed the desert south and early one morning rolled into Hit from behind. White platoon took up a breaking position on the west side of the city, and Red, HQ, and Blue platoons took up spots in the palm groves to the east, just across the Euphrates River and around the only bridge across for miles. It was there that our fun began.

At Red Platoon's OP on the south side of the bridge, we pulled a few of our vehicles right up to the river, facing directly into the city. A few hours after we set in, we got mortared. Hit is, after all, the Mortar Capital of Iraq. The Mouj go there to get trained, and the teams are supposed to be pretty good. Luckily, the first two 120mm rockets landed about 100m away. I was on watch in the turret, and in defiance of the 8,000 people that constantly tell me to keep my head down, I stayed standing because it was my job to find where these guys were shooting at us from before they could do it again. I saw some people on a rooftop but I couldn't tell if they were the ones or not. About 20 minutes later, Ahmad saw someone poke his head around a wall and shot an RPG right at me. It fell about 10m short of the vehicle and exploded in the water, but by then our Iraqis had already opened fire and the rest of us knew where to shoot. We got into a pretty big firefight, but you really just can't compete with the 25's.

That night, through the TOW's thermals, Voelker spotted six guys low crawling through the bushes and weeds on the other side of the river, with AK's and mortar tubes. We watched them set up for almost five hours before we opened up on them, and Voelker shot a guided missile under the power lines and across the water that hit right on target. We spent about $15,000 in less than two minutes.

The second morning we again got into a firefight across the river, but after that, things slowed down. The Freedom Guard - Red Platoon got the four guys: Hosham, Ahmad, Shamal, and Kazim. Hosham is the team leader and the only one with a long military history. He is 27 and was a captain in Saddam's army, an anti-air gunner who shot down three Turkish spy planes. He's got a scar on his left arm and leg from shrapnel from a Kurdish gas missile. Ahmad is 21 and he's always off the wall hyped up. He's one of the funniest guys I have ever met in my life. Shamal is I think 22 and Kazim is 19 – I'm actually older than him. They are the quieter ones, but they're both pretty nice.

Ahmad is the only one who speaks a little bit of English. But even then he would say things like "You in go home and food me" which is supposed to mean "Can you get me an MRE?" (I had to translate the menus for them). It took me about an hour one day while we were interrogating a guy by a house where we found some 25mm anti-air rounds to figure out that "You in maybe" means "He doesn't know". Fortunately, I knew a bit more Arabic than he did English, so I could talk with all four of them and they could talk with us. That's why the team was attached to Red Platoon, and later it turned into them being attached to me. The CO and XO had the five of us running all kinds of crazy missions, and there were times it was only the five of us in patrols. Together, Ahmad and I were one pretty fluent translator, and since I'd done intelligence work already in Fallujah, Ramadi and Seqlawia, I knew what kinds of things we needed and wanted to know. We left Sgt Paul and Chad in Ramadi, so my team and I became the company's only HIET asset. It was pretty cool.

The Iraq Freedom Guard is screened and trained by United States Marines. They go through extensive training that puts them on a level with the Iraqi Special Forces, way above the standards sometimes set by the IP and the ING. The reputation of these four preceded them. You have to be sure you can trust your guys, though, in a deeper way than you might trust a close friend. And there's something about surviving a firefight next to a guy that can create that trust immediately. We were chasing down some guys one night and it was just me in charge of the four Iraqis clearing houses in the city by ourselves; Sgt Collins had the rest of the team down the street. I have to know that these guys are capable of doing their job so we can cover each others' backs while I focus on my job, and more importantly, I have to know that they're really on my side, right? But competence and loyalty were never questioned with these guys, especially Hosham and Ahmad – there was something about them and me that just clicked together. And if someone dares question my judgment on that one I am obviously a stranger to you, and I would like you to take that up with me next time I see you face to face.

After a 15 day field op we left Hit, dropped off the Freedom Guard at the FOB outside the city, and headed back to Al Asad. Hosham told me to look for them in a week or so, as they were eventually heading that way as well. Actually two days later, I ran into them in the chow hall, and we were all clean and shaven with haircuts and clean uniforms. They were staying at Camp Ripper as well so their tents were pretty close to ours. It was good to see them, and I went over there and talked with them for a while and met some of their other friends. The next morning, though, Comanche set out on our last road march back to the dreaded base of KV. And here I am now (uh oh OPSEC), until turnover is complete with 2nd Lar. From here the company flies back via Chinooks to Al Asad, and then another C130 to Kuwait. In less than 20 days Comanche should be back on base in the United States of America.

It's amazing how close you can grow to a person in just 15 days. It's even more amazing when you don't speak the same language, and half the time you don't know what each other is saying. I actually miss these guys, and with two of them I know whatever paths our lives take, I will see them again someday.

But that's why I say I wonder if it's really worth it. You meet people, make new friends, grow close, and split your separate ways. Everywhere I go I meet new family, but then we split and it's all good byes and faded memories again. The more people you meet, the more people you know you'll never see and only miss. Is there a point?

That's it for now. Until next time

– Jarod

I wrote to Jarod at least twice after this, but I never heard from him again. The pictures I have in my book of him and his Iraqi friends are amazing, and Jarod if you ever read this, and remember me, you are always welcome to come to visit us on Orcas Island.

Around the same time I first heard from Jarod, I found on a website an address for some soldiers that said they weren't getting any mail. That's the one thing I just can't tolerate, so I wrote, and sent some goodies. Here's the response I got:

22 January 2005
Hello

My name is Sgt Alberto 36 years old from Puerto Rico. I'm here at Camp Victory, Baghdad, Iraq with the 165th ASG unit, a Garrison Command. I'm a cook, but here I work with the force protection, giving security and guard to the base. I'm proud of you for your letter and your support. Keep that up, we need you. We are a Reserve Unit. In Puerto Rico I work with the Puerto Rico Police Dept. I work scenes crimes.

Thank you, I see you.
–Alberto

17 February 2005
Hello Mrs. Karey–

I am Sfc Israel from Puerto Rico. I'm working with Sgt Alberto, Mrs. Thank you for support our troops. Thanks you also for give to us moral support that we need. Puerto Rico is a beautiful place, if you look in your computer www.topuertorico.com and www.gotopuertorico.com

This time Baghdad is cold, but the weather still change soon. We are proud having people like you that think we are important. Probably we finish this mobilization on December. Well, is time to go away.

See you,
Sfc Israel

I continued to support Sgt Alberto and Sfc Israel until October this year, when they said their tour was finished. They sent me a wonderful picture of them with one of Saddam's palaces in the background. Shortly after I had adopted Sgt Alberto and Sfc Israel, I came across yet another request from Marines on a web site. This Sgt Tyler was stationed at Abu Grhaib (sp?) with 3 other Marines, and they had very little access to goods. They were attached to an Army unit, and sort of at the end of the supply line, so they needed some TLC. That was enough for me, so I adopted Sfc Tyler and his Marines. The initial request was for reading material, but me being a mom; I could hardly let it stop there. Sgt Tyler became on of my most favorite Marines, because he always wrote back to me. I think his first letter touched me the most, so here it is.

Early April 2005
Ma'am

Thank you so much for your prayers. I sit here writing this letter to you today because of them. 2 hours ago we were attacked and I had metal fly by my head not six inches away. I know that it is because of your prayers that I am alive today. Sorry for being too graphic, but I am overwhelmed that I am still alive. I am here with 3 other Marines attached to the 306th MP BN, which is an Army unit. We "interview" prisoners and such.

As soon as I get the chance, I will email a picture of us to show you who you supported. We are really enjoying the stuff you sent. The letter stuff is perfect for writing because we are getting so much support and needed them.

Thank you so much from the bottom of our hearts.
Sgt Tyler

And from one of his Marines . . .

Early April 2005
Dear Mrs. Keel-Stidham

I am Sgt Tyler's newly appointed Cpl and I just wanted to thank you for your package (the magazines were great). I saw your address after Sgt Tyler had written you and I, too am from Washington State. I grew up in Bellevue and my folks live in Sammamish (just between Redmond and Issaquah). I miss home with its green trees and fresh water. Iraq is an ugly place, it makes it all the more magnificent that God made the Garden of Eden here. Anyway thanks again so very much for your care and support. It's people like you that make our job worthwhile.

Semper Fi, Cpl Paul

I received at least 3 more letters and several emails from Sgt Tyler, who always was so grateful for the little bit of stuff I sent. He emailed me some pictures, and the best part of this story is the end. Before Sgt Tyler and his Marines were to come home, they emailed their friends to see if anyone knew about going to Alaska. That's where they wanted to go for a fishing trip when they got home from their tour in Iraq. As Sgt Tyler put it "We are in about the hottest place, so we'd like to go someplace cool." Well I didn't know a thing about Alaska, but my son's former girlfriend's dad, he himself a former Marine, lived in Anchorage, so I got in touch with Megan. Megan in turn emailed her dad and he set the whole thing up for these Marines. It was incredible to be able to help them with their vacation, and Steven Boyle deserves a lot of credit for taking care of these Marines.

Semper Fi, Steve. I didn't get to meet Sgt Tyler or his Marines, but Steve did, and they both sent me pictures of them fishing. I hope Sgt Tyler will visit us on Orcas one day.

This is the email Sgt Tyler sent to those of us who supported him as his tour was winding down.

17 June 2005
Dear Friends

It has been 4 months since I arrived into country and began my first deployment in Iraq. Over the past 4 months I have encountered things

I never thought I would, and experienced feelings I didn't think I had. With all of this happening, there have been many people who have stood by my side, and whom I am very proud and thankful for. Everyone receiving this email falls into this category.

Speaking on behalf of my unit, it is hard to find the words to express our feelings of gratitude and thankfulness we have for each and every one of you. Through your support we have been able to set up a library in the middle of the desert over half-way around the world. We have everything including Western, Romance, Language books, Thrillers, Song Books, Comedy, Bibles and so much more. I have enclosed a picture of the library for your memories and to show you what you have accomplished. It may not look like much, but we have run out of room to put the books, and they are stacked three and sometimes four deep. There are over 130 books in this picture and we are waiting to get a bookshelf that will hold and display them properly.

When we first arrived here there was a lot of talk about how this war might turn into another Vietnam, and how eventually the people in the States would get "bored" with the war and forget about us. What I soon discovered was precisely the opposite. This War (and it is a war) has taken on a shape of its own. There are those in the states who disagree with this war and those who accept it. The odd thing is, both sides have come together to support the men and woman of their country. With every letter, package and email of encouraging words, we have come to the realization that America is proud of her sons and daughters, and will stand behind them through anything.

There are over 60 names on my mail TO: line and those are only the people whom I have email addresses for. In a little over four months, my command has been bombarded with packages. Here is a small list of some of those items: candy, cooling head bands, SO . . . MUCH . . . FOOD, squirt guns, a kiddy spa (which came in handy by the way), coffee pots, gourmet coffees and creamers, jerky, magazines, uniform items. Socks, pens, headphones, envelopes, hygiene items, oh and don't forget, BOOKS, BOOKS, And MORE BOOKS!!!!! As you can see, we have much to be thankful for, and that is not including the words of encouragement and numerous letters we have received from people.

This letter is coming from someone who has truly been humbled by your actions. Instead of talking to my wife about home, I find myself in a one-way conversation describing how people all over the United States are showing their unselfish support for my unit. I can only hope that someday I will be able to touch someone's life as much as you have been able to touch all of ours.

Like I said, I don't know how to say thank you for the items, words, thoughts and prayers you have so freely given, I guess the only thing I can say is . . .

Thank you
Sgt Tyler
USMC

Sgt Tyler you certainly touched my life, I'm forever grateful for your service and your letters.

Early in 2005, a marine, 1st Lt Ilario Pantano, was being charged with 2 counts of murder for defending himself in a war. I rallied behind him and his organization that he and his mother started. Defend the Defenders.org. I made a small donation, and Lt Pantano was later acquitted. He emailed me a couple of times to thank me for my support, and the last time he did, he gave me the name of one of his buddies, who had recently deployed to Iraq. I promptly wrote to his friend Lt Frank, and adopted him. I'm still currently supporting Lt Frank, and he's never failed to write to me, or answer my emails. Here are a few letters from 1st Lt Frank. Incidentally, he is writing a book himself about his experiences in Iraq and with his Marines. I'm looking forward to it!!!

27 May 2005

Thank you so much for the care package!! That was such a wonderful surprise! My Marines were so happy to get the snacks. They love it. We

are a Motor Transport/Convoy Security Platoon. We are part of MHG –
Marine Expeditionary Forces Headquarters Group. It's a mouthful, so we
use the abbreviation MHG for short. Most of our days are spent escorting convoys on the roadways of Iraq. We travel all over the country, but
are based out of Fallujah. As you can imagine, my Marines are exposed
to some serious dangers, but when they return to base and see the care
packages and kind words that you send they are re-charged and moti-
vated by the generous and selfless support. We all send our gratitude.
People like you, Karey, make us proud to serve and we all do it happily.
It is an honor to protect our nation and help the people of Iraq. Marine
Moms is a wonderful organization and I applaud your efforts and support to the troops. You'll never know just how much it means to us. Tell
your son Tim, I said Semper Fidelis and Thanks for serving.
God Bless and Semper Fi

Lt Frank and Marines of IMHG

26 June 2005

Thank you so much for the care package! As always, we really appreciate your
generous support. I read your letter to my platoon. We all enjoyed the beautiful
pictures of your view. What I would give to be there enjoying the green grass
and majestic views of the water! I can't wait to get back to the good ol' USA.

You live in a beautiful part of the country. I checked the map to see where
exactly Orcas Island is. I am planning a Pacific coast trip with my wife when
I return. My Marines and I will be deployed to Iraq for a year. We have been
here for 5 months already, so we are almost half way done. It is a long time
to be away from loved ones, but these Marines do it proudly and honorably.
I am happy to serve with them. Being a Marine Mom, you know the caliber
of person that makes the sacrifice. Thank your family from me.

Thanks Again.
SEMPER FI
Lt Frank and the Marines of IMHG Motor T

9 August 2005
Karey,

Thanks for the letter and pictures. I was shocked to hear that someone had the audacity to spit on your truck and give you the finger?
Especially when there is an Eagle, Globe and Anchor proudly displayed.
The next time that you run across that pitiful person please inform him
that there is a platoon of pissed off Marines in Iraq that highly disapprove of his actions and will be happy to "fix" him. Remind him that
"Marines" – No better friend, No worse enemy" – Gen Mattis, USMC.

Glad to hear that you and your husband are able to fully enjoy the
beautiful outdoors that surrounds your property. That really is a blessing. I took a "mental hike" after looking at the pictures that you sent.

Please don't worry about sending food. We have plenty. The DFACs
(chow halls) are fully stocked and serve plenty of good food to your
Marines. It is all you can eat once you get inside. There are not starving
Marines here, in fact, it's just the opposite really. Some units that are
always forward or "outside the wire" have to eat MREs on occasion as
the mission dictates, but rest assured they also have the opportunity to
eat in the chow halls after the missions.

I hope that your son is doing well. Where is he headed off to? If he
comes here, I will look out for him and make sure he is taken care of.
Thank you so much for all that you do. We always appreciate everything. I hope that you will focus your efforts on your son now (don't
worry about us).

Thanks Again
SemperFi,
Lt Frank

*Lt Frank has become very dear to me. He's never neglected to write back,
and I think I have more correspondence from him than any other of my
"adoptees". I truly hope that Lt Frank will take his Pacific Coast road trip
and come see us.*

. . . Every single letter I've received is special, but sometimes there's just a little more to a letter that touches you in a special way, and this next letter certainly does that, it is from my first female Marine, Sgt Cristina. I was given the email address for someone in the woman Marines Association, and she had a few names of deployed women Marines, two of which came to me. I wrote and sent packages to the other woman Marine as well, but I never heard from her. Sgt Cristina, however, sends me lots of emails. It is this first one though, that is so special. I have since learned that Sgt Cristina is a very special person, and I hope, as with all my "adoptees," we can meet in person someday.

17 July 2005
Good Morning Ma'am,

First off I want to start by thanking you and your family for the kind gesture of adopting me. It is very exciting. Well, second of all I want to describe myself a little. I am 23 years old. I have been a Sergeant for almost a year now. I did not know it would have brought on so many responsibilities but it did and I love it. I am in charge of 12 Marines. They are all great, but of course like me not even close to perfect. We try our best to keep our spirits up since most really miss their families. It's all new; some of them are 18, 19 year-old boys, just left home, so it tends to be harder on them.

As for myself, this is my second time over here and you can say I am a veteran when it comes to Iraq. My poor mother is finally getting used to the idea that I am a Marine and I chose this life. My sister is in the Air Force and my brother is in the Army. My brother is also in Iraq, I don't know where exactly, he does very dangerous missions and all I can do for him is pray. My sister, the one in the Air Force is also going to be deployed but nothing like us, she has it easy in the Air Force which I thank God for. I couldn't see my younger sister here. It's too dangerous sometimes. My little brother who is 8 is very proud of us and I know for fact that he is my real true motivation to go on. Everyday he wakes up, gets ready for school and tell them (other kids and teachers) about his sisters and brother. I know there are more innocent younger brothers and sisters, and that is why I know we are here, so we can protect them.

I love serving my country, even though at first I wasn't too happy about America. I was originally born in Peru, South America and I am mixed Asian descent. But, America has given me so many opportunities to succeed. I can never regret it.

Well Ma'am, I have written plenty for now. As for your son, he is a very lucky man. Where exactly is he stationed? The Marine Corps is very small, and eventually we all know each other. We are after all the Few and the Proud.

Greetings to you and your family,
–Cristina

March 16, 2006

He's back in the USA! Sgt Tim got in to Cherry Point, NC yesterday morning, and called me at 8:15!! It was so awesome to talk to him without the satellite delay!!
I'm smiling!

Thank you all for keeping him in your thoughts and prayers!
–Karey

9

LETTERS TO AMERICA

Major Eric Rydbom
Deputy Division Engineer
4th Infantry Division
Iraq, 2003

M ajor Eric Rydbom
Deputy Division Engineer
4th Infantry Division

OPEN LETTER TO FIRST LUTHERAN CHURCH OF RICHMOND BEACH

It has been a while since I have written to my friends at First Lutheran

---

★ AUTHOR'S NOTE: This letter written by Major Eric Rydbom, U.S. Army, to his fellow parishioners at his church in Washington State became known world-wide when his friends, so touched and, in some cases, angered by his words, passed it on in what became a chain reaction. Its authenticity has often been called into question, but having contacted Major Rydbom (now LTC Rydbom) and not only receiving his approval to print it verbatim and in its original form, he also gave us two other letters to his church, which are reprinted here as well. They are a remarkable and honest account from the frontlines.

Church about what's really going on here in Iraq. The news you watch on TV is exaggerated, sensationalized and selective. Good news doesn't sell.

The stuff you don't hear about? Let's start with electrical power production in Iraq. The day after the war was declared over, there was nearly no power being generated in Iraq. 45 days later, in a partnership between the army, the Iraqi people and some private companies, there are now 3200 mega watts (Mw) of power being produced daily, 1/3 of the total national potential of 8000 Mw. Downed power lines (big stuff, 400 kilovolt (Kv) and 132 Kv) are being repaired and are about 70% complete.

Then there is water purification. In central Iraq between Baghdad and Mosul, home of the 4th Infantry Division, water treatment was spotty at best. The facilities existed, but the controls were never implemented. Simple chemicals like Chlorine for purification and Alum (Aluminum Sulfate) for sediment settling (The Tigris River is about as clear as the Mississippi River) were in short supply or not used at all and when chlorine was used, it was metered by the scientific method of guessing. So some people got pool water and some people got water with lots of little things moving in it. We are slowly but surely solving that. Contracts for repairs to facilities that are only 50% or less operational are being let, chemicals are being delivered, although we don't have the metering problem solved yet (It's only been 45 days).

How about oil and fuel? Well the war was all about oil wasn't it? You bet it was. It was all about oil for the Iraqi people because they have no other income, they produce nothing else. Oil is 95% of the Iraqi GNP. For this nation to survive, it MUST sell oil. The Refinery at Bayji is at 75% of capacity producing gasoline. The crude pipeline between Kirkuk (Oil Central) and Bayji will be repaired by tomorrow (2 June). LPG, what all Iraqi's use to cook and heat with, is at 103% of normal production and WE, the US ARMY, at least 4th ID, are insuring it is being distributed FAIRLY to ALL Iraqis.

You have to remember that 3 months ago, ALL these things were used as weapons against the population to keep them in line. If your town misbehaved, gasoline shipments stopped, LPG pipelines and trucks stopped, water was turned off, power was turned off.

Now, until exports start, every drop of gasoline produced goes to the Iraqi people, crude oil is being stored, the country is at 75% capacity now, they need to export or stop pumping soon, thank the UN for the delay. ALL LPG goes to the Iraqi people EVERYWHERE. Water is being purified as best they can, but at least it's running all the time to everyone.

Are we still getting shot at? Yep.

Are American Soldiers still dying? Yep, about 1 a day from the 4th ID, most in accidents, but dead is dead.

If we are doing all this for the Iraqis, why are they shooting at us?

The general population isn't. There are still bad guys, who won't let go of the old regime. They are Ba'ath party members (Read Nazi Party, but not as nice) who know nothing but the regime. They were thugs for the regime that caused many to disappear in the night and they have no other skills. At least the Nazis had jobs they could go back to after the war as plumbers, managers, engineers, etc … these people have no skills but terror. They are simply applying their skills … and we are applying ours. There is no Christian way to say they must be eliminated and we are doing so with all the efficiency we can muster. Our troops are shot at literally everyday by small arms and RPGs. We respond and 100% of the time, the Ba'ath party guys come out with the short end of the stick. The most amazing thing to me is that they don't realize that if they stopped shooting at us, we would focus on fixing things and leave. The more they shoot at us, the longer we will stay.

Lastly, realize that 90% of the damage you see on TV was caused by IRAQIS, NOT the war. Sure we took out a few bridges from military necessity, we took out a few power and phone lines to disrupt communications, sure we drilled a few palaces and government headquarters buildings with 2000 lb laser guided bombs (I work 100 yards from where two hit the Tikrit Palace), he had plenty to spare. But, ANY damage you see to schools, hospitals, power generation facilities, refineries, pipelines, was ALL caused either by the Iraqi Army in its death throes or the Iraqi civilians looting the places. Could the army have prevented it?

Nope. We can and do now, but 45 days ago the average soldier was lucky to know what town he was in much less be informed enough to know who owned what or have the power to stop 1,000 people from looting a building by himself.

The United States and Britain are doing a very noble thing here. We stuck our necks out on the world chopping block to free a people. I've already talked the weapons of mass destruction thing to death, bottom line, who cares, this country was one big conventional weapons ammo dump anyway. We have probably destroyed more weapons and ammo in the last 30 days than the US Army has ever fired in the last 30 years (Remember, this is a country the size of Texas), so drop the WMD argument as the reason we came here, if we find it GREAT, if we don't, SO WHAT? I'm living in a "guest palace" on a 500 acre palace compound with 20 palaces with like facilities built in half a dozen towns all over Iraq that were built for one man. Drive down the street and out into the countryside 5 miles away (I have) and see a family of 10 living in a mud hut herding two dozen sheep, then tell me why you think we are here.

Respectfully,

ERIC RYDBOM
MAJ, ENGINEER
Deputy Division Engineer
4th Infantry Division

OPEN LETTER TO FIRST LUTHERAN CHURCH OF RICHMOND BEACH
3 July 03

To all the wonderful people of First Lutheran Church from Iraq, Greetings.

This will be my last letter as my time here is quickly coming to a close. I would like to provide some final thoughts on my time in Iraq.

First, you need to understand that, in general, the Iraqi people are industrious, resourceful and eager for a new life. The news, again, has been bad, and this time, things have gotten a little worse. There has been more disorganized hostile activity against US forces AND Iraqi civilians. We are taking fewer casualties than before, even with the increased attacks. The Iraqi civilians, specifically businesses, are being threatened and even bombed or burned out, for dealing with coalition forces. These are the same people as before, Fedayeen and Ba'ath Party members who are now officially out of a job forever. They will not go away quietly, but with these methods, they will gain no new recruits and will not stay alive long either. We send out forces on raids to capture major Fedayeen and Ba'ath Party leaders everyday, mostly on information from Iraqis and we are more often than not, successful. Time is on our side.

There have also been attacks against Iraqi infrastructure by these terrorist forces as well, that again, does nothing but hurt the Iraqi people. Oil pipelines and electrical power transmission lines have been the main targets. What do we do about it? We hire Iraqi companies to go out and fix them and pay top dollar and help the Iraqi economy, that's what we do. Then we train Iraqi security forces to secure the pipelines and the power lines, paying more Iraqi people and creating jobs where there were none before. That's what we do too.

Are we making progress? Overall? Yes. There has been a little back-sliding. When the power lines go down, the power grid fluctuates wildly and the power plant shuts down. When the power plant shuts down, the oil refinery shuts down and when the oil refinery shuts down, the oil flow has to stop because there is only so much storage capacity and there is no LPG produced for people to cook with. So you see, it's all interconnected. So how can I say we are progressing? Easy. We are contracting to repair two key 400Kv Ultra-high voltage lines as I type this. It'll be 60 days until they are complete, but this will stabilize power for the entire country. We have companies going to the Bayji Thermal Power plant to repair the last 2 of 6 turbines adding 250 Mega-watts to the grid in the next 2 weeks. We have another company going to the Bayji Gas Turbine plant to repair 2 of its 4 turbines in the next two weeks adding ANOTHER 250 Mega-watts to the national power grid. I have personally signed two contracts with local Iraqi companies to repair and upgrade water treatment plants in 2 cities. The Al Dour water facility contract is $23,000 worth of pumps and chlorination equipment and the Baqubah water treatment facility is $99,795 worth of pumps, laboratory testing equipment, pipes, chlorination metering and injection equipment and upgrade of their distribution towers. The work at these two facilities will be complete within the next 30 days and provide CLEAN and TREATED drinking water to 100,000 people for the first time in their lives.

THAT'S HOW I CAN SAY WE ARE MAKING PROGRESS . . .

People have to remember, the 4th Infantry Division has been in central Iraq for a total of 96 days now, 3 months and 1 week. Patience is a virtue. 96 days to both secure an area the size of West Virginia, defeat remaining terrorist forces inside that area AND fix things destroyed in a war, looted by the local population to survive and keep an economy functioning at some level. Yes, patience is a virtue, and most news channels and many Americans need to be more virtuous.

What about the UN? We are all persons of faith, please don't waste it on the UN. I may elaborate in person when I get back.

Respectfully,

> ERIC RYDBOM
> MAJOR, ENGINEER
> Deputy Division Engineer
> 4th Infantry Division, Tikrit, Iraq

OPEN LETTER TO FIRST LUTHERAN CHURCH OF RICHMOND BEACH, WA

17 JULY 2003

Hello all. I anticipate this to be my last letter from Iraq.

I have stopped watching the news, even when it's available, because I now have so little respect for the journalists. They refuse to leave the relative safety of Baghdad, Mosul, Irbil or Kirkuk to go get the real stories. Additionally, the stories are always slanted to the bad side. Are soldiers being killed? Yes, a total of 220 since the war began. While that is tragic, especially for the families that have lost mothers and fathers, sons and daughters, husbands and wives, and while I would never make light of it, that many soldiers were killed every day in World War II (and more), that many soldiers were killed every week in Korea and Vietnam. Since when has war been deemed a fair and clean sport? It is the dirtiest of all games, and that's the rub, it's not a game, and the winner wins by not playing fair. We play fairer than most, we don't use women and children, we don't engage those who don't engage us or who don't have weapons. While there are late night curfews, people are very free to go about their daily business to make a living with no harassment by US forces. When we are engaged, we come down on them with overwhelming firepower like crushing an ant with a hammer. It is at that point, not a fair fight, but it's not supposed to be, is it?

I sit in or listen to the battle update brief with the Commanding General everyday, and I can assure you that the small pockets of Ba'ath Party loyalists, Fedayeen, and occasional Iranian troublemakers are getting the worst of it. This is NOT Vietnam. This is NOT a repeat of the Soviets in Afghanistan. There is NOT popular support among the population, therefore no recruiting base like the Afghans or the NVA and Viet Cong had. As we engage and kill Ba'ath party and Fedayeen, there is no one stepping up to take the place of those killed. Resistance will ultimately die due to lack of interest.

So what kind of progress is really being made?

Power: The national capacity as designed is about 10,000 Mega Watts (Mw). The system has NEVER produced more than 6,000 Mw due to poor design, construction, maintenance and management. Currently, the ARMY in conjunction with the IRAQIs (note how I left out the UN and all the big and blustering US and foreign mega-corporations like BECHTEL) have restored an average of 3,400 Mw per day, over 50% of what was being produced, in 90 days. The target is 4,000 Mw by the end of July. 400Kv Ultra-high voltage lines are being repaired (the ones looted by Iraqis who melt down the cables and sell them for scrap to make a living, talk about shooting yourself in the foot!) and substations are also being upgraded, hydroelectric dam turbines are being repaired or are scheduled for repair or upgrade. The plan is to get through the summer, then ramp power back down to 3,000 to 3,500 Mw to do upgrades and repairs, then add 1,200Mw of capacity each year for the next 5 years, actually bringing the REAL power production in Iraq up to 10,000 Mw. Are there power outages? Yes, MANAGED outages so EVERYBODY gets some power at regular intervals, like California. Why have you never heard this before, because it's boring, a bunch of facts and numbers, but it's the truth and you'll never hear it reported on the news . . . because it's boring. Soldiers dying, even a few, is NOT boring.

Water: Prior to the war and under UN sanctions, chemicals such as chlorine and alum were banned (potential precursor chemicals for chemical weapons). The problem with that is that they are exactly the chemicals used to purify drinking water in every water treatment plant in the world. The water treatment plants themselves had fallen into disrepair through total neglect and mismanagement by regime appointed managers that knew nothing about what they were managing, and, as I've said in the past, almost all the income of Iraq went to building Palaces and buying weapons and ammunition. That sounds incredible, but if you could see what I have seen traveling around the country, you would agree. Anyway, I digress. This month alone, we will have repaired two complete water treatment plants in Al Dour (AD Dwar on many maps) and Baqubah serving about 300,000 people. That includes pumps, filtration systems, chlorine metering and injection systems and even laboratory equipment for testing water samples. A third plant will start within two weeks and will serve another 50,000 people with clean, even by US standards, water. Why have you never heard this before, because it's boring, a bunch of facts and numbers, but it's the truth and you'll never hear it reported on the news . . . because it's boooorrrrring. Soldiers dying, even a few, is NOT boooorrrrrring (you may have heard this last sentence before J).

Sewage Treatment is another issue. Most of Iraq is on septic systems because the composition of the soil in many areas does not lend itself to running miles of sewer pipes, they break continually due to the shifting soils and rock. In the areas that DO have sewage treatment plants, the plants are generally inoperable. Pre-war, an average of about (I'll write it out because it's so huge) 500 million cubic meters (picture 500 million 3-foot by 3-foot boxes) of raw sewage to include medical waste was dumped directly into the Tigris River annually. That, by the way, is the same river that the inoperable water treatment plants get the drinking water from that's distributed to the population, which is why we have focused on FIXING the water treatment plants. So what are we doing about sewage treatment, outside of Baghdad which has a working sewage treatment system? We are fixing what exists, the city of Tikrit will be the first within the next 30-45 days, and we are soliciting designs and bids from contractors to build plants where they don't exist now. This will take TIME. Ask yourself when was the last time you saw a project in the United States like building a sewage treatment plant take 90 days or less??? Why should it be any different here? Why have you never heard this before, because it's boring, a bunch of facts and numbers, but it's the truth and you'll never hear it reported on the news ... because it's boooorrrrrring. Soldiers dying, even a few, is NOT booooorrrrrring (Wow, it's like an echo J).

We are buying so much stuff for schools and hospitals everywhere that it's mind boggling. Books, chalk boards, desks, medical supplies of all types, medical equipment of all types, operating tables, exam tables, MRI machines, the list is endless. We are paving roads, or, more precisely, we are hiring Iraqi contractors to pave roads, thereby injecting money into the Iraqi economy and putting Iraqis to work. Is there a lot of unemployment? OF COURSE! Half the population used to work for the regime! The army was 3 million soldiers, they are a little short of work right now and thankfully so! But guess what? We will begin establishing the New Iraqi Army, downsized and better trained, within the next few days and they'll have three divisions within the next year. Who do you think is going to be in the new Iraqi Army? THE OLD IRAQI ARMY! Except they'll be on our side now. Why have you never heard this before, because it's boring, a bunch of facts and numbers, but it's the truth and you'll never hear it reported on the news ... because it's boooorrrrrring. Soldiers dying, even a few, is NOT booooorrrrrring (Handy little line, isn't it J). Plus, most journalists are not thinking beings in a common sense sort of way anyway. I can't think of one journalist today of the stature of Edward Morrow, Walter Cronkite, David Brinkley, Chet Huntley, who when they spoke, it was the words of truth, where personal integrity was more important than selling the story and when you saw them on TV, you instantly knew they were men of honor and integrity. They reported facts, not sensation. They kept their opinions to themselves because they looked at their audience as thinking beings capable of forming their own opinions from the facts.

Who the hell am I to spew all this out. Well, nobody really. Some of this is obvious fact from experience and direct involvement (I find and hire contractors and see the work is completed and QC'ed). Some, is obviously, just the opinion of one Major with 21 years in the Army speaking for himself, not the Army. Several things I can say for sure though. 1: we are doing good things here with the best of intentions and it is generally appreciated. 2: America has the finest Army in the world, capable of waging a major combat operation, establishing security and continuing to eliminate bad guys while beginning to rebuild a nation . . . IN 100 DAYS. While not asked for, a little appreciation is due.

My friends at First Lutheran, I hope that all the soldiers here are remembered in your prayers, and the Iraqi people as well. They are the most industrious and innovative people I have ever seen. For 25 years, they have kept things running by bubble gum and bailing wire. Now we are giving them a lot of new stuff at a lot of cost to each one of you in dollars and a much greater cost to some, in blood. Failure is not an option, as you can see, we are not failing, despite what many may say.

On a side note, please be prepared when I finally get home, the last molecule of political correctness left my body several days ago. See you soon.

Respectfully,

ERIC RYDBOM
MAJ, EN
Deputy Division Engineer (for a little while longer)
4th Infantry Division

BOOK THREE

*Logistics, Transformation
and the Art of War*

10

THE VIEW FROM HERE — PART TWO

Vice Admiral J. D. (Dan) McCarthy SC, USN
Director, Material Readiness and
Logistics (OPNAV N4)
with Capt. Kurt Kunkel, SC, USN

H ello Stuart:

When you asked for my thoughts on OIF and what the view was from my berth as the Director of Material Readiness and Logistics, I thought of what I would say to our future procurement personnel on that very question. It sums up the logistical efforts required to bring our Naval Power to the battle and to sustain them there. I hope that it shows the value and logic of supporting and maintaining a strong, well-equipped, well trained Navy during peacetime, as well as during periods of conflict.

Dan

U.S. Naval Forces remain arrayed around the globe in support of National Strategic Policy objectives just as they have been throughout much of the past 60 years, and certainly since the end of World War II. Naval Forces provide both a powerful deterrent role through their forward presence, as well as the nation's quick response capability to National Command Authority decisions. These same Naval Forces require minimal host nation support and can be sustained at sea almost indefinitely.

The capabilities resident in these naval forces are sustained through a dedicated team of logistics professionals. Their work is not accomplished by accident or through some magic formula. It is achievable because our military dedicates a significant amount of time, money and personnel resources to ensuring they can do just that. We plan, procure and train to support our Naval Forces at sea and increasingly, ashore. This sustainment is executed during wartime just as it is practiced during peacetime using focused and experienced leadership at all levels of the supply chain and chain of command.

The carrier strike group or expeditionary strike group training off of the Virginia Capes (VACAPES) or Southern California (SOCAL) operating areas is sustained in virtually the same way as that provided to our forces in the more hostile environment of the Middle East. Replenishment of fuel, ordnance, food, mail, personnel, and repair parts can happen at sea either from ships alongside or via aircraft and helicopters. In concert with the Defense Logistics Agency (DLA), key Classes of Supply have been pre-positioned to enable more timely replenishment of these Forces in potential hot spots. Friendly ports, when available, offer opportunities for replenishment and more extensive maintenance actions than can be done at sea. It is through these foreign ports, military airfields and in conjunction with forward-assigned US military personnel resident in our diplomatic missions around the world, that our logistics sustainment, training and exercises are enhanced.

Behind all of this sustainment and this thing called "logistics" is a cadre of professionals who work tirelessly to bring all of the pieces together in support of our Navy and Marine Corps operating forces. These professional logisticians come from all walks of life. Many wear the uniform and serve in various afloat, policy, planning and fleet support positions throughout their careers. They move from logistic job to logistic job in between training opportunities and professional education.

U.S. Civil Service personnel are a key component of our logistics team. In addition to their critical skills sets, they provide long-term continuity to shore-based organizations and units.

U.S. contractors, many of whom have prior active or reserve duty experience, are also part of the "workforce" that sustains our Navy and Marine Corps team. With so much emphasis being placed on the use of advanced technology and deploying systems ahead of traditional organic logistic support, contractor expertise has been and will continue to be an integral aspect to seamless logistics sustainment of our operational Forces.

Another group of logistics professionals who provide a key component in our support structure is foreign government employees and local foreign contractors. Our Fleet and Fleet Marine Force are supported around the globe by a vast network of husbanding agents and supporting personnel. These men and women tap in to local supply sources and, utilizing their invaluable local knowledge, obtain all manner of items required to support our forward deployed forces.

This group of Sailors, Marines, civil servants, contractors and foreign nationals has made logistics in a difficult environment appear easy. This may be the untold story of Naval Logistics in Operations Enduring Freedom and Iraqi Freedom – logistical challenges met at all levels by a variety of personnel from diverse backgrounds and nations who have pulled together to achieve a common goal of sustained superior support of afloat and ashore operational forces. Around the globe, 24 hours a day, 7 days a week, these are the people who sustain our forces.

When our forces operate in the traditional areas of responsibility these people maintain the logistic pipeline supporting operations. When something like Operations Desert Storm, Enduring Freedom and Iraqi Freedom occurs, these same logistics professionals step forward to make things happen, allowing operational commanders to focus on bringing the flexible combat power of our forces to bear on our enemies. It is difficult if not impossible to recognize all of the individuals whose sacrifices contributed to the success of Operations Enduring Freedom and Iraqi Freedom. As is often human nature, individuals will accept the challenge, making the difficult seem effortless, all the while toiling out of the limelight to ensure that products and services are provided in a timely manner, whenever and wherever needed. The vast majority of the recipients of this support, our frontline war fighters, will rarely know of this daily activity.

Such was the case of a retired Air Force Master Sergeant, working for the Navy in the Civil Service. This career logistics professional, supported by dedicated professionals from the worldwide air cargo specialists at DHL, solved the problem of the volume of high priority material flowing into the CENTCOM AOR through Bahrain. DHL reorganized their facility to pre-sort inbound material and passed it through the Navy Air Terminal on it's way to the final end-user. Sailors and Marines both afloat and ashore had no visibility of this, only seeing the end result—priority material requirements showing up in a timely manner in support of combat operations.

Naval Reservists made significant contributions across the entire spectrum of operations. The Naval Expeditionary Logistics Support Force (NAVELSF), headquartered at Williamsburg, Virginia, provided manpower to augment the Bahrain Airhead, and continues to provide Navy Cargo Handling Battalion support to the critical surface lift port of Ash Shuaybah, Kuwait. It is through Ash Shuaybah that a majority of the equipment required by the land forces passes. NAVELSF personnel also continue to provide fuel support to U.S. and Coalition Forces ashore and are serving as U.S. Customs Inspectors for material flowing back to the United States.

Innovation and visionary solutions cut across all pay grades and skill sets. In Bahrain, during the high point of operations in Iraq, it was a Navy Reserve Second Class Petty Officer, assigned to NAVELSF, who decided that the way to process and distribute the overwhelming flow of mail to FIFTH Fleet units was to establish a parallel processing center in the Bahrain International Airport parking lot. Manpower and machinery were then more efficiently utilized to keep the mail moving and to prevent system failure due to massed volume. Other than a very small group of people involved specifically with that operation, most will never know what steps were taken to ensure the uninterrupted flow of parts and personal mail; they only knew that their mail made it to them when and where they needed it.

Besides the stress of the job, the stifling heat, the ever-increasing support requirements and shorter deadlines these logistics professionals also had to cope with the age-old problem of leaving loved ones behind. Babies were born, parents passed away, marriages were stressed, but the mission always got done. Regardless of the conflict, ours is a history of the profession of arms having had to balance this additional stress to the tasks at hand, and although an ageless problem, it is of little comfort to the Sailor or Marine who knows that life back home has continued on without him or her. Somehow, whenever times have gotten tough, our people have reached inside and found the fortitude to persevere, working through personal and professional adversity in order to accomplish the mission.

As modern warfare evolves and the logistical requirements and specialties required to support the next generation of warfare become known, it is our people who we must count on to keep the Fleet and Fleet Marine Force, and our Joint and Coalition partners, ready for action at any time and any place. It is the logistics professional, practicing his or her art with equally well-applied technological enhancements, who will continue to keep our Forces sustained, ready and responsive.

11

TRANSFORMATION — PART ONE

RADM Robert Conway Jr
Commanding Officer ESG-1, USN
Operation Iraqi Freedom/
Operation Enduring Freedom

D ear Dad,

If it is true that the peaks and valleys of human experience are a good measurement of one's life, then my life's account must surely include Commanding the first Expeditionary Strike Group (ESG-

---

★ AUTHOR'S NOTE During this early part of the twenty-first century, the American military is undergoing a sea change. This transformation is preparing us for how we will fight wars in the coming decades. This chapter is from RADM Robert "Bob" Conway, Jr. to his father, Captain (Ret.) Robert T. Conway, Sr., and, as well as recording a piece of US Naval history, it illustrates quite well the process of transformation during wartime. Expeditionary Strike Groups are intended to extend the reach and the striking power of Navy assets onshore as well as at sea. ESG 1 was the prototype of this new force, and it is, at the time of this writing, still a work-in-progress. RADM Conway was the plank owner (original crew-member) Commander of ESG-1.

1) during Operation Iraqi Freedom and Operation Enduring Freedom. Why? Because it was during that time I encountered some of the highest moments of my entire Naval career.

As you know from your experiences during World War II and Korea, letters by their very nature are portholes into history, so in this letter I want to share with you some of my own personal thoughts about Expeditionary Strike Group One (ESG-1), and I want to respond to your question about where in Naval history ESG-1 fits. Honestly, I'd have to say ESG-1's place in history is still being defined and needs to mature more before I can answer that, but to give you a more comprehensive response, I've included with this letter an excerpt of a draft that I crafted, along with copies of three letters I received from others who were there with me. In CDR Carol Hottenrott's letter for example, she asks a very telling question: "What else could be expected from a maritime force, inclusive of the traditional amphibious forces, coupled with naval combatants, with a flag (or general officer) in charge, tasked with experimentation and innovation?" In Captain Randy Morgan's letter, he cites that ESG-1's primary task was to improve "the Navy's role in response to the Global War on Terror – make us more relevant." And finally, in CMDCM Ron Downs' letter, he provides the Enlisted perspective of ESG-1's contribution to Naval history. Each of these letters is filled with germane information that I am sure you will find of interest.

Concerning my firsthand experience with ESG-1, as you well know, Dad, command is a line officer's ultimate goal, so learning that I was about to become the plank owner Commander of ESG-1 put a smile on my face that remains to this day. I was to take command of ESG-1 and tackle a daunting challenge: how to bridge the Sea/Land interface as it applies to the war on terrorism. Those were some exhilarating and challenging days as we prepared to get underway.

I don't think you would have seen this before so what follows is an excerpt from ESG-1 material I previously wrote:

ESG-1 was the product of a new approach to our Navy's war fighting. Before ESG-1, the United States Navy had traditionally fought wars from a blue-water setting. The enemy was almost always a clearly recognizable and organized group positioned within a general area of engagement. War-fighting capabilities, while not always equal in firepower, were somewhat similar in form and purpose. More often than not, civilians, especially women and children, were not deliberately targeted.

However, all of that changed on 9/11 when America and her allies went to war against terrorists who have the ability of blending into their environment to the point of being almost transparent. These terrorists use unconventional weapons that can be made in their homes, and clearly, they do not adhere to George Patton's theory that nobody ever won a war by dying for his [or her] country. Also, these terrorists give us miniscule windows of opportunity that might not open again for months or even years, if ever; therefore, speed and agility have become critical factors to executing our new strategies. What am I talking about?

Allow me to expand on the above thoughts.

War-fighting capability is "the main thing" for Navy alignment, and expanding war-fighting capabilities across the spectrum of conflict is the Strike Group purpose. Essentially, ESGs give the Navy the capability of rapidly delivering Sailors and Marines to the littoral battlefronts anywhere in the world, thereby bringing the Navy into 21st century war-fighting and keeping the Navy relevant.

So what is the difference between an ESG and a Carrier Strike Group (CSG)? The ESG can place significant Marine Corps forces ashore far quicker and provides the Navy and Marine Corps team with additional offensive capabilities and increased agility. ESGs can respond rapidly to last-minute changes and get boots on the ground to meet a plethora of challenges.

For those who were paying attention, there was a realization long before September 11, 2001, that this war is being fought along coastlines and inland, more so than in deep water. As a sidebar, 80% of the world's population lives within 60 kilometers of the coastline. Clearly, the Global War on Terrorism (GWOT) has expanded the Navy's area of responsibility (AOR), and in response to that, we had to change. Leading change isn't easy, especially when it crosses cultures (Navy and Marine).

There were those individuals who dismissed ESG-1 as an anomaly that would go away, even when rigorous data showed that the Navy absolutely had to include littoral areas and land-based installations in its AOR. If the Navy was going to be relevant in the Global War on Terrorism, it simply had to find a new way to bring a highly mobile and self-sustaining force capabilities across the entire spectrum of operations.

ESGs provide those capabilities in spades. Specifically, ESG-1 brought multiple capabilities in comparison to the traditional Amphibious Ready Group (ARG), including a precision strike capability Tomahawk Land Attack Missile (TLAM), Intelligence, Survey and Reconnaissance (ISR), Air-Defense and surface-to-surface defense for the amphibious ships, Anti-Submarine Warfare (ASW) capability, non-compliant boarding, CHEM/BIO capabilities to evaluate cargo discovered on smuggling vessels, and most importantly, a command and control capability from the Joint Operations Center on PELELIU. This afforded the Group a capability to operate in distributed operations throughout the Horn of Africa (HOA), the Red Sea, the Arabian Gulf, and the Indian Ocean.

When the initial anticipated friction subsided, ESG-1 became a reality. Let there be no doubt about it; when ESG-1 conducted its pilot deployment in 2003, it met and exceeded the objectives in which it was allowed to engage. The bottom line is that ESG-1 provided the mobility, agility, and lethality desired. Perhaps the best piece of evidence in support of this bottom line is Vice Admiral Michael McCabe's statement: "No longer will I just ask about those carriers, but rather . . . Where is Expeditionary Strike Group ONE?" (Ref. D).

Currently there are five Expeditionary Strike Groups, with a concept that allows the Navy to field seven more, but it was ESG-1 that laid the groundwork as its seven ships and 5,000 Sailors and Marines deployed in support of operations in Iraq, the Arabian Gulf, the Red Sea, and the Horn of Africa.

Dad, never in my career have I been as proud as I was when commanding ESG-1. For six and a half months, the group consisting of USS

GREENEVILLE (SSN 772), USS PORT ROYAL (CG 73), USS PELELIU (LHA 5), USS OGDEN (LPD 5), USS DECATUR (DDG 73), USS JARRETT (FFG 33), USS GERMANTOWN (LPD 42), Amphibious Squadron Three, and 13th Marine Expeditionary Unit (MEU) conducted humanitarian assistance and security and stabilization missions.

During that time, there were three peak moments that stand out above the rest. The first was during November 2002, when ESG-1 was involved in two separate interception operations in the Persian Gulf, seizing a total of $21 million dollars worth of narcotics. The second was in January 2003, when ESG-1 served as command and control for Exercise Sea Saber, a coalition maritime interdiction training exercise, arguably the group's most complex coalition mission on deployment, and the last was on 1 February, 2003 when I pinned on my second star. You asked about lessons learned. My answer: it isn't so much what we learned from ESG-1 but rather what the Navy and Marine Corps team learned from ESG-1. The primary lesson learned is that the U.S. Navy's war-fighting style has changed, permanently. With ESGs, we are prepared to fight into the littorals where significant combat power can be delivered with speed and agility. I could drone on, but suffice to say, ESG-1 was only the beginning of the journey; therefore, the lessons learned will become more evident with time.

It was an honor of a lifetime commanding ESG-1, but the story is not about me. It was all about the outstanding Sailors and Marines who made it happen. For your interest I'm including several additional war letters that expand on that. The letters are from people who were a part of the ESG-1 Team and who were strategically and operationally involved during the training cycle and deployment. Each letter is, in essence, a historical record that I think you will enjoy reading.

Here are two closing thoughts, Dad. First, ESG-1 is an exceptional piece of Naval history that – to this day – stands as a first-rate model for complexity of change. And second, ESG-1's legacy can be described by quoting for you the words inscribed on an Arlington monument: "They have no place in history, for theirs is a date with destiny." As far as I'm concerned, that applies to ESG-1 and to the remarkable men and women who were a part of it.

Bob

Dad:

Captain Morgan is a former U.S. Navy Seal and his most recent assignment was as my Special Operations Warfare Commander for ESG-1. I asked him to give you his thoughts on our efforts and some background from his viewpoint.

On Oct 16, 2003, the Secretary of Defense sent a Global War on Terrorism memorandum to his combatant commanders. He asked, is DoD changing fast enough to deal with the new 21st century security environment? In amplification he stated that DoD has been organized, trained and equipped to fight big armies, navies and air forces. It is not possible to change DoD fast enough to successfully fight the global war on terror; an alternative might be to try to fashion a new institution, either within DoD or elsewhere – one that seamlessly focuses the capabilities of several departments and agencies on this key problem.

Now, why is that important?

Well, my first encounter with RADM Conway was a January 2003 briefing in North Island Naval Base to leadership of the West Coast Fleet Commands and the Type Commanders. RADM Conway was currently assigned to his job as Naval Region Hawaii, and was laying the groundwork for command of the First Expeditionary Strike Group (ESG). His orders from the Navy leadership for ESG 1 were a blank piece of paper, spoken orders were something in the line of," Improve the Navy's role in response to the Global War on Terror – make us more relevant." RADM Conway posed questions in January of 2003, which closely matched the strategic questions of Secretary Rumsfeld in October of 2003.

• The Navy owns the blue water; can we transform our deploying Amphibious, Maritime SOF, and Marine Corps combat power to apply pressure in the littorals?

• The Navy is challenged in the joint environment. How do we integrate the Joint Command and Control functions to optimize synchronized operations with established Joint Task Forces?

• How does the Navy transform to make an impact in the Global War on Terror?

• What Command and Control methodology is best for integrating amphibious sealift, Marine Corps and Special Operations combat capability, and USN Maritime dominance capabilities with its assigned submarines, Cruiser/Destroyer assets, and Maritime Patrol Aircraft?

From the start I knew those involved with the First Numbered Expeditionary Strike Group were in for wild ride - a journey that will be critical to transforming the U.S. Navy. That is why I was excited about being assigned as the Special Operations Warfare Commander. I also realized that I could contribute to the transformation efforts by establishing a Plans (N5) directorate for RADM Conway. So we started the journey which would challenge "rice bowls" of current assigned forces, force transformation, and generally make people "uncomfortable" by doing things that they have never been doctrinally tasked.

It was very evident that the Navy picked the right leader for this daunting task. In early 2003, he had to pick the right staff and shape it to meet the expected tasking. From our immediate boss, Commander Third Fleet, I knew we had a tough road ahead. In the process of transformation and developing new doctrine for the Global War on Terror – we would be expected to accomplish in training ALL THE TASKS that have been assigned a Carrier Strike Group and an Amphibious Readiness Group to be certified for deployment. Concurrently, we had to apply a "New brand of Expeditionary Warfare" and based on Chief of Naval Operations tasking discover how we could best impact the Global War on Terror.

Early on, RADM Conway realized shaping the ESG staff was critical in execution. In his subtle manner, here are some items that enforced team building, challenged our thinking, and increased communications. He stated:

"We are all about transformation – and you all are part of something important in Naval History." His office had a full library of books on transformation that quickly became required reading for all.

"We are one team – and we must all speak the same vision." His morning staff meetings included the whole staff, from the senior directorates to the Staff Sergeant and Radar operators assigned. This challenged many – but had its impact.

• "Engage at the senior Commanders level – and keep communications open." All subordinate commanders input mattered, and they were part of the ESG team.

• "Rely on the genius of our senior enlisted." We wrapped our arms around the senior enlisted – not only to communicate change, but also to resolve issues at the proper level of command.

• "Set high standards, and ask Why, Why, Why?"

So, the journey began – and the initial guidance at those early staff meeting served well throughout the training and deployment. Of utmost importance – those consistent themes and guidance stayed consistent and were driving business processes that took us through training, combat operations, to the Change of Command. As you can see, RADM Conway's leadership had a direct impact on the staff assigned and all component commanders that worked for him. The direct impact on the small staff assigned and to the senior leaders of the Marine Expeditionary Unit, Ship CO's, Amphibious Squadron, Naval Special Warfare Squadron, and other assigned Naval Expeditionary Units is small compared to the impact on the U. S. Navy's relevance to the Global War on Terror. One of RADM Conway's edicts was – "Do not use the word ARG (Amphibious Ready Group) any more" You see, part of the Global Strategy prior to ESG 1 was how we deployed our Carrier Strike Groups and Amphibious Ready Groups. As of April 2005, both the Chief of Naval Operations and Commandant of the Marine Corps talk to our Forward deployed presence and strategy in terms of how many Carrier Strike Groups and Expeditionary Strike Groups are required.

And how did we do this? I believe it all starts at the top. RADM Conway had to take the "heat" from his peers and communicate at the highest level - we were the executors. He developed consistent themes for operating that served well in not only preparing us for combat operations, but set standards for future Naval Operating Forces. These standards that apply to all deploying Navy forces were evident in his daily Staff guidance and updates. A few phrases that we all remember from deployment are:

- "PILE IT ON"
- "MOBILE, LETHAL AND AGILE RESPONSE"
- "WE WORK AT THE OPERATIONAL LEVEL OF WAR"
- "JOINT OPERATION COMMAND CENTER – THAT IS WHO WE ARE"
- "TAKE CARE OF YOUR PEOPLE, THEY WILL TAKE CARE OF YOU"

PILE IT ON. When tasked to develop new doctrine for Expeditionary operations and do all the things expected of Carrier Strike Groups and Amphibious forces, the "whine factor" increased. We were a small staff, and still had to execute the administrative, operational and other things staffs did. RADM Conway's guidance was "Let them Pile it on!" He knew we were doing the right thing, and had a relentless pursuit to execute Naval Expeditionary operation in the sea-land interface. This is where the action was. He led from the front and interfaced with senior British, Iraqi, and Coalition leaders in Southern Iraq to execute combat operations in that critical oil infrastructure support mission. Additionally, he synchronized the maritime campaign with ongoing ground and special operations. This sea-land interface and sharing of Command and Control have become the standard for Fifth Fleet operating in the Northern Persian Gulf. We still executed the mission in the sea-land interface, concurrently while assuming Command and Control of all the Carrier forces in the Northern Persian Gulf - a task historically assigned to the CSG Commander (oh by the way they were on a liberty port call in Dubai).

MOBILE, LETHAL AND AGILE RESPONSE. What does the ESG give

you? RADM Conway firmly believed the ESG brought a capability that no other previous Navy warfighting group brought. "Mobility, lethality and agility" became our trademark and were guiding principals in executing our mission. Some Navy leaders do not like to talk about it, but it was a consistent message by RADM Conway – we are about applying combat power to destroy the enemy's infrastructure and putting lead in their heads. How do you apply the right combat power, in the right place, at the right time against the right enemy? Again, RADM Conway provided commander's guidance that would make an impact to Navy doctrine and our impact on the Global War on Terror. Early in the training, we developed an Adaptive Planning Process that has been adopted by all deploying ESG forces. It is based on Sensing the Environment, Interpreting the Enemies' Intent, Deciding on the Proper Course of Action, and Acting with Mobility, Lethality and Agility. This Sense, Interpret, Decide, Act applies to all facets of warfighting and were adopted by component commanders. In fact, the sensing part became a critical step in developing new missions that even the Fifth Fleet Commander did not know were executable. While deployed in the Southern Persian Gulf, RADM Conway convinced the operational leadership that ESG forces could execute distributed operations that influenced the region; stretching from the Red Sea, to Kenya, to the Southern Persian Gulf and interdiction of Terror linked shipping off Pakistan and the Straits of Hormuz. Additionally, we continued to "Pile it on" and executed the Command and Control of a Department of State sponsored Counter Proliferation exercise involving 14 coalition partners.

WE WORK AT THE OPERATIONAL LEVEL OF WAR. Early in our training we were tasked to execute a scripted Schedule of Events. RADM Conway had the confidence in his subordinate commanders that they would execute the training schedule with success. He challenged the staff and commanders with "We work at the operational level of war" and based on the higher headquarters desired effects – what would really do? This risk taking at the Flag level became evident in our first encounter with the ComThirdFlt staff during our certification exercise.

To apply the firepower of the ESG in a complex problem, we distributed the forces from San Francisco to San Diego to execute the battle problem. Although our intentions and actions were communicated in required reports and reflected in the Common Operational Picture – no one really got word to the Senior Exercise director that ESG 1 force lay down was "different" from previous commanders. When they deployed from San Diego, fully expecting to see the ships of ESG 1 on the horizon – it was quite the surprise when COMTHIRDFLT requested – "ESG ONE – WHERE ARE YOU." Nevertheless, our response was the right one and we were praised for our efforts. Proving we could work at the Operational Level of War continued to be a challenge in both the Pacific and Central Command. RADM Conway's continued pursuit of excellence and pushing the envelope set the standard. We were certified for the first time as a Maritime Joint Task Force, and he continued to challenge the deployed Fleet Commander and our staff with Expeditionary solutions that met the Combatant Commander's Desired Effects. This effects based planning and working at the operational level of War are evident in the new CNO's (ADM Mullen) 2006 Guidance to the Navy.

JOINT OPERATION COMMAND CENTER – THAT IS WHO WE ARE. The forces assigned to Expeditionary Strike Group ONE are not joint by doctrine – but they are. They can control airspace and apply indirect/direct fires, they can occupy and control ground battle space, they are the pros on Maritime dominance, and with the assignment as Special Operations Warfare Commander as a component commander, they can execute the full realm of special operations. Additionally, RADM Conway realized the outstanding air and sealift capabilities in supporting the theater Combatant Command from a Sea Basing concept. A senior Navy Logistics Commander was hand picked for the staff and coordinated Army, Air Force and Commercial logistics efforts in conducting the myriad complex operations ESG 1 executed. The most evident application of this lesson learned was the capability the next ESG 1 deployed with and missions executed. They were assigned responsibility of all Joint logistics response to the latest earthquake in

Pakistan – and executed from a Sea Based platform. And how do you do this – RADM Conway stated from the beginning that we needed a JOINT OPERATIONS COMMAND CENTER. We built it, operated from it and during the deployment had senior Army, Air Force and Coalition Commanders integrated into the Command Structure. Again, this did not sit well with many of the senior Navy leadership which have continued to develop a Tactical Fleet Command Center (TFCC). This continues to be a doctrinal step that will challenge deploying Carrier Strike Group and Expeditionary Strike Group commanders of the future. To make an impact on the Global War on Terror, the deployed Navy response will have to work at the Operational Level of War and have an organic Joint Task Force capability. These are the primary lessons learned briefed by RADM Conway to the CNO and Commandant of the Marine Corps. It is true transformation – and will become more evident as we are challenged with distributed operations and our new Navy Expeditionary Command capability that we are fielding in 2007. For your information - the Joint Operations Center (JOC) survives – it is an integral part of two of the three ESGs that have deployed and I anticipate will be the future capability that the Navy will grow to.

TAKE CARE OF YOUR PEOPLE, THEY WILL TAKE CARE OF YOU. I think everyone assigned to the First Numbered Expeditionary Strike Group will attest that they have never worked harder in their careers. The hardest working person on the staff was RADM Conway himself – balancing the details of training and pushing the "new way of warfighting" against a resisting Navy and Marine Corp leadership. This leadership from the front and setting the standards were key indicators from RADM Conway that "people are our most important asset." He stated this in his commander's guidance and challenged the Senior Enlisted leadership to take on leadership roles historically assigned to officers. The most telling truth in taking care of your people was preparing them for the uncertainty of combat operations and ensuring they had the tools and skills to bring them to the fight with the highest chance of success. This requires discipline and pushing the limits in a training environment as well. It paid off – we left the Central Command area of operations with a full muster. As part of the personal staff, I realized that RADM Conway had a great sense and caring of all the people problems that exist in any large organization. He counted on his senior enlisted and staff to be aware of all the operational and warfighting facets – but also to take care of the troops. The senior Medical Officer and Chaplain had direct access to him and daily advised him of personnel issues. He let his Commanders and senior enlisted lead their people and was focused on developing them as leaders. His open door policy and 24 hour access to the smallest of problems served well in handling personal conflicts that will exist over a 7 month deployment. When a personnel decision had to be made, he would err on what is best for that individual, as long as no impact on warfighting readiness is realized. This deep sense of caring for the expeditionary warfighters is one aspect of RADM Conway that is his most important trait, but most unrealized. I think he would like it that way and let the component commanders and senior enlisted take credit.

The First Numbered Expeditionary Strike Group was all about Transformation and pushing the envelope. The successes of the deployment speak for themselves in conducting combat operations in Southern Iraq, influence and Special Operations in the Horn of Africa, and maritime dominance operations conducted concurrently over a water space at least 4 times the size a Carrier Strike Group has controlled. The real impacts will be realized as the Navy challenges itself on the Global War on Terror in Distributed operations, Joint execution at the operational level of War, and providing a Mobile, Lethal, and Agile response from a Sea Based environment. All this will be on the back of our most important asset – the U.S. Navy Sailor. Like RADM Conway said from the beginning – "We are about 10 years ahead of our time!"

Dad: Command Master Chief Downs was my CMDCM for ESG-1

Admiral,

Having returned from ESG1 Deployment under your command, I've had some time to realize the impact it will have on Naval History and I would like to share with you some observations from the Enlisted perspective. This was truly a transformation for the Navy and Marine Corps team. In the beginning, ESG-1 was the catalyst for an emotionally charged transformation; however, it is clear that as we continue to monitor things in the 5th fleet AOR, we were a part of something special that has had a lasting impact on the Global War on Terrorism.

As we began the ESG-1 journey, the resistance to change was remarkable. At times the opposition seemed impossible to overcome and even with the fact in mind that ESG-1 would make our Marines and Amphibious ships more relevant in the GWOT, the resistance continued, often from the highest levels. You stuck by what you believed, based on your prior war fighting experiences and carried the day. Even as we started our work-ups as a group, the trainers defaulted to the std CSG/ARG training model in spite of your efforts to change the status quo. So it was even more impressive that we met all those wickets and started training ESG-1 in transit to the 5th fleet AOR. Your years of experience in that Region proved to be invaluable in what we were undoubtedly going to face in our deployment. Your gut call to use Force Recon for non-compliant boarding was just one of the highlights. Watching the Sailors and Marines on the DDG and GG combine to do boardings was flawlessly executed, in spite of all the naysayers. I also recall that we were concerned about being picked apart as we in-chopped to the 5th fleet AOR, but as we arrived and learned on the fly of having the Flag Officer connected via technology, we saw that we could operate simultaneously in the NAG, SAG, HOA, Red Sea, and have Marines on the ground in Iraq, with a group half the size of a CSG. Your insight to look at capabilities versus platforms proved to be an Operational and

Tactical victory. You set the bar high for all ESGs to come.

The Senior Enlisted of ESG-1 were initially skeptical as well, but they quickly learned their role, and more importantly, they started to understand the operational role. It became clear that their tactical contributions would make ESG-1 a success, regardless of what order came down. Comments were made like, "Wow, this is Sea Basing." I would also say the Senior Enlisted had several joint lessons as well as a little taste of the politics within the Navy and Marine Corps team. As SGTMAJ Jeff Morin and I traveled extensively throughout the ESG visiting with Sailors and Marines, whether on the ships or on the ground in IRAQ, we could watch the transformations taking place. The more we operated the more they understood the mission and capabilities of ESG-1 and the need to continue with ESG's in the future. While talking to Sailors and Marines, we often used that period in history to explain that we were starting to make the shift from Battleships to Carriers. We were starting to see the Amphibian, Crudes and Marine mentalities coming together as a team. It was a sad day when the GNNFP changed to send us home at the 7 month mark of our deployment. We were engaged and operating like a well oiled machine, and although we all looked fwd to seeing our families, it was kind of unspoken that--hey we're here and ready to go, so "Put us in Coach!"

In closing, Admiral, I think you and all of us involved in ESG1 made our mark on Naval and Marine Corps history. The lessons learned on Dist OPS, Sea Basing, (HOA) and the agility and speeds at which we could strike the enemy in a very small window of time will be a part of our 21st century Navy and Marine Corps team. The pirates and smugglers, along with the Terrorist, will soon learn that ESG will be a large part in their demise as we continue to not only keep the sea lanes open in the blue water for our global economy but also reach into the Brown or Green water to seek out and destroy the enemy. I've only scratched the surface of what we accomplished as ESG-1, but the lessons we all learned and the things we proved that could be done well will, undoubtedly, be used to continue the GWOT. Admiral, I think I speak for the majority of the Enlisted Sailors and Marines when I say it was a true honor serving as part of ESG1 under your Command.

Very respectfully,

Ron Downs
CMDCM ESG1

Dad:

CDR Carol Hottenrott, USN, served as the Current Operations/Surface Operations Officer from the initial establishment of ESG-1 until May 04

Much has been written about leadership and change and yet the topic, stemming from leading business management techniques of the day, does little to describe the realities of military change, of leadership attempting to implement innovation in long held doctrine, such as that of amphibious warfare. The announcement of the establishment of Expeditionary Strike Group ONE (ESG-1), under RADM Bob Conway in April 2003, signaled such a leadership and change opportunity: it not only addressed some recognized shortcomings of amphibious operations, but also posited a maritime response to some of the new asymmetric threats presented by global terrorism. The Marines had always succeeded in getting ashore, but since Korea, they moved ashore against enemies who did not oppose them in the littoral – or from the air. What else could be expected from a maritime force, inclusive of the traditional amphibious forces, coupled with naval combatants, with a flag (or general officer) in charge, tasked with experimentation and innovation?

ESG-1 truly began as an experiment with RADM Conway attempting to deliver a more relevant and responsive force to the combatant commander, capable not only of tactical contributions, but of creating operational level of war impact. As the staff came together in the Spring of 2003, the scope and complexity of questions raised by the tasking proved more numerous than the answers, including the composition of the staff itself: how many officers were needed, what should be the mix of services and warfare specialties, how much support staff was required? How would the existing staffs (Commander, Amphibious Squadron THREE and the 15th Marine Expeditionary Unit's (MEU) command staff) be integrated and what would be their role and responsibilities? The Admiral's thought process centered on keeping the staff "manageable" and the staff size smaller than a carrier strike group staff, keyed perhaps on a core of about twenty-five officers. Specific officers on the PHIBRON staff or from the flagship were also dual-tasked. And a final element of the staff strategy focused on the expectation that with today's technology, "reach-back" capability could be employed. "Reach-back" implied gaining synergies from using research and planning teams ashore at other staffs, rather than afloat. The concept proved insightful, if not slightly ahead of its time. In order for ESG-1 to achieve this capability at the time, relationships had to be fostered – if not staff members themselves assigned to the organizations expected to be utilized.

Then, too, came the problem of organization of the larger strike group. The ESG concept sought to expand the Navy's capabilities in the littoral where the amphibious ships and the Marines operated. RADM Conway implemented a command and control concept based on the existing Composite Warfare Commander (CWC) doctrine necessary for multi-ship war fighting at sea, coupled with the ability to integrate with a Carrier Strike Group to form a truly powerful Naval Expeditionary Task Force. Unique to the ESG, the CWC concept was expanded to encompass a landing component (the MEU) as the strike force, coupled with new Special Operations Warfare Commander – empowered by a staff Special Warfare Officer and the ability to coordinate with regional special operations forces, and finally, a much more invigorated Information Warfare Commander. (This warfare area rose in importance in the ESG due to the opportunities created to influence events due to the interaction of ground forces and boarding teams with foreign nationals.)

Also integral to the Admiral's vision of capability for the ESG, was the creation of a Joint Operations Center (JOC). The carriers had always been configured with a flag command center to monitor the battle-space and associated evolutions. Though the helicopter carriers (LHAs and LHDs) had been configured with numerous command and control spaces for amphibious operations inclusive of air, landing force, and supporting arms coordination, there was no adequate space for establishing a watch and controlling air, surface, land, and special operations. With the clear vision that an ESG would prove an ideal joint platform expanding to Army and Air Force use, RADM Conway fought for and won funding to augment USS PELELIU (LHA 5) with a Joint Operations Center, complete with large screen displays, multi-functional computer workstations, and several C4I upgrades. The JOC became the focal point of ESG operations – a command center where all shipboard warfare commanders could manage their operations, receive the latest intelligence, or communicate with higher authority. The space primarily supported the ESG flag watch, an intelligence support desk, and also significantly, the Sea Combat Commander.

The Sea Combat Commander (SCC) executed the operational and tactical employment of all surface ships and assigned missions. Traditionally a role executed by the Destroyer Squadron Commander in a Carrier Strike Group, it was such an important role – fused closely with the planning of the MEU, that RADM Conway believed the SCC needed to reside on the "big deck" for planning and execution efficiency. As such, the Amphibious Squadron staff expanded its role – they kept their traditional amphibious warfare duties as a subset of the overall maritime mission of surface and undersea warfare commander duties. This was no easy task, and the ESG concept in reality challenged the current distinct roles and specialized staffs, specifically the distinction afforded amphibious warfare, to integrate and adapt to the realities of the littoral – which centered not merely on getting the Marines ashore, but in defending those assets at sea.

Throughout the stand-up of ESG-1 and the group's first deployment, cultural and ideological barriers also presented leadership challenges. The Navy and Marine Corps amphibious team did not welcome the ESG experiment, particularly the West-coast model superimposing a flag or general officer over the existing structure. Amphibious doctrine, they argued, was simply not broken, and though the addition of combatants to the mix understandably increased their capability, it also added the responsibility to execute more missions and missions with which they were unfamiliar. In the absence of having assets to deal with undersea, air, and surface threats in the littoral, the ARG tended to focus on what it did best--the ship-to-shore movement. A scenario in which Marine assets were required for the defense of the Amphibious Task Force was known as the "Emergency" Defense of the ATF. Yet in the post USS COLE and 9/11 environment, force protection simply had to recognize a larger scope of threat, with a shorter timeline.

RADM Conway recognized this and challenged everyone to think "out of the box." He challenged his staff, his warfare commanders, his ships and the MEU. The group had to do more; it could do more. We needed to develop new capabilities and missions and we needed to be able to know at all times what potential threats existed. ESG-1 relied on traditional HSL surveillance, but sought to augment that support with Air Command Element (ACE) assets more frequently, and for the surface and air defense commanders to be able to employ the Harriers and Cobras. Marines were integrated with sailors in Visit, Boarding, Search and Seizure take-downs – from Navy RHIBS (Rigid Hull Inflatable Boats), as well as the Marines' traditional use of insertion via helicopters. ESG-1 trained for raids and reconnaissance operations to be launched from FFGs and DDGs vice the LPD or LSD. Joint USMC-Navy ISR was conducted, with the emphasis on real time collection, and possessing a near real-time reaction package poised to strike.

Though the ESG-1 model has not been officially accepted as doctrine, it remains the most viable of the ESG staffs, capable of the widest range of coherent mission planning and distributed execution. The staff manning and staff interrelationships have been fine-tuned, the JOC standardized as an official ship alteration, and the accomplishments and capabilities of an exceptional Navy-Marine Corps team continue to expand to confront the challenges of our time. ESG-1 proved itself relevant and up to the task, largely as a result of RADM Conway's vision, persistence, dedication, and decisive leadership. Such are the qualities required of those who take risks for the sake of improvement, and who convince and inspire others to follow. Time will tell how important the ESG-1 experiment was under RADM Conway, but I believe the Navy and Marine Corps is certainly better for his leadership and innovation.

12

TRANSFORMATION — PART TWO

Brigadier General Mike Regner
USMC ESG-1
Operation Iraqi Freedom/
Operation Enduring Freedom

S tuart – I sent you a brief summary of ESG ops/issues … what I did not provide you (and I'm not sure if it is of value or not) are a few one liners.

Just over 2 months after returning from my deployment with ESG 1, I reported to Iraq (One Marine Expeditionary Force Headquarters or I MEF HQ in Fallujah) to assume the duties of the MEF G3-Operations Officer (Marine Expeditionary Force Operations and Plans-Operations Officer). During my 10 months in Iraq as the G3, I was quite busy. During this time 3 separate MEUs (Marine Expeditionary Units, the 15th, 22nd and

---

★ AUTHOR'S NOTE: The following material is excerpted from a series of emails sent to the author from Brigadier General Mike Regner. They provide a rare look at the creation of new training, tactics and procedures being employed by our military. The lessons learned and the bonds forged from the transformational experiences of ESG-1 (Chapter 11) flowed directly to the troops in Fallujah and Najaf.

31st) deployed to Iraq (previously, MEU's had not normally deployed ashore for greater than a few months) and, along with the 1st MARDIV (First Marine Division), 3rd Air Wing and 1st FSSG (1st Force Service Support Group) participated in the liberation of Najaf and Kufa from Sadr and his terrorist thugs; as well as the liberation of Fallujah and the first Free Iraqi Elections.

"No better friend, no worse enemy", as spoken by then MajGen Mattis, Commanding General of the 1st Marine Division (1st MarDiv CG) was indeed being borne out.

I also had the rare challenge of replacing a highly trained, equipped and very effective warfighting/peacekeeping/enabling organization, the 22nd MEU which was a SOC MEU, SOC being Special Operations Capable, with a fresh from the States, Mississippi National Guard, that had logistical issues from the start. I deployed down to the Southern Babil (Sunni/Shia fault line) AO (area of operations) along with Operations experts, comm techs, aviation fire reps and a team of ISF (Iraqi Security Force) trainers (Marines) to lend a hand to the Army CO and his Mississippi National Guard unit; to this day we are good friends. His unit performed well and had a fine reputation with the Iraqis from Najaf, Kufa, Al Hillah, Al Musayibb and Al Mahmudiyah. They quickly became proficient and, were the 1st units in the I MEF AO to actually turn over the security responsibilities of the area (Kufa and Najaf) to the local Iraqis.

Suffice it to say – working beside my former MEU COs (Marine Expeditionary Unit Commanding Officers) in Iraq – I clearly knew their Special Ops skill sets and, this provided the CG's (Commanding Generals) with valuable tools in their kit.

Concerning the decision to establish / evaluate the ESG Construct: In 2001 the USMC and USN started to discuss the benefits of reinforcing ARGs (Amphibious Ready Group) by way of adding surface combatants/subs to force ratio. (The discussions may have taken place way before this but I became aware of this in 2001.) The reason was simple – lightly defended amphibious ships (except for their Marine contingents – aka the MAGTF – Marine Air Ground Task Force), and in the locations they traditionally operate – the littorals – could be a very lucrative target to a terrorist org/cell. Thus, the USN and the USMC elected to evaluate the inclusion of surface combatants into this amphibious mix. Thus, during open ocean transit or operating in the littorals, the ARG (appropriately renamed Expeditionary Strike Group or ESG) would have the protection and capabilities of these additional ships/sub. This was spelled out fairly well in the NOC (Network Operations Command); what was not spelled out were all the "issues" we were to face during this transformation.

RADM Conway, RDML Cullom and I had the task to put this concept into reality. From my view, I believed that neither RADM Conway or Cullom had much experience in MAGTF operations let alone amphib ops and, due to this, these leaders would attempt to change the warfighting equation. But then too, these admirals believed the gator navy and her Marines were not aware of all the possible threats in the littorals/open ocean and worse yet, it may have only been a matter of time before this "target rich environment (gators)" was the subject of a terrorist strike.

In both cases – the USN and USMC had a lot to learn – after a few meetings and training events, we started to bond towards a highly capable warfighting team (although ... this was not easy!) The Cruiser/Destroyer (CRUDES) community had COMCARTRAGRU and the Amphib / USMC had EWTG LANT/PAC [Expeditionary Warfare Training Group. (Atlantic/ Pacific)] ... neither of which had similar training. The Carrier training community wanted the MAGTF / LHA (Marine Air-Ground Task Force / Amphibious Assault Ship) assets to perform in an air guard role (w/ the CG) and the USMC wanted to do business as usual; neither of which was the right answer. In sum – through realistic training scenarios, a better understanding of each community and their complementary warfighting capabilities and, the breaking/bending/remodeling of the ARGs / CRUDES / CARRIER ops, we formed a team which was relevant and effective in the GWOT.

The challenge of maintaining flying proficiency and maintenance readiness was a concern for the MEU's ACE (Aviation Combat Elements).

In fact, initially (during work-ups), it did have an impact which was not favorable. But during our deployment, due to command involvement, we became most effective. This was proven out during multiple ship (dhows) boardings as well as during "distributed operations". It was also evident when the MAGTF deployed ashore into the Al Faw peninsula and the ESG served as a "sea based" for ISR, reinforcement, medical, maintenance, logistics as well as security (against smugglers/ potential terrorists/pirates and providing security to Iraq's sea based oil terminals). Without discussing classified TTPs (Tactics, Techniques and Procedures), let me just say that not a single ship/dhow left the Shat al Arab w/o RADM Conway knowing what was heading his way (he remained at sea most of the time).

Throughout the deployment to Iraq, Djibouti, the Red Sea, Kenya and the Gulfs/Seas in this region the USN and the USMC received/provided frequent updates. All were pleased with "test / experiment" – some still did not fully understand the value of this new construct but RADM Conway and I knew we were breaking the paradigm and the results were worth the cost.

Whether it was the press or the families back home – we stayed in touch, kept all abreast of our situation and progress and I look back now and clearly state it was worth the investment.

I recently spoke at a SEABASING conference and stated how ESG 1 really conducted its ops as a DO (Daily Operations) Seabase, had all the pillars and the dedicated men and women to make changes and history. So where to now? Do we need a GO (General Officer) or FO (Flag Officer) and their staff on a forward deployed ESG? Yes, to train up with but not necessarily to deploy with … it is situation ally dependent … more to follow on this from our CNO / CMC. In the NAG – no question – the GO / FO has value. What must the USN / USMC complete in the immediate future to make an ESG more relevant? Treat every LHA / LHD (Amphibious Landing Ship) as a command ship and build the FORCE NET (a network of sensors, analysis tools, and decision aids supporting naval operations) capabilities into the C2 architecture of these ships (as far as I know, there are only one or two ships in 3rd Fleet with this capability).

An ESG with her main battery – the MAGTF – truly performs as a rheostat. You can address multiple missions – HA / DA / MIO / STOM … in sum about 25 plus missions. Turn up the heat – disperse – provide protection and training to our allies and in the end, you truly have a "1000 ship naval force" operating in any region of the world and doing so w/o shore basing (needing host nation support) for your MAGTF. Terrorists will never really know where you will pop up next, they will not have the impact and impunity of the past and, I believe these are the offshoots of the ESG construct.

I support the ESG construct, know it still must be improved (training (TTPs), equipping and manning) but, is that not exactly what a relevant warfighting team must do to remain successful, especially in the GWOT?

Hope this helps.
Semper Fi – Brig. Gen. Mike Regner

13

EIGHT MONTHS IN THE PALACE

Major General Kevin Kuklok
USMC Ret.
Baghdad, Iraq
November 2003 – June 2004

TO: STUART PLATT

FROM: KUKLOK

Stuart: Although working in the Office of Policy, Planning and Analysis (OPPA) was a seven day a week, 12-15 hour per day assignment with many memorable challenges, I had opportunity to work with outstanding personnel and significant accomplishments were achieved by them along with our Iraqi hosts. There are several excellent books written that highlight these adventures, but none of this progress would have been possible without the patriotism and dedication of the young men and women in our armed forces who, by force of might, overthrew the totalitarian regime of the previous government.

There were many highlights during the time I spent in the Palace from November 2003 through June 2004 working for the CPA (Coalition Provisional Authority) on the planning and reconstruction of Iraq. There was the sense of accomplishment of being part of a unique group. Coalition members I often had contact which included British airmen, professional (civilian) nation builders, some very seasoned specialists in capacity building, and a couple of outstanding professionals from the United States Army.

Our job was to develop a strategic plan to help restore Iraq to its leadership position in the world as it had been often in history, most recently in the 1960s, prior to the 30 year reign of terror and decimation of the Hussein era. Focusing on security, essential services, governance, and the economy and then putting these into a coherent strategic message for the soon to be elected Iraqi government, allowed us to interface with a wide array of United States and other Coalition nation service members who had the same goal: restoring the capacity of the new Iraq to regain its rightful place among the free nations of the world.

My daily interaction with U.S. Forces occurred on three levels in the Palace and each level had its own special meaning with respect to the young men and women in uniform in Baghdad. The first was the weekly Joint Planning group meetings and daily interface with the Coalition Joint Task Force (CJTF-7) personnel who were involved in the Nation building process, leading to Sovereignty with Sustainment through the Strategic plan. Although many of these service members had never previously been engaged in a nation building process, as they typically faced the "tyranny of the immediate", these professionals brought a wide array of skill sets to bear that were invaluable to the development of a plan that was easily adaptable in the transition to an Iraqi based government.

The second level of interface with service members was a personal one. As a retired Marine reservist in Baghdad, I was able to rekindle friendships with many Marines with whom I had served throughout my reserve career and including a recent 20 month stint on active duty completed prior to my arrival in Baghdad. Nothing keeps an old Marine younger than being around his fellow Marines at the tip of the spear!

The third, and most important service members encountered in the Palace, were the young soldiers and Marines, active, reserve and National Guard, who by example, set the tone for the entire Palace. These included Fleet Anti-terrorism Security Team (FAST) Marines who would spring into action when rockets were in the Baghdad skies and who always provided solid invisible security for the civilians of the many nations temporarily located in the Green Zone. There were also Army reserve and Guardsmen and women, some from my own community in Southern California, providing public affairs, security, trucks, vehicles, and a wide array of services to support the transition to the new and free Iraq.

These young men and women made the rewards of the rebuilding of the nation of Iraq ever more meaningful as it reinforced the reality that the best of our young citizens are actively engaged in making the world a better place. They reflect the best characteristics of our nation and I was proud to play a minor role in their efforts and accomplishments in the reconstruction of Iraq.

Good luck with the book, I look forward to reading it.

Kevin Kuklok
Maj Gen USMC Retired

GLOSSARY

1 MEF HQ – *One Marine Expeditionary Force Headquarters*

1st MARDIV – *First Marine Division*

1st FSSG – *1st Force Service Support Group*

3d ACR – *Third Armored Cavalry Regiment*

3DMAW – *Third Marine Aircraft Wing*

56th BCT – *56th Brigade Combat Team (Texas National Guard)*

ACE – *Aviation Combat Element*

AO – *Area of Operations*

ARG – *Amphibious Ready Group*

C2 – *Command and Control*

CCC – *Central Criminal Court (Iraq)*

CG – *Commanding General*

CMC – *Commandant of Marine Corps*

CO – *Commanding Officer*

CPA – *Coalition Provisional Authority*

CRUDES – *Cruiser/Destroyer*

CSM – *Command Sergeant Major (Army)*

DDG – *Guided Missile Destroyer*

DO – *Daily Operations*

ESG-1 – *Expeditionary Strike Force - One*

EWTG LANT/PAC – *Expeditionary Warfare Training Group (Atlantic/Pacific)*

FFG – *Guided Missile Frigate*

FO – *Forward Observer*

FOB – *Forward Operating Base*

FORCENET – *A network of sensors, analysis tools, and decision aids supporting naval operations*

GNFPP - *Global Naval Force Presence Policy*

GPS – *Global Positioning System*

GWOT – *Global War on Terrorism*

HOA – *Horn of Africa*

ICDC – *Iraqi Civil Defense Corps*

IED – *Improvised Explosive Device*

JAG – *Judge Advocate General*

LHA / LHD – *Amphibious Landing Ships*

LPD – *Amphibious Transport Dock*

LSD – *Landing Ship Dock*

Lt. Col. – *Lieutenant Colonel (Marine Corps, Air Force)*

MAG-11 – *Marine Aircraft Group 11*

MAGTF – *Marine Air-Ground Task Force*

MAGTF / LHA – *Marine Air-Ground Task Force / Amphibious Assault Ship*

Maj. Gen. – *Major General (Marine Corps, Air Force)*

MALS-11 – *Marine Aviation Logistics Squadron 11*

MCAS – *Marine Corps Air Station*

MEF G3 – *Marine Expeditionary Force – Operations and Plans*

MEU – *Marine Expeditionary Unit*

MEU(SOC) – *Marine Expeditionary Unit – Special Operations Capable*

MRE – *Meal Ready to Eat*

MS NG – *Mississippi State National Guard*

NAG – *Northern Arabian Gulf*

NBC – *Nuclear Biological Chemical*

NOC – *Network Operations Command*

OHRA – *Office of Reconstruction and Humanitarian Assistance*

OPNAV – *Office of the Chief of Naval Operations*

PHIBGRU – *Amphibious Group*

POM – *Program Objective Memorandum*

RCT2 3/6 – *Regimental Combat Team Two – 3rd Battalion, 6th Marine Regiment*

RPG – *Rocket Propelled Grenade*

R&R – *Rest and Recreation*

SAG – *Southern Arabian Gulf*

Sgt – *Sergeant (Marine Corps)*

SOC – *Special Operations Command*

SSG – *Staff Sergeant (Army)*

TOC – *Tactical Operations Center*

TT – *Transition Team*

TTP – *Tactics, Techniques and Procedures*

USMC – *United States Marine Corps*

USN – *United States Navy*

BIOGRAPHIES

General Dennis Reimer – Foreword

General Dennis J. Reimer was born in Medford, Oklahoma, and is a graduate of the United States Military Academy at West Point, New York. General Reimer retired from the United States Army in 1999 as the 33rd Chief of Staff of the Army.

After graduating from the Field Artillery Officer Orientation Course at Fort Sill, Oklahoma, and the Ranger Course, U.S. Army Infantry School, Fort Benning, Georgia, Lieutenant Reimer was assigned to the 20th Artillery, 5th Infantry Division (Mechanized), Fort Carson, Colorado, where he later served as the Executive Officer.

Lieutenant Reimer then served as the Assistant Battalion Advisor, Advisory Team 60, U.S. Military Assistance Command in the Republic of Vietnam. From Vietnam, he entered the Artillery Officer Advanced Course, U.S. Army Air Defense Artillery School at Fort Bliss, Texas. Upon graduation, Captain Reimer became the Commander, Company C, 11th Battalion, 3d Brigade, U.S. Army Training Center at Fort Benning, and later, became the Executive Officer of the Battalion.

By 1970, he had been promoted to Major and he served as an instructor at the United States Army Field Artillery School before going on to the Command and General Staff College at Fort Leavenworth, Kansas.

After completion of the Command and General Staff College, he was assigned to the Personnel Management Office, in the Assignment Section of the Field Artillery Branch, Office of Personnel Operations, Washington, DC. He was next assigned as the Assistant Executive/Aide, Office of the Chief of Staff, United States Army in Washington.

Major Reimer served as the Executive Officer and, after promotion to Lieutenant Colonel, became the S3 (Operations), Division Artillery, 4th Infantry Division (Mechanized) at Fort Carson, Colorado. In July

1976, Lieutenant Colonel Reimer became the Commander of 1st Battalion, 27th Artillery, also in the 4th Division and then became the Commandant, Training Command, in the Division.

Lieutenant Colonel Reimer became a student at The United States Army War College, Carlisle Barracks, Pennsylvania, in 1980. Upon graduation, he was assigned as Deputy Commander, and later, Special Assistant to the Commander, V Corps Artillery, United States Army Europe. Colonel Reimer then took command of the Division Artillery, 8th Infantry Division (Mechanized), United States Army Europe. After completing command, he became the Chief of Staff of the Division.

Colonel Reimer became the Assistant Commandant, United States Army Field Artillery School and was then promoted to Brigadier General, and later, became the Commanding General, III Corps Artillery at Fort Sill. General Reimer left Fort Sill to become the Assistant Chief of Staff, C3/J3, United States Army Element, Combined Field Army, Republic of Korea and was named Assistant Chief of Staff for Operations for Combined Forces Command/United States Forces, Korea/Eighth U.S. Army in December 1986.

In June of 1988, Major General Reimer assumed command of the 4th Infantry Division (Mechanized) and Fort Carson.

In May 1990, he became the Deputy Chief of Staff for Operations and Plans for the Army during Desert Storm. He then became the Commanding General of the United States Army, Forces Command, Fort McPherson, Georgia.

He was then nominated by President George H. W. Bush to become the Vice Chief of Staff of the Army and on 20 June 1995, General Reimer became the 33rd Chief of Staff, United States Army.

General Reimer's awards include the Defense Distinguished Service Medal, two Legions of Merit, the Distinguished Flying Cross, six awards of the Bronze Star Medal (one with "V" device for valor), the Purple Heart and the Combat Infantryman Badge. He also wears the Parachutist Badge, the Aircraft Crewman Badge and the Ranger Tab.

He graduated from the Military Academy with a Bachelor of Science degree and earned a Master of Science degree from Shippensburg State University, Shippensburg, Pennsylvania.

CHAPTER ONE
THE VIEW FROM HERE — PART ONE

Sgt. Chris McCarthy
United States Marine Corps
MALS-11, MAG-11, 3DMAW
Kuwait - Iraq
January 2003 – May 2003

Sgt Chris McCarthy was born into a military family at Tripler Army Medical Center in Honolulu, HI on July 21st, 1978. His father is a career Naval Officer.

In the early years of his life he lived at various times in San Diego, Los Angeles, Rhode Island, Washington, Virginia, Georgia, Indiana, and Florida before leaving home to study at Purdue University in 1996. Chris withdrew in good standing from the University to enlist in the Marine Corps, and graduated from the Marine Corps Recruit Depot, San Diego in August, 2001. From there he went on to Aviation Electricians Mate school in Pensacola, Florida where he finished as Honor Graduate in June, 2002.

He arrived on station at MCAS Miramar in July of 2002 and deployed to Al Jaber, Kuwait from January to May, 2003. He is now married to the beautiful Rachel Schmidt McCarthy and they celebrated their wedding on December 23rd, 2005. Sgt McCarthy is currently on Temporary Assignment of Duties to I Marine Expeditionary Force (Forward) at Camp Victory, Kuwait. His deployment has interrupted his studies for a degree in Computer Information Systems, but after he completes his deployment Sgt McCarthy plans to finish his degree and then attend Officer Candidate School in order to receive his commission as an officer in the Marine Corps.

3DMAW

The Third Marine Aircraft Wing was established on November 10, 1942 and these Marine aviators flew in combat in WWII, Korea and Vietnam. More recently the wing has served in Operation Desert Storm, Somalia, and in Operation Iraqi Freedom. 3DMAW is stationed at MCAS Miramar in Southern California.

MALS 11

Marine Aviation Logistics Squadron 11 is the oldest Squadron in the USMC, formed in 1921 in Quantico, Virginia. The squadron has seen heavy action throughout its history including the battles for the Solomon Islands, New Britain, Peleliu, and the Philippines during WWII and Vietnam from 1965 through 1971. Most recently the squadron has been in action during Operation Desert Shield, Operation Desert Storm and Operation Iraqi Freedom.

Ahmed Al Jaber Air Base

Sitting 75 miles from the Iraqi border inside Kuwait, Ahmed Al Jaber Air Base is a Kuwaiti Airforce facility which served as a principal base for American and allied forces in the 1990's and was a major staging point for OIF. During Operation Southern Watch and in the build up to OIF, Ahmed Al Jaber became known as the "base that never sleeps" due to the nonstop activity of some 7000 people trying to operate from a base designed for 2000!

CHAPTER TWO
LAW AND ORDER

Captain Brian Baldrate
3d ACR U.S. Army
Al Anbar Province, Iraq
May 2003 – March 2004

Captain Brian Baldrate grew up in Guilford, Connecticut and graduated from the United States Military Academy in 1995. After graduation, he served as

Armor officer in the First Cavalry Division. Brian returned to school and in 2000 received a Law Degree and a Masters in Public Administration from the University of Connecticut. Following school, Brian served for over three years as a trial counsel for the Third Armored Cavalry Regiment.

Deployed to Operation Iraqi Freedom, Iraq in April of 2003, Captain Baldrate served as the Third Armored Cavalry Regiment's lead legal advisor. He was responsible for all international and military law issues including: the proper application of the law of war during combat and foreign occupation, identification and investigation of war crimes, and writing and advising on the rules of engagement for combat operations.

Specific responsibilities during Operation Iraqi Freedom included arranging the terms of a surrender of an Iranian terrorist force (MeK), interrogating captured Iraqi detainees in determining their status under the Geneva Conventions, and leading the restoration effort of the Iraqi judicial system in western Iraq. Other deployments with the Regiment included The National Training Center, Fort Irwin, CA., 8/02-9/02, and Operation Bright Star, Egypt, 9/01-11/01.

Brian currently works as a trial attorney for the Army's Litigation Division, in Arlington, Virginia, where he now lives with his wife, Christy, and their son, Jackson.

CHAPTER THREE
THE OTHER SIDE OF THE SANDBOX

SSG Bryan Catherman
3d ACR U.S. Army
Al Anbar Province, Iraq
October 2003 – April 2004

In Iraq, I was SSG Catherman; now I'm just Bryan. I was activated to Fort Carson, Colorado the first week of January, 2003. I volunteered to deploy to Iraq with the 3d Armored Cavalry Regiment and received orders to do so in September of that year. Upon my homecoming to Utah in April of the following year, I returned to my life as a Reservist. Shortly thereafter,

I finished my eight years with the military, so I picked up my schooling again and earned a Bachelor's degree. After being accepted into a graduate program at the University of Utah, I realized my pre-activation and deployment plans of government work in the legal arena just didn't fit me anymore. Instead, I reactivated my real estate license to pay the bills and to spend my time chasing down my dreams.

I still enjoy motorcycling the backcountry highways with my beautiful wife. I read much more, and it's mostly for fun too. Hiking trips and exploration happen occasionally, but I find it difficult to find the time. Lisa and I have two Labrador Retrievers – one golden and one black and we spoil them rotten.

I witnessed the best and worst of Iraq. I hate it when people ask me, "So Iraq, is that a good thing or a bad thing?" I struggle with these questions all the time. I no longer have the luxury of the simple black and white. Much of my answers fall somewhere in the gray or go completely unanswered. I am proud to have served, there is no question, and Iraq will forever be a part of me. In Iraq, I served on the forward edge of freedom. Throughout the remainder of my life, I pray I am blessed to continue in the service of my community, because there is no endeavor which is more noble.

3d ACR - Third Armored Cavalry Regiment

The Regiment was established by Act of Congress in 1846. The main task for the Regiment was to be the establishment of military outposts on the route to Oregon, but prior to that deployment they were sent south to participate in the Mexican War.

Troopers of the Third U.S. Cavalry have since gone in to battle in ten major conflicts: the Mexican War, as mentioned above, the Indian Wars, the Civil War, the Spanish-American War (including the famous charge on San Juan Hill in Cuba), the Philippine Insurrection, WWI, WWII (as the spearhead of General George Patton's Third Army), the Persian Gulf War, Bosnia and OIF. In its proud history the Regiment has earned 39 campaign streamers, a Presidential Unit Citation, and 23 troopers of 3d ACR have been awarded the Medal of Honor.

Baghdad had already been taken when boots from 3d ACR finally hit the ground in Iraq. Their task was to secure Al Anbar province, a highly volatile region, bypassed during the assault on Baghdad, which includes the Sunni Triangle, the tribal heartland of Saddam Hussein. This area had been bypassed during the assault on Baghdad and the Regiment faced a difficult task. Al Anbar was the biggest piece of territory assigned to any unit in Iraq.

As in days long past, the 3d ACR established outposts known as Forward Operating Bases, 20 of them in Al Anbar, with 140,000 square miles of hostile territory surrounding them. Terrorists were frequent on the long supply routes to each FOB and 31 troopers from 3d ACR and 18 attached troopers of the Task Force died in OIF 1 and over 200 were wounded.

Northern Palace
Rifles Base
Camp Blue Diamond

Formerly a palace complex that was home to Saddam Hussein, 3d ACR took over what then became known as Rifles Base.

Al Anbar Province, Iraq

Al Anbar is a province in Iraq. Ramadi is the capital of the province, which is the largest in Iraq. It also shares a border with Syria, Jordan and Saudi Arabia. The route to Mecca in Saudi Arabia passes through Al Anbar province and the tens of thousands of pilgrims who pass through the area each year pose a daunting security problem. The province may be best known for the city of Fallujah and as the heartland of the Sunni Triangle. Tribal and religious traditions are powerful influences in this volatile region.

CHAPTER FOUR

A LINE IN THE SAND

Sgt. Chris Missick
319 Sig Bn, C Co
U.S. Army
Iraq
April 2004 – March 2005

Chris Missick enlisted in the Army Reserves in January of 2001 and did his basic training at Fort Leonard Wood, MO. Chris enlisted to fulfill a commitment he made to himself while working on the Bush campaign in California in 1999. Being asked to serve as Director for Youth Outreach for Northern California in the Bush for President Campaign, Chris found himself in the middle of a major national presidential campaign. His hard work paid off, and in early June of 2000, he was promoted to Deputy Director for the Northern California campaign effort. The culmination of his work on the Bush Campaign came when he attended the Republican National Convention in Philadelphia. Chris was instilled with the greatest sense of pride in his nation, and humbled with an even deeper desire to serve America.

In the aftermath of that tumultuous election in November 2000, Chris went ahead and fulfilled his obligation. Only days before President George W. Bush was inaugurated, Chris signed on the line to enlist in the US Army Reserve. He shipped out to Iraq on May 31, 2001, and began what he could not have known then, would be the experience of a lifetime. The following months changed both Chris and the country, as the nation experienced one of the most horrific events in its history.

Returning from active military service in December of 2001, and beginning his remaining 5-year reservist commitment, Chris was intent on finishing school and preparing for his next stage in education. Above anything else however, the tragic events of 9-11 forged a commitment to his country and his community. September 11 inspired many people to do not just good things, but to begin remarkable endeavors. Thus inspired, with a continued commitment to America's communities, he filed the necessary papers and ran for office on the Sacramento Central Committee. However, in the midst of his term, his unit, the 319th Signal

Battalion, was called to service by the President to support the war effort in Operation Iraqi Freedom.

319th Signal Battalion

Formed on June 25, 1943 as the 984th Signal Service Company and activated at Fort Dix, N.J. The 319th Signal Battalion served in Europe throughout the latter part of the war and through the early post-war period and was deactivated May 29, 1946. Like many military units of the era, the Battalion was activated several times over the next decades and in its current incarnation they are now based in California.

CHAPTER FIVE
WHO'S YOUR BAGHDADDY?

Captain John Upperman
56th Brigade Combat Team
Texas National Guard
Talil, Iraq
January 2005 – December 2005

Captain Upperman lives in Round Rock, Texas with his wife and 4 children. He works at Dell as a marketing professional and he is a member of the HHC, 3-112 Armor, 56th Brigade of the Texas National Guard. His unit was activated for deployment to Iraq in August 2004. He is a modern soldier in every sense, using the internet to blog about his experiences in Iraq both during and after his return.

56th Brigade Combat Team, Texas National Guard

More than 8,000 members of the Texas Army National Guard and Air National Guard have served on military missions since Sept. 11/2001. During the mobilization of the 56th BCT, from January 2005 to December of 2005, the Texas National Guard had more than 4,900 Soldiers and Airmen deployed on active duty.

The 56th Brigade evolved from the historic 56th Cavalry Brigade, which was established in the early 1920's. The brigade, based in Fort Worth, Texas, is a component of the 36th Infantry Division.

Talil AFB, Iraq

Talil Airbase is located approximately 310 kilometers southeast of Baghdad and 20 kilometers southwest of the city of An Nasiriyah in the Euphrates River valley. The base had not been in full use since the first Gulf War in 1991. It was often attacked by American and British forces during the 1990's as part of the enforcement of the established "no fly zone".

This is also the location of the ancient city of Ur, thought to be the birthplace of the biblical patriarch Abraham and perhaps the oldest city in the world, flourishing since 4000 years BC. The Ziggurat of Nanna is located there also.

Camp Adder

Camp Adder is part of the sprawling complex of Talil Air Base. It has served as the major resupply center for the U.S. military in Southern and Central Iraq.

CHAPTER SIX
DEVIL DOG

Sgt David S. Bateman
RCT2 3/6 USMC
Western Iraq
September 2005 – December 2005

Sgt David Bateman was born in Orlando, Florida. He served as the assistant Radio Chief in his communications platoon, which is part of the 3rd Battalion of the 6th Marine Regiment. He had recently re-enlisted in the Marines when his unit was ordered to Iraq. He had served until 2001 in a Communications Company of the 2nd Marine Division. He then found out that he had not only a love of golf but also a talent for it and with the help of a Montgomery G.I. Bill and a student loan he enrolled in a Golf Academy where he learned the finer points of the game. After graduation and while working as a golf pro he realized that he was, at the age of 25, much younger than his peers on the course and his thoughts turned back to his service in the USMC. The birth of his son Ethan confirmed for him that he had to pursue something more than golf. He re-enlisted in Mid-July 2004 and the unit received orders for their deployment at the end of August.

While serving in Iraq, just prior to Christmas of 2005, Sgt. Bateman received a non-combat related injury to his hand and was flown back to the United States for surgery and rehabilitation. He is now re-united with his wife Robin and their son Ethan and Sgt. Bateman will be applying to join the Marine Enlisted Commissioning Program in order to become an Officer in the USMC.

RCT2 3/6 USMC

The 3/6 Marines were originally activated on the 14th of August 1917 at Quantico, Virginia. They were subsequently deployed during October-November 1917 to France as part of the 4th Brigade of the American Expeditionary Force of WWI. The Marines saw action throughout WWI and then formed part of the occupation force post war from December 1918 through July 1919. They then returned to the United States and were disbanded in August of 1919.

The 3/6 Marines were activated and deactivated a number of times during the 1920's and were deployed to the Dominican Republic and to China during that period. The unit was deactivated once more in the late 20's and did not reform until a year before American involvement in WWII began.

The Regiment was initially assigned to Iceland and then redeployed following the U.S. entry into the war, to the Pacific where they saw action in most of the major engagements of the war in that theater including Guadalcanal, Solomon Islands, Tarawa, Saipan, Tinian, and Okinawa.

The 3/6 then served with the occupation forces from September 1945 to February 1946 and then returned to Camp Pendleton in California where they were deactivated yet again.

With the onset of the Cold War, the 3/6 was reactivated in 1949 and for most of the next decade they served in the Caribbean and the Mediterranean. Then, during the next 40 years the 3/6 Marines served across the globe including Lebanon in 1958, Cuban missile crisis in 1962, the intervention in the Dominican Republic, 1965, Guantanamo Bay, Cuba, 1979, Operation Just Cause, Panama, December 1989-January 1990, Operations Desert Shield and Desert Storm, Southwest Asia, December 1990-April 1991 Operation Enduring Freedom & Swift Freedom, Afghanistan & Pakistan from November 2001-Febuary 2002, defense of the American Embassy Kabul Afghanistan, December 2001, and Sept 2002-present, Joint Task Force Horn of Africa, Nov 2001-present. The latest deployment was Operation Iraqi in 2005.

CHAPTER SEVEN

CITIZEN SOLDIERS

Lt. Col. Dan Hokanson
National Security Fellow
Harvard University

Lieutenant Colonel Dan Hokanson was born in Happy Camp, California, and is a National Security Fellow at Harvard University. He holds a Bachelor's Degree in Aerospace Engineering from the U.S. Military Academy at West Point, New York, a Master's Degree in International Security and Civil-Military Relations from the Naval Postgraduate School in Monterey, California, and a Master's Degree in National Security and Strategic Decision-making from the Naval War College in Newport, Rhode Island.

Lieutenant Colonel Hokanson served as an Aviation officer in the U.S. Army before joining the Oregon National Guard. He has served in Air Cavalry, Attack Helicopter, Aero medical Evacuation and Aviation

Testing units. He has also served as a Strategic Planner at National Guard Bureau Headquarters and has commanded at the Platoon, Company and Battalion level. Lieutenant Colonel Hokanson is a Command Pilot with over 2500 hours in five different aircraft and ten different series. He was a member of the 1996 U.S. World Helicopter Team, has flown twenty-nine combat missions, forty-five search and rescue missions, two major forest fires, and was awarded the Soldiers Medal for Heroism as well as the Nation Guard Association's Valley Forge Cross for Heroism.

Lieutenant Colonel Hokanson developed and founded the first National Guard Military Air Rescue Team (MART) and has command-ed over one-hundred air rescue operations. He and his wife, the former Kelly Triplett of San Lorenzo, California, and their three children live in Massachusetts.

CHAPTER EIGHT
DEVIL DOGMA

Karey Keel-Stidham
Marine Mother
Orcas Island, Washington, USA

I'm the nearly 47 year-old very proud mom of a United Sates Marine, who will hopefully be Sgt T.W, Stidham when this book goes to print (he's Cpl Stidham right now). I live on beautiful Orcas Island in Washington State, but lived in Bellingham and Ferndale, WA for the past 45 years.

My son joined the Marines on his 17th birthday, July 25th 2000. He spent his senior year of high school as a Marine "poolie" in the Delayed Entry Program. Two days before his 18th birthday he headed off to boot camp, and that's where he was on September 11, 2001. It took about 3 days for it to sink in to me what 9/11/01 was going to mean to the moth-er of someone in the military, and it was a harsh reality.

Fast forward to February of 2003, and my son was in Kuwait for the beginning of Operation Iraq Freedom. At first he was able to call us pret-ty regularly, I think about once per week, and he was writing to us and we were writing to him. Once the combat operations actually began, the communication pretty much ceased. I was a wreck and was glued to the news 24/7. And then the most wonderful thing happened. Tim told us that someone had "adopted" him. Some complete strangers cared enough about my son to write to him, send him packages and recruit others in the group to do the same! I was so touched by the mere thought that all I could do was cry. The group was the Hollywood Chapter of the DAR (Daughters of the American Revolution) in Los Angeles, CA and the person who ultimately had the most impact on me was Nancy Daniels, who was the Hollywood DAR National Defense Chair at the time. Nancy's sister, Laurie. was an art teacher at a private school and all the kids in Laurie's class wrote wonderful letters to Tim as well, thanking him for protecting us, and telling him to stay safe. I was so overwhelmed by this that I vowed I would do the same for someone else's child. Nancy and I have since become very good pals, and though we've never met in person, I know one day we will.

After Tim came home from his first deployment, I looked around on the Internet and found Adopt-A-Platoon (www.adoptaplatoon.org); I got in touch with them and said I wanted to "adopt" a soldier or Marine. That was in the fall of 2003, since then I've adopted a total of about 30. More recently I've found my "adoptees" more by word of mouth. All the ones I've lost contact with have come home as far as I know and not one of the moms has adopted me as I did with Nancy, but if I helped even one of our fine service members get through their deployment, then that's what matters. I have wonderful letters from many of these "adopted" troops to share, and I'm awed every time they thank me for writing to them and sending them packages.

Tim's second deployment wasn't nearly as traumatic as the first for me. And we had email nearly everyday from him. Tim's job was working on the CH-16 Sea Knight Helicopters, so I knew he was relatively safe. I still worried and prayed a lot, and having the "adopted" troops helped me to cope. I had others to worry about besides my own. I also became an email junkie with other Marine moms and that helped immensely.

There were some very difficult moments, too though. As a part of the Marine Moms group (bandofmothers.org) supporting other moms, there were often condolences to write, and the first time I did that, I thought I'd never stop crying. Imagining the pain of losing a Marine son was just too real, too close to my own heart. But, I got through the first one, and have written many since, each just as difficult as the first.

Its late 2005, as I write this and my son is back in Iraq for his 3rd tour. This time he's not with the helicopter squadron. He volunteered (you never volunteer for anything in the Marine Corps!!) to go back and work security at the base in Al-Asad where he'd been before. This time, I'm worried more again since I know he's not just working in the helo's. He's a guard at roadblocks and checkpoints. We don't have email with him every day, but maybe once or twice a week or so. I'm praying for the time to quickly pass, and am thankful for every minute of every day that he is safe. He told me before he left that he didn't know if he'd be lucky 3 times. God willing, he will.

I'm currently supporting 8 other Marines in Iraq, 8 in Afghanistan, and 6 soldiers in Iraq. Two of the Marines in Iraq are the sons of moms I became acquainted with before they deployed, and these moms are also writing to my son. My brother-in-law Jeff, a Lt. Col in the Army Reserve, has also just finished a year in Kuwait working on reconstruction efforts. We are all one big family (except for the Cindy Sheehan types).

My father served in Okinawa and China as a Marine during WWII, and then re-enlisted to serve in the Korean War. He is Tim's example and Tim had aspirations of being a Marine since he was nine years old. My father-in-law Major Jerry S. Stidham was also in WWII, he flew P-38's over Europe and was a hero in his own right. My collection of letters in this book are being shared to honor the service of my dad, my son and my father-in-law as well as all who have served past and present. Without the sacrifice and service of true heroes like these none of us would be free to read a book like this. I thank RADM Platt and Duffrey Sigurdson for including my letters. I hope they will help others to realize how much the simple act of writing a letter can mean to someone who is serving so far from home, not to mention the mom who loves that someone serving so far from home!

CHAPTER NINE

LETTERS TO AMERICA

Major Eric Rydbom

Lieutenant Colonel Rydbom graduated from the Pennsylvania State University in May 1983, receiving a commission as a Second Lieutenant of Infantry in 1982. Following the Infantry Officer Basic Course at Fort Benning, GA, he served as Rifle Platoon Leader, Anti-Armor Platoon Leader and Company Commander, C Company, 1/112th Infantry Regiment, 28th Infantry Division, Pennsylvania Army National Guard from 1982 through 1987. In 1987 he transferred to the Utah Army National Guard where he served as Executive Officer and Company Commander of B Company, Company Commander of C Company, deployed in support of Operation Desert Storm, and Assistant Battalion S-3, 1457th Engineer Battalion (Combat)(Corps)(Wheeled) from 1987 through 1991. In 1992 he transferred to the 163rd Separate Armor Brigade, Montana Army National Guard where he attended the Reserve Component Tank Commanders Course at Gowen Field, Idaho and in 1993 attended the Armor Officer Advanced Course at Fort Knox, KY. While in the 163rd SAB, he served as Brigade LNO, Assistant Brigade Engineer, Commander, B Company 1st Battalion, 163rd Armor, Executive Officer of the Brigade HHC, and Commander HHC, 1st Battalion 163rd Infantry between 1992 and 1996. After completing CAS3 and the Engineer Officer Advanced Course, he transferred to the United States Army Reserve and served as S-4 for the 379th EN BN in Missoula, Montana and as Commander of the 50th Military History Detachment in Helena Montana until being assessed into the Active Guard and Reserve program in 1998. From 1998 through 2000, LTC Rydbom was assigned as the Unit Training Officer for the 70th Regional Support Command in Seattle, WA and served as Deputy Brigade S-3 for the 4th Brigade, 91st Division (Training Support) at Fort Lewis, WA. from 2000 through 2002.

After completing CGSC in 2003, LTC Rydbom was assigned as Deputy Division Engineer, 4th Infantry Division from February through August 2003 in Kuwait and Tikrit, Iraq. In December 2003, he was assigned as G-3 Operations Officer for the 416th Engineer Command in Darien, IL. with responsibility for Installation Related Troop Construction projects at five USAR Installations nationwide. In August 2004, he assumed the duties of Assistant Garrison Commander, Fort Hood, Texas and served there through October 2005. He arrived at the University of Montana as the Executive Officer and Assistant Professor of Military science on 7 November 2005.

His awards and decorations include the Bronze Star, Meritorious Service Medal with OLC, Army Commendation Medal with 3 OLC, Army Achievement Medal with 2 OLC, National Defense Service Medal with Bronze Star, Armed Forces Reserve Medal with 2 device, Global War on Terrorism Expeditionary Medal, and Global War on Terrorism Service Medal.

CHAPTER TEN
THE VIEW FROM HERE

Vice Admiral J.D. McCarthy SC, USN
Director, Material Readiness and Logistics
(OPNAV N4)

Vice Admiral McCarthy became Director, Material Readiness and Logistics in August 2004. As such, he is responsible for the strategic planning for all Navy Fleet readiness and logistics programs.

A native of Auburn Hills, Mich., Vice Adm. McCarthy earned his commission through Officer Candidate School, Newport, R.I., in October 1969. He holds a Bachelor of Science degree in Engineering from Oakland University and is a distinguished graduate of the Naval Postgraduate School, where he earned a Master of Science degree in Management with subspecialties in financial management, weapon system acquisition management and materiel management. He is also a distinguished graduate of the Naval War College and a graduate of the University of Michigan Executive Education Program.

Vice Adm. McCarthy has served in a variety of sea and shore duty assignments providing him extensive logistics and financial management experience. At sea, his assignments have included Assistant Supply Officer, USS Holland (AS 32); Supply Officer, USS Newport (LST 1179); Supply Officer, USS New Orleans (LPH 11); and Recommissioning Supply Officer, USS Missouri (BB 63). Ashore his assignments have included duty as Planning Officer, Naval Supply Center, Pearl Harbor; Special Assistant to the Stock Control Director, Navy Ships Parts Control Center; Executive Assistant to the Commander, Naval Supply Systems Command; Comptroller, Naval Surface Force, U.S. Pacific Fleet; Head, Spares Program and Policy Branch on the staff of the Deputy Chief of Naval Operations for Logistics; Commanding Officer, Navy Supply Corps School; and Comptroller, Defense Logistics Agency.

Since his promotion to flag rank in November 1996, Vice Adm. McCarthy has served as Deputy Director for Material Management, Defense Logistics Agency; Deputy Chief of Staff for Logistics, Fleet Supply and Ordnance, U.S. Pacific Fleet; and as Commander, Naval Supply Systems Command and 42nd Chief of Supply Corps.

Vice Adm. McCarthy's personal decorations include the Defense Distinguished Service Medal, Navy Distinguished Service Medal, Legion of Merit (four awards), and the Meritorious Service Medal (two awards). He is a qualified Surface Warfare Supply Corps Officer, a member of the Navy Acquisition Professional Community, and a Certified Government Financial Manager.

CHAPTER ELEVEN

TRANSFORMATION — PART ONE

RADM Robert Conway Jr.
Commanding Officer ESG-1, USN
Operation Iraqi Freedom/Operation Enduring Freedom

Rear Admiral Conway was commissioned an Ensign in 1972 and served in various leadership positions onboard USS VESOLE (DD 878), USS TOWERS (DDG 9); USS BAINBRIDGE (CGN 25), and USS GRIDLEY (CG 21). He also served as Chief Staff Officer for Commander, Destroyer Squadron Seventeen and as senior examiner for steam propulsion on the staff of Commander-in-Chief, U.S. Pacific Fleet Propulsion Examination Board.

Rear Adm. Conway commanded USS JOHN YOUNG (DD 973) from April 1992 to January 1994. During his command tour, John Young was awarded the Navy Unit Commendation for Operation Desert Storm and the Battle Efficiency "E". Rear Adm. Conway also served as Commander, Destroyer Squadron Seven from January 1996 to July 1997. During this command tour he deployed as the "Sea Combat Commander" for the Constellation Battle Group in the western Pacific and Arabian Gulf. He also commanded Naval Surface Group Middle Pacific, Pearl Harbor, Hawaii. From April 2003 to October 2004, he served as the plank owner Commander of Expeditionary Strike Group One, San Diego, Calif., and deployed to the Arabian Gulf and Red Sea in support of the Global War on Terrorism. Rear Adm. Conway assumed duties as Commander Task Force Warrior in August of 2004.

Leadership duties ashore include Naval Facility Cape Hatteras (SOSUS); Officer Candidate School, Newport, R.I.; Deputy Commander, Operational Test and Evaluation Force Pacific, as the senior test director for the Tomahawk Cruise Missile Project; Head, Surface Commander Assignment Branch, Bureau of Naval Personnel (PERS 410) and Deputy to Assistant Chief of Naval Operations for Distribution (PERS 4), Bureau of Naval Personnel, Washington, D.C.; Chief, Simulations and Analysis Management Division, J-8 directorate, Joint Chiefs of Staff, Washington, D.C.; Director, Surface Officer Distribution, Bureau of Naval Personnel (PERS 41), Millington, Tenn. From September 2000 until March 2003, he was the unofficial "Mayor of Hawaii" while serving as Commander, Navy Region Hawaii.

Rear Adm. Conway earned a Master's degree in education from Providence College and a post-graduate degree from the National Defense University's Industrial College of the Armed Forces.

Personal decorations include Defense Superior Service Medal, Legion of Merit (five awards), Meritorious Service Medal (four awards), Navy Commendation Medal (two awards), and various service medals and unit awards.

OTHER CONTRIBUTORS TO CHAPTER ELEVEN

Captain Charles R. Morgan, USN
Special Operations Warfare Commander ESG-1

Born in Kansas City, Kansas, Captain Morgan was later raised in Pittsburgh, Pennsylvania. He graduated from Plum High School in 1975 and also was awarded Eagle Scout with the Boy Scouts of America. He graduated from Penn State University in 1980 in the Naval Reserve Officer Training Corps. In 1995, he received his an advanced degree in National Security and Strategic Studies from Naval War College.

His first assignment was as a Surface Warfare Officer on the USS Spiegel Grove (LSD-32). He attended Basic Underwater Demolition SEAL (BUD/S) Training in 1984. His operational tours were at SEAL Team ONE and THREE. He was the Executive Officer of SEAL Team THREE in 1993 to 1994. From 1998 to 2000, he was Commanding Officer of SEAL Team FIVE. He has deployed to the Pacific, the Persian Gulf, South America, Africa and has been involved in Operation Earnest Will, Operation Just Cause, and Operation Promote Liberty.

Staff assignments have been Chief Staff Officer for Special Boat Squadron ONE, Chief Staff Officer for Naval Special Warfare Group ONE, Chief of Staff for Naval Special Warfare Command, and Chief of Staff for Expeditionary Strike Group ONE. Other sea duty assignments were as the Special Operations Officer for Commander SEVENTH and THIRD Fleet.

He most recent assignment was as Special Operations Warfare Commander and Staff Plans for the first Numbered Expeditionary Strike Group deployment to Operation Iraqi Freedom and Operation Enduring Freedom.

Captain Morgan is married to the former Mary Jo Coulston of San Diego and has a two year old daughter, Grace "Xena the Warrior Princess."

Commander Carol A. Hottenrott, USN
Surface Operations Officer ESG-1

Commander Hottenrott was born in Poughkeepsie, New York. She attended the University of Pennsylvania, earning both Bachelor and Master of Arts degrees in Political Science/International Relations and received her commission through the Naval Reserve Officer Training Corps in 1987.

Following basic training as a Special Operations Diving and Salvage Officer, Commander Hottenrott reported to USS HOIST (ARS 40) in Little Creek, VA where she consecutively served as Supply Officer, Main Propulsion Assistant, and Operations Officer. USS HOIST conducted diving, towing, and salvage operations throughout the Second and Sixth Fleet areas of operation. For her second division officer assignment, she served as Executive Officer in USS PAPAGO (ATF 160), also based in Little Creek, VA. She then attended Department Head School in Newport, RI, and subsequently reported as Executive Officer to USS BRUNSWICK (ATS 3), home-ported in Sasebo, Japan.

In 1994, Commander Hottenrott transferred to the Surface Warfare community and was detailed as Operations Officer to USS KINKAID (DD 965), then deployed to the Persian Gulf. Following this tour, she then served as the Operations Officer on the staff of Commander, Destroyer Squadron SEVEN, which also deployed to the Persian Gulf in 1997, embarked in USS CONSTELLATION (CV 64). In August 2000, Commander Hottenrott assumed command of USS PELICAN (MHC 53) in Ingleside, TX, and her tour encompassed the ship's first operational deployment in support of fleet exercises on the East Coast. Commander Hottenrott most recently served as the Current/Surface Operations Officer on the inaugural staff of Commander, Expeditionary Strike Group ONE, which deployed to the Persian Gulf in support of OPERATIONS ENDURING and IRAQI FREEDOM in 2003-2004. Commander Hottenrott currently serves in command of USS HOWARD (DDG 83), homeported in San

Diego, CA.

Commander Hottenrott's shore duty assignments include a tour on the Joint Staff, assigned to the J-3 Directorate as a Senior Operations Officer at the National Military Command Center, and as a Congressional Liaison for Appropriations Matters on the staff of the Assistant Secretary of the Navy (Financial Management and Comptroller).

Commander Hottenrott's personal decorations include the Defense Meritorious Service medal, the Meritorious Service Medal (three awards), the Joint Commendation medal, and the Navy-Marine Corps Commendation medal (four awards).

Master Chief Ron Downs, USN
Command Master Chief ESG-1

Master Chief Downs assumed duties as Command Master Chief for Task Force Warrior in May 2004. Prior to reporting to Task Force Warrior Master Chief Downs served as Command Master Chief for ESG-1. This historical transformation included the first 9580 assigned to the battle group construct. Master Chief Downs has been instrumental in "Leading Change" and the success of ESG ONE while deployed in support of OEF/OIF.

Master Chief Downs hails from Mt. Vernon, Missouri where he enlisted in the Navy in August 1981. Upon completion of Fireman Apprenticeship training as an Honor Graduate in November of 1981, he reported to USS CALOOSAHATCHEE (AO 98) in Norfolk, VA. After two Mediterranean deployments and a UNITAS deployment, he volunteered for recruiting duty. Upon acceptance, he reported to Navy Recruiting District, St. Louis in November of 1985 and following his highly successful tour, he returned to the Norfolk area to serve in USS BARNSTABLE COUNTY (LST 1197), completing a Mediterranean deployment and a WATC/UNITAS deployment. During a routine West African Training Cruise, BARNSTABLE COUNTY was tasked with the evacuation of Monrovia, Liberia and supported Operation DESERT STORM and DESERT SHIELD.

In February of 1995 he reported ashore to Naval Weapons Station,

Yorktown, VA where he served as Pier Safety Loading Officer. He terminated shore duty early to take orders to the newest Combat Logistics Force platform, USS SUPPLY (AOE 6), assuming duties as Engineering Department LCPO and collateral duty CMC.

While in SUPPLY, he was advanced to Master Chief Engineman. Master Chief Downs was selected for the Command Master Chief program in December of 1997, next he served as Command Master Chief in USS MITSCHER (DDG 57) from April 1998 to April 2000 where he completed a Mediterranean deployment in support of the EISENHOWER Battle Group and earned two Battle Efficiency Awards and four consecutive CINCLANTFLT Retention Honor Roll Awards, resulting in the coveted Golden Anchor Award.

Master Chief Downs reported to Norfolk Naval Shipyard in May 2000. During this assignment, he spearheaded several long-term quality of life improvements, including galley renovations, barracks improvements, Single Sailor project and excellent liaison with home ported ships and ships undergoing extended availabilities.

From September 2001 to June 2003, Master Chief Downs was a CNO Directed Command Master Chief for CNR Hawaii where he was responsible for numerous quality of life improvements throughout the Region and initiated a Region wide Command Master Chief Professional Development Program. Served as a valuable member of the CNO/ MCPON Leadership Panel.

Master Chief Downs' awards include the Meritorious Service Medal (3 awards), Navy and Marine Corps Commendation Medal (5 awards), Navy and Marine Corps Achievement Medal (3 awards), Navy Unit Commendation, Meritorious Unit Commendation (2 awards), Battle Efficiency Award (4 awards), Good Conduct Medal (6 awards), Navy Expeditionary Medal, National Defense Service Medal, Armed Forces Expeditionary Medal (2 awards), Sea Service Deployment Ribbon (8 awards), Military Outstanding Volunteer Service Medal, and Navy Recruiting Service Ribbon.

Master Chief Downs graduated from the Senior Enlisted Academy in Newport, RI in May 1999 and is a graduate of Norfolk State University where he completed his BS degree in Interdisciplinary Studies.

CHAPTER TWELVE

TRANSFORMATION — PART TWO

Brigadier General Mike Regner
USMC, ESG - 1
Operation Iraqi Freedom/Operation Enduring Freedom

Brigadier General Regner is serving as the Deputy Director, Programming Division, OPNAV Staff, Washington, D.C.

Brigadier General Regner was raised in Charleston, SC. He graduated from The Citadel with a Bachelor of Science degree and received his commission through the Naval Reserve Officer Training Corps Program in 1976.

After completion of The Basic School in 1977, Second Lieutenant Regner was assigned to Charlie Company, 1st Battalion, 8th Marines, 2d Marine Division where he served as a Rifle and Weapons Platoon Commander and deployed with the 24th Marine Amphibious Unit to the Landing Force 6th Fleet Area of Operation. Upon his return from deployment, First Lieutenant Regner was reassigned to Kilo Company, 3rd Battalion, 8th Marines and served as a Company Executive Officer and deployed to the Landing Force 6th Fleet Area of Operation with the 22nd Marine Amphibious Unit.

In 1979, First Lieutenant Regner was transferred to Recruiting Station Little Rock, AR where he served as the Operations and Executive Officer. In March of 1983, he attended The Infantry Officer's Advanced Course and completed Jump School at Fort Benning, GA.

Captain Regner was then assigned as the Commanding Officer of Lima Company, 3rd Battalion, 3rd Marines, 1st Marine Brigade. In June of 1984, Captain Regner deployed with Battalion Landing Team 3/3 to the Landing Force 7th Fleet Area of Operation. He was reassigned as the Battalion S-4 and deployed to Okinawa, Japan in January of 1986. After his return from deployment, Captain Regner was transferred to Headquarters Marine Corps where he served in Manpower and Reserve Affairs. In June of 1988, Major Regner was assigned to Bravo Company, Headquarters Battalion, Headquarters Marine Corps as the Commanding Officer. In 1990, he attended the Marine Corps' Command and Staff College in Quantico, VA.

In 1991, he was transferred to 2d Marine Division to serve as the Executive Officer to Battalion Landing Team 1st Battalion, 8th Marines. During this time, he deployed to Landing Force 6th Fleet and Landing Force 7th Fleet Areas of Operation where he participated in Operation DESERT STORM, the United Nations Operations in Somalia and NATO Operations in and around the Former Republic of Yugoslavia. He was later reassigned as the Staff Secretary, 2nd Marine Division.

In February of 1995, Lieutenant Colonel Regner assumed command of the 2nd Battalion, 8th Marines and deployed to the Landing Force 6th Fleet Area of Operation in support of Operations in and around Bosnia. He was then transferred to the NATO Defense College, Rome, Italy and graduated in 1997. Upon graduation, he was then reassigned to Supreme Headquarters Allied Powers Europe, Mons, Belgium where he served as the Joint Amphibious Operations Planner and Partnership for Peace Staff Officer.

In May of 1999, Colonel Regner reported for duty to Head Quarters Marine Corps, Office of Legislative Affairs, where he served as the Director, United States House of Representatives, Marine Corps Liaison Office. In July 2002, Colonel Regner assumed command of the 13th Marine Expeditionary Unit, Camp Pendleton, CA. From August 2003 to March 2004, General Regner deployed to 5th Fleet's Area of Responsibility in support of Operations ENDURING and IRAQI FREEDOM and participated in Operation SWEENEY in the Al Faw peninsula in southern Iraq. After his return from deployment, he was ordered back to Iraq where he served as the Operations Officer for I Marine Expeditionary Force throughout Operation IRAQI FREEDOM II. As the I MEF G-3, he participated in the liberation of Najaf and Fallujah as well as securing the first free elections in the Al Anbar and Karbala Provinces of Iraq.

Brigadier General Regner holds a Master's Degree in Public Administration from Webster College.

His personal decorations include the Bronze Star, Legion of Merit with gold star in lieu of second award, Defense Meritorious Service Medal, Meritorious Service Medal with gold stars in lieu of third award and the Navy and Marine Corps Commendation Medal with gold star in lieu of second award.

CHAPTER THIRTEEN

EIGHT MONTHS IN THE PALACE

Major General Kevin Kuklok
USMC Ret.
Baghdad, Iraq
November 2003 – June 2004

Major General Kevin B. Kuklok completed 35 years of commissioned service in August 2003 retiring as the Assistant Deputy Commandant for Plans, Policies, and Operations, Washington D.C.

Kevin was born in Fargo, ND. He attended the University of North Dakota, graduating with a Bachelor of Science degree in Chemical Engineering. General Kuklok received his Master's Degree in Business Administration from the United States International University in San Diego, CA.

Lieutenant Kuklok served in the Republic of Vietnam in 1970-71 with HML-367, flying the AH-1G Cobra. He also served as a Forward Air Controller with 2d Battalion, 7th Marines at Camp Pendleton. He was the Commanding Officer of H&MS-41, Det B and HMM-764, CH-46 squadron. During the latter tour, HMM-764 was activated for five months in support of Operations Desert Shield and Desert Storm.

As the Commanding General, Reserve Marine Air Ground Task Force East, (Command Element), Camp Lejeune, NC, Kevin commanded a Combined NATO exercise, Battle Griffin-96 in northern Norway. Concurrently, he served as the Chairman of the Secretary of the Navy's Marine Corps Reserve Policy Board. He also served as Commanding General, 4th Marine Aircraft Wing from 1997 through 2000. He was then reassigned as the Commanding General, Marine Corps Reserve Support Command. He served in this capacity until November 2001 when he was once again called to serve on active duty in support of Operations Noble Eagle, Enduring Freedom and Iraqi Freedom. His decorations include: Distinguished Service Medal, Air Medal with Numeral "66", Meritorious

Service Medal, and Navy Achievement Medal with Combat "V".

Kevin joined the Coalition Provisional Authority as a planner for the Essential Services reconstruction effort in Iraq in the Office of Policy Planning and Analysis and completed his 8 month tour as the Director reporting to AMB Paul Bremer.

Kevin is currently the Site Manager for Dayton Operations for S&K Technologies. He resides in Centerville OH with Diana, his wife of 33 years. They have two children.

INDEX

(as